The Blackfoot Confederacy, 1880–1920

The Blackfoot Confederacy 1880-1920

*

A Comparative Study of Canadian and U.S. Indian Policy

*

Hana Samek

University of New Mexico Press
Albuquerque

Library of Congress Cataloging-in-Publication Data

Samek, Hana, 1953–
  The Blackfoot confederacy, 1880–1920.

  Bibliography: p.
  Includes index.
  1. Siksika Indians—Government relations.
2. Indians of North America—Alberta.
3. Indians of North America—Montana. I. Title.
E99.S54S14 1987 971.23'00497 87–13947
ISBN 0-8263-1002-8

First paperbound printing, 2011
Paperbound ISBN: 978-0-8263-5069-5

15 14 13 12 11   1 2 3 4 5

To my mother,
"v kostce"

Contents

Illustrations following page 86

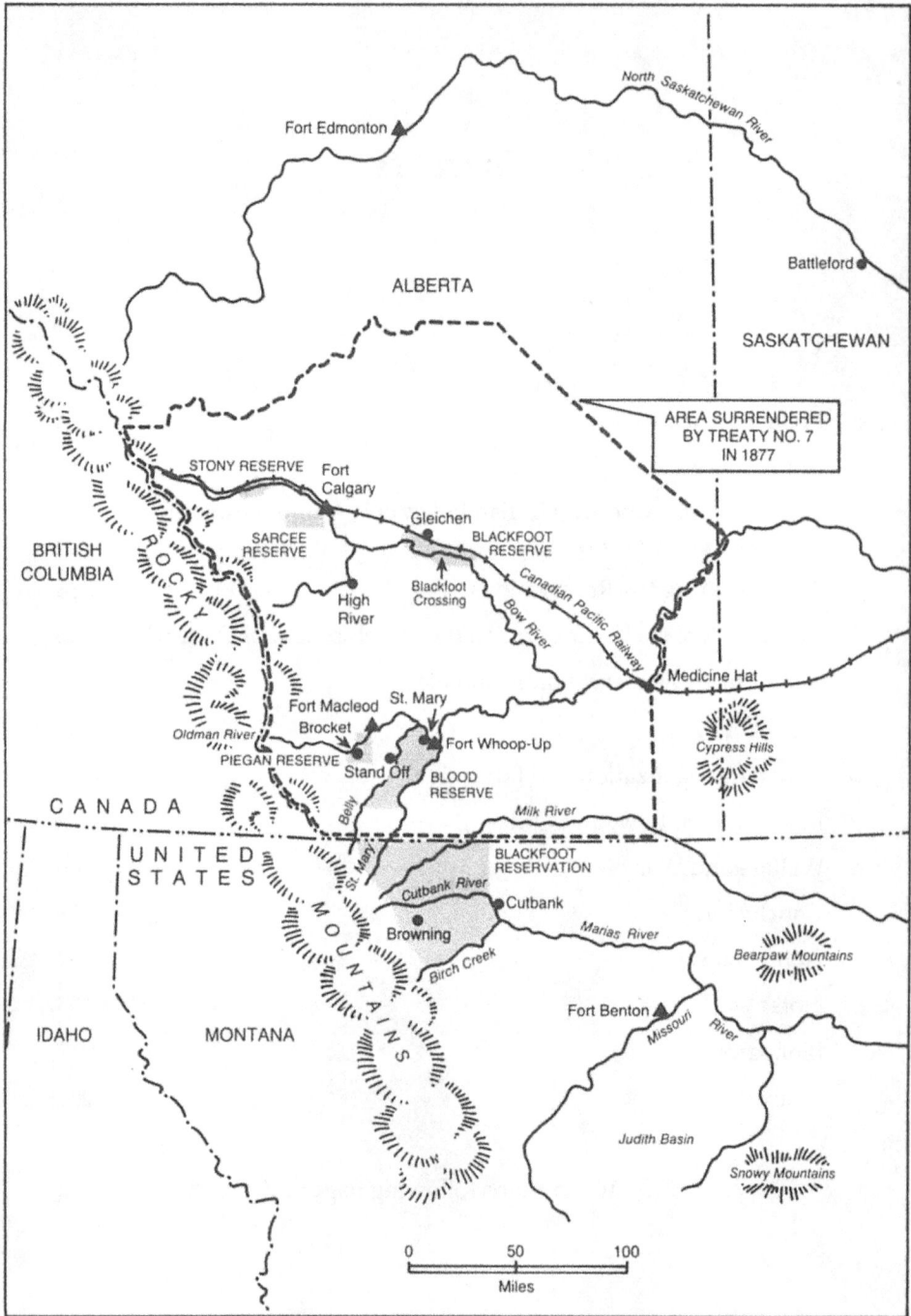

Historical Map of Blackfoot Country

viii

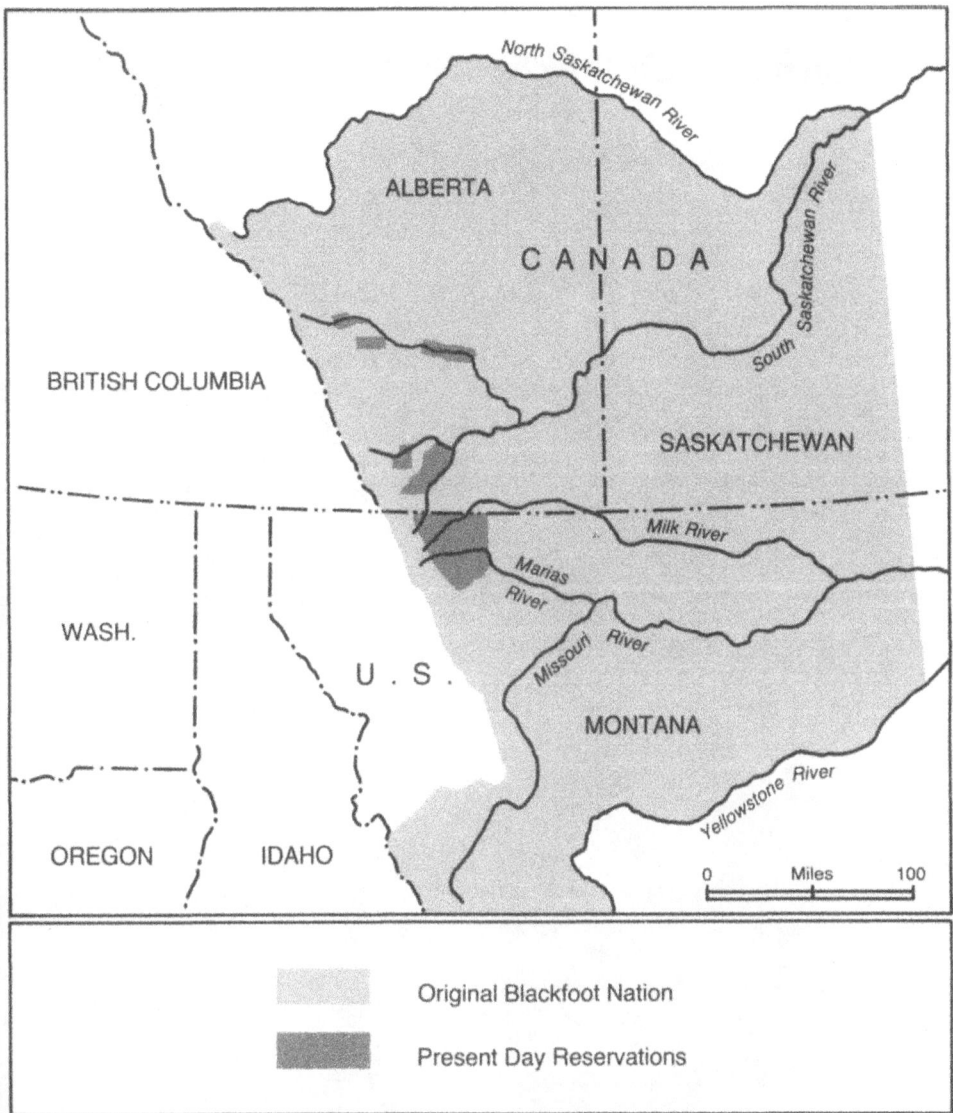

Regional Map of the Blackfoot Indians

Preface

To the casual observer, it must seem that white men in Canada and the United States have tried to find the solution to the "Indian problem" for centuries. In fact, barely a hundred years have passed since the last of the western nomadic tribes were confined to reservations where government officials, teachers, and missionaries could undertake the tribes' civilization and assimilation. Furthermore, despite the popular impression that native people have been historically the subjects of a massive, unrelenting campaign by the government to destroy their culture, in truth the campaign has consisted of periodic sallies announced with and accompanied by a great deal of noise, and actually fought by poorly trained and even more poorly supplied individuals. As a result, the most noteworthy part of the history of native management in Canada and the United States is not that the policies of the two nations were aimed at the destruction of a native culture and the substitution of a different life style, but that in many instances they have failed to achieve either end. For better or worse, native people in both countries live everyday with the consequences of these failures.

This comparative, historical study of a forty-year span in the life of the Blackfoot Confederacy examines some of the reasons for the overall failure as well as some of the unheralded successes. Although I have offered my own evaluations of native policies in the two countries, I have tried to present a portrait of Indian administration within the context of its time, rather than from an ideological perspective currently in vogue in either Canada or the United States. If I have learned anything from this study, it is that those who condemn past architects of Indian policy for shortsightedness, or just plain stupidity, are likely to find themselves condemned by a new generation of individuals who believe they have found the answer to the "Indian problem."

I wish to thank Dr. Douglas Leighton, Department of History, Huron College, London, Ontario, for originally sparking my interest in "Indi-

an" history; and Dr. Richard N. Ellis, Department of History, University
of New Mexico, for suggesting the Blackfoot Confederacy as a subject for
a comparative study in Indian policy. Throughout the years, both individuals have served as my mentors, and both have earned my deepest
respect for their scholarship and dedication to the profession. Dr. Richard
Barrett, Department of Anthropology, University of New Mexico, has
provided many insightful comments and helpful suggestions.

My research in the United States was greatly facilitated by Mr. Joel Bark-
er of the Denver Federal Archives and Records Center, and by the staff
of the Seattle Archives and Records Center. Mr. Bill Russell and Mr. Bob
Armstrong of the Public Archives of Canada guided me through Indian
Department records and made available microfilm copies through inter-
library loan. Dr. John Leslie, director of the Treaties and Historical Research Center, Indian and Northern Affairs, Ottawa, gave me access to
the center's collections. Dr. Hugh A. Dempsey, assistant director, Glen-
bow-Alberta Institute, generously offered his critical comments; Mrs.
Georgeen Klassen, assistant chief archivist at Glenbow, provided me with
some of the illustrations.

Last, but not least, I owe a debt of gratitude to my mother, Mrs. Marie
Samek, who remained a good-humored, steadfast supporter throughout
what seemed interminable student years abroad. As always, any shortcomings of this work are not the fault of those mentioned above.

Hana Samek
Albuquerque, New Mexico
May 1986

Introduction

On 25 June 1876, on a ridge overlooking the Little Big Horn and the Rose-bud rivers in Montana, the Sioux and their allies annihilated part of the Seventh Cavalry under the command of George Armstrong Custer. Over the next several months, as the United States army pursued the hostiles, the warriors and their families retreated north. During the winter and spring they crossed the "medicine line," the boundary separating the land of the bluecoats from the land of the Great Mother. There, out of the reach of the vengeance-seeking Americans, the Sioux asked for a sanctuary, promising to live in peace in British territory.[1]

Thus, the young Dominion of Canada became once again a haven for American Indians escaping oppressive treatment in their homeland, where General William T. Sherman's often-quoted remark that the only good Indian was a dead Indian seemed to sum up the attitude of the general public. But the Sioux exodus to Canada was prompted not only by a desire to escape, but by the belief that the Dominion would accord to the Indians a just and fair treatment—a treatment she had already extended to her own native people.[2]

The defeat of the Seventh and the subsequent escape of the Sioux, including Sitting Bull, again focused the attention of the American public on national Indian policy. A popular publication echoed the musings of many Americans in observing that

> the British Crown in America has not since our separation from it expended treasury in Indian wars, lost its subjects by massacre or mourned desolate settlements. As the general form and professed objects of the two systems are almost identical, can the explanation of the discordant results be found in any details of their execution [?][3]

Indeed, many Americans asked the same question with increasing frequency as reports of mismanagement and corruption in the Bureau of

1

Indian Affairs (BIA) and news of periodic clashes between whites and Indians on the frontier filled the front pages of newspapers. These events prompted some Americans to call for a reexamination of their management of the aboriginal population and to urge the study of Canadian Indian administration. These individuals and philanthropical organizations concerned about Indian welfare found in Canada what they were looking for: the absence of warfare, a simple administrative system, and a generally amiable relationship between whites and Indians. Not surprisingly, therefore, during the last decades of the nineteenth and the first decades of the twentieth century, Canada came to enjoy a reputation among humanitarian reformers and the American public for devising a far better Indian policy than the United States.

In their meeting halls, American humanitarians extolled the virtures of Canadian Indian adminstration, and these favorable reports appeared regularly in the American press, in reform literature, and in government studies. By learning from the Canadian example, and in adopting completely or partially Canada's "Indian system,"[4] American reformers hoped to rectify, albeit belatedly, what domestic critics of American Indian policy labeled "a century of dishonor."

American fascination with Canadian Indian policy persisted into the late 1940s, but the interest peaked between 1880 and 1920.[5] Although those who administered Indian affairs in both countries undoubtedly could have profited from knowing what programs had been successful or which ones had failed in the other country, to date scholars have not produced a detailed comparative history of Indian policy in the two countries. As a result, many Americans continue to see their country's Indian policy as having an especially disgraceful history, while regarding Canada's experience as a success. Until recently, Canadians shared the belief that the Dominion had followed a just and honorable course in Indian affairs.

Although the comparative approach to the study of Indian policy emerged in the United States during the latter part of the nineteenth century, scholars largely abandoned this area of inquiry even as they continued to pursue the study of the American West and Indian–white relations. Nevertheless, some historians have recognized the need for students of the American West to broaden their conceptualizations by examining frontier experiences in other countries, including the area of interracial relations. One scholar commented that "one sometimes gets the impression that the American experience in dealing with the native inhabitants was unique in the United States, that bureaucratic confusion as well as humanitarian dedication relative to aboriginal policy existed only in this country." Although a handful of early comparative frontier studies considered the Canadian experience, Indian policy as a part of frontier development has received only perfunctory attention. Current comparative works on frontier history tend to concentrate on South Africa, Australia, Siberia, New Zealand, and New Guinea, while overlooking Canada as an obvious choice for comparison to the United States in the area of Indian management.[6]

At the same time, the reluctance of scholars to engage in comparative inquiry is understandable, since comparative studies of Canadian and American Indian policy pose a plethora of problems. Some of the difficulties stem from the current status of comparative studies in general, others from the status of American Indian historiography, and still others from the infancy of the study of Canadian Indian policy. While in the last few decades American scholars have produced a considerable body of work examining their country's Indian–white relations, they tend to focus almost exclusively on policy formulation and development while neglecting the study of the implementation of policy on reservations.[7] Moreover, the role of the Indian agents, reservation management, and the institutional development of the Bureau of Indian Affairs have remained topics that are largely ignored. In addition, historians often conclude their studies in 1887, with the passage of the Dawes Allotment Act; consequently, the period from the 1880s through the 1920s remains to be explored in greater detail.[8]

Despite gaps and deficiencies in the historiography of American Indian policy, these studies are virtually comprehensive when compared to Canadian scholars' coverage of Indian policy in their country. One historian observed that even though Canadian Indian policy evolved over a period of four centuries, the field has attracted little attention from historians and other scholars.[9] Although this situation is slowly beginning to change, and several recent publications and an increasing number of dissertations and theses have begun to explore the history of Canadian Indian policy, the subject in general remains a neglected aspect of Canadian history. Moreover, much of the new literature is generated by scholars other than historians—sociologists, anthropologists, political scientists, and journalists—who often evaluate Canadian Indian policy without understanding its roots or historical context.[10]

This lack of interest in Canadian Indian policy by historians is a reflection, in part, of the historical lack of concern about Indian matters by the Canadian public generally. By contrast, the numerous studies by American scholars of their country's Indian policy stem naturally from the process of American westward expansion, in which the aboriginal population played a highly publicized role. But while Americans bemoaned their country's history of Indian–white relations, the presence of native people on Canadian soil seemed to slip completely from the mind of the Canadian public during the nineteenth and most of the twentieth century. One student noted that Indians in Canada assumed a position of "irrelevance" from which they did not emerge until the 1960s.[11]

This lack of interest among Canadians in their native people also stemmed from a general conviction that the Dominion always conducted a benevolent and fair Indian policy. If one ignores the two Riel rebellions—which were comparatively tame affairs—Canada, in comparison to the United States, has indeed enjoyed a largely nonviolent contact with her aboriginal population. Comparative frontier studies sometimes single out the largely orderly and peaceful nature of the Canadian western settlement process as one of the reasons for the differences between Indian–white relations in Canada and the United States. It is hardly surprising, therefore, that the history of Canadian Indian policy has not excited much scholarly or public attention, although Canadian newspapers frequently made disparaging comments on the Indian policy of the United States.[12]

The different attitudes of the two countries toward native people and their treatment is further illustrated by the highly visible role played in American Indian administration by the various movements for reform of federal Indian policies. In Canada, similar reform movements were, and are, virtually nonexistent. One American official even summed up the basic difference between Indian administration in the two countries in terms of the absence of a strong Indian reform movement in Canada. "In Canada," he wrote, "the British traditions of reticence, of letting well alone, of hushing up 'scandals,' of trusting officials, are stronger, so that there is apparently not so much interest on the part of the public in the so-called Indian question."[13] Reform movements in the United States, on the other hand, grew out of perceptions of the aboriginal population as a "problem," and culminated in the reformers' "enthusiastic, optimistic, and panacean approaches to Indian policy." Constant self-criticism and the conviction that remedies lay in implementing the proper legislation produced a staggering body of federal American Indian laws and regulations.[14]

Clearly, then, a basic difference between American and Canadian Indian policy is revealed by the frequent changes and experimentation in the management of native people in the United States, and a more constant, conservative approach employed in Canada. These different approaches are especially noticeable during the period from 1880 to 1920. During this time, Americans passed voluminous legislation designed to do away with their "Indian problem." The period began optimistically with the belief that the nomadic tribes of the West could be assimilated into American society in a relatively short time. As years passed, however, it became obvious that measures designed to facilitate assimilation did not work, and humanitarians reacted by agitating for the passage of more legislation. Ironically, the Indian legislation passed between 1880 and 1920 with the best of intentions proved to have disastrous consequences for the native poeple—a conclusion reached by the Meriam Report, published in 1928. These forty years, therefore, form both the apogee and nadir for American Indian policy and its administration.[15]

During the same period, Indian affairs in the Canadian West settled into a matter of routine administration, interrupted only by the short-lived North-West Rebellion. In fact, the activities of the Department of Indian Affairs (DIA) drew virtually no public attention, much less calls for reform. After consolidating laws concerning Indians under the Indian Act of 1876, the Canadian government peridocially revised and updated the statute, which provided a clarity and basic consistency in Indian administration that American reformers found enviable. Canada, therefore, did not experience the periodic agitations of reformers that occurred so often south of the border.

By contrast, in the United States the public's perception of the deficiencies in Indian policy shaped Indian administration. Swamped with stories of Indian and white clashes on the frontier, Americans generally criticized their government for its corrupt and ineffectual treatment of Indians. Most of these accusations came from frontiersmen who thought that eastern do-gooders caused the government to be too lenient with belligerent savages. Reformers, on the other hand, blamed corrupt management and avaricious frontiersmen for goading the Indians into armed resistance. After the transfer of the BIA from the War Department to civilian jurisdiction in 1849, efforts persisted to return the bureau to the army. At least the army, many thought, was not riddled with graft and incompetence and possessed a firsthand knowledge of Indians. Such knowledge was more than the largely eastern-born, civilian administrators and philanthropists could claim; and though the bureau remained under civilian jurisdiction, pleas for the return of Indian administration to the army remained a controversial proposal among reform circles into the early twentieth century.[16]

Meanwhile, Canadians could contrast their experience on the western prairies to the lawlessness and strife that periodically gripped the American West, and conclude that the general absence of Indian–white conflict stemmed from the establishment of law along with a benevolent and fair-minded treatment of the Indians. In time, this belief became, as a Canadian historian observed recently, "one of those self-congratulatory myths which bind a nation together."[17]

Not coincidentally, then, American interest in Canadian Indian affairs mounted during the years following the Civil War, just as American Indian affairs had reached their nadir. In 1869, the year that Americans sent out a "Peace Commission" to end Indian warfare on the plains, the chairman of the House Committee on Indian Affairs asked for information on the treatment of Indians in British America and "the means employed to bring them into habits of civilization." A thirty-eight-page report subsequently submitted to the committee concluded that the Dominion "will be known in history as having striven to do justice to the aborigines, . . . and that they have so far founded their empire or dominion upon the principles of humanity and true civilization."[18] This report set the tone for virtually all queries about Canadian Indian administration over the next several decades.

For instance, when the discovery of gold in the Black Hills in 1874 prompted American newspapers to predict another removal of the Sioux, the editors reprinted a letter from a Canadian praising his government's treatment of the Indians. This writer felt that harmony between the races could be accomplished only by dealing fairly with the Indians. In commenting on the letter, the American editors urged Washington to follow the Dominion's example in scrupulously adhering to the Indian treaties as the surest way of keeping the Indians pacified.[19]

Washington, however, paid little attention to such exhortations and broke the Sioux treaty. The action forced the Sioux to fight and then seek refuge in Canada, and their flight catapulted this latest embarrassing failure of American Indian policy into an international arena. In 1879, David Mills, Canada's minister of the interior, came to Washington to persuade the American governement to repatriate the Sioux. Mills took the opportunity to lecture to the American president on the shortcomings of his country's Indian policy, just as another group, the Nez Percé, made a desperate bid for Canada.[20] The spectacle of a British subject pontificating to the president of the United States irked some Americans who were otherwise sympathetic to the Canadian approach. A writer in *The Nation* commented that "while our statescraft is by no means so perfect that it cannot learn something from our friendly rival, we cannot safely copy any system that has been successful elsewhere, unless it be applicable to our conditions and environment."[21]

Some Americans attempted to put a better face on the disaster by stressing the differences between the two countries. General Nelson A. Miles, for instance, argued that the Canadian West experienced far less demographic pressure than the American West. Miles, however, admitted at the same time that the Canadian Indian system was "permanent, decided and just." The Canadians, Nelson wrote, punished only the culprits, not the entire tribe for the action of a few. Carl Schurz, who as secretary of the interior was responsible for the embattled Bureau of Indian Affairs, contrasted the bloody Indian wars in the American West with the peacefulness of the Canadian prairies. Schurz credited the differences to Canada's better management of her Indian affairs, but he also maintained that the slow growth rate of Canadian settlement prevented clashes between Indians and whites. When railroads, settlers, and miners came, Schurz predicted that Canada would face similar difficulites.[22]

Other Americans refused to explain away their country's blunders. In his preface to Helen Hunt Jackson's *A Century of Dishonor*, Bishop H. B. Whipple, a longtime advocate of a humane Indian policy, simply pointed to the blood shed on American soil at a time when "Canada [had] no Indian wars." Whipple also praised Canada for her honorably kept promises and the high moral character of her Indian agents.[23]

Canadians generally accepted such positive images of their Indian administration. Only the events of the North West Rebellion briefly shattered this vision. In the House of Commons, a scathing attack on the government's Indian policy as the cause of the rebellion pointed out that Canadians, in effect, labored under the illusion of practicing an efficient, honest, and fair-minded Indian policy. During an emotional session, one member of Parliament, M. C. Cameron, exclaimed: "It was our proud boast a few years ago, when our neighbors on the other side of the line had their turmoils, unrest, and massacres among their Indians, to say that it was due to their agents taking advantage of the government, and to point to our own country where we had no such difficulties." Cameron declared that "we are not in a position to point to our Indians as proudly as we did before."[24]

A similar incident in the United States would have signaled an all-out attack on the government by the press from the afflicted territory. One western Canadian newspaper, however, rose to defend the government, its personnel, and its Indian policy. The newspaper compared this rebellion to similar situations in the United States, where, the writer argued inaccurately, "Indian uprisings are regarded as the chronic outbreaks of political sores, and administrations are not censured for them—so much are they dependent upon uncontrollable causes." The implication that no one was to blame for the rebellion was surely one of the most interesting comments on Canadians' perceptions of their Indian policy. Others in the East, however, expressed support for Cameron's charges and voiced the nation's shock about the true state of Indian affairs.[25]

But since "peace, order, and good government" shortly returned to the territories and the area experienced no further unrest, Canadians quickly returned to their former complacency. In 1892, a noted Canadian missionary praised his country for her treatment of Indians and contrasted

Canadian policy with that of the United States. A short-lived journal devoted to Canada's native people, *The Canadian Indian*, held an equally
positive view of the Dominion's policy. Identical views appeared in a
British journal's lengthy paen entitled "The Treatment of the Canadian
Indians," whose author contrasted the Canadian perception of Indians
with that of the Americans, who, he claimed, saw Indians "as we see
rats." He blamed the American government for violence against Indians,
stating that, by contrast, the Canadians thought that the only good Indian
was an alive one.[26]

Even after the American Indians were conquered and confined to the
reservations, however, the "Indian problem" remained unsolved. This
time, humanitarian reformers had to find solutions to the problem of inte-
grating native people into the dominant society. Again, many turned to
the study of Canadian Indian administration, and Canadians became welcome guests at various gatherings of American philanthropists. The lis-
teners must have been intrigued by statements such as those by the
Reverend Egerton Young of Toronto, who told an audience gathered in
1900 at the annual Lake Mohonk Conference of Friends of the Indian: "I
come from Canada where we have no Indian question. We get along very
nicely with our Indians."[27]

Over the next several years, other and more prominent Canadians lec-
tured on Canadian Indian administration at the Mohonk conferences.
In 1912, Frank Pedley, the deputy superintendent of the Department of
Indian Affairs—an office similar to that of the American commissioner of
Indian affairs—gave an address that was generally self-congratulatory in
tone, although he avoided pressing the point.[28]

In 1914 and 1916, Duncan Campbell Scott, the poet–administrator who
headed the Indian department from 1913 to 1932, came to Lake Mohonk.
During his first appearance, Scott addressed the question of his department's policy and personnel. In contrast to complaints by Americans that
their Indian policy vacillated and the Indian service's untrained staff made
it inefficient, Scott pointed out that Canada had an established policy and
an administrative framework developed over a century and a half. He also
maintained that the employees of his department enjoyed the security of
tenure and could not be removed without good reasons. Political appointments, Scott stressed, were not as detrimental to the Canadian service as
they were in the United States because his department tempered patronage
with considerations for the applicant's necessary qualifications.[29]

When Scott returned to Mohonk two years later, he focused on the
praise that Americans had showered on Canada for her Indian administration. He felt unsure "that we are quite worthy of all the commenda-
tions we receive," reminding the audience that the American public tended

to take far greater interest in Indian affairs than did Canadians—the Mohonk meetings, he said, served as a good example. In Canada, according to Scott, the public was content to let government and religious bodies deal with native people. Although Scott maintained that no great differences existed between the two countries in managing governmental Indian policies, he thought that "caution and prudence" were the guiding principles of his department. Scott alluded to the American tendency to create a plethora of legislation to bring about the end of Indian wardship, and he stressed that the Dominion was far less impatient with her Indians. He granted that some Americans might label the Canadian approach too slow and conservative, but indicated that he would not emulate the American approach.[30]

The Americans, on the other hand, were interested in precisely those aspects of Canadian Indian policy they could emulate. An article in *The Red Man*, a publication of Carlisle Indian School, commented on the "impression that . . . seems to prevail among the friends of the Indians in America that Canada has handled her Indian problem more wisely than we." The author singled out two features as especially noteworthy— the absence of reservation allotment and the apparent greater personal and tribal liberty enjoyed by Canadian Indians.[31] Such persistent and positive publicity about the superiority of the Canadian Indian administration led a group of American reformers to decide to launch a formal investigation.

At the Lake Mohonk conference in 1914, members of the Board of Indian Commissioners, a citizens' committee watching over the Indian bureau, became so intrigued with Duncan C. Scott's presentation that they decided to send the board's secretary, Frederick H. Abbott, to make "a first hand study of the methods and policies of Indian administration in Canada." The board's chairman asked Scott to allow an American emissary to study the Canadian system, assuring him that the information gathered "would be laid before the Secretary for the United States Department of the Interior with hope that the methods of legislation and administration in connection with Indian affairs in this country might be improved thereby."[32]

Abbott spent seven weeks in Canada, including six days at the Indian department in Ottawa and the rest of his time in the field, visiting reserves and Indian schools from Quebec to Alberta. At the end of his visit he produced a 150-page report, half of it appendices, entitled *The Administration of Indian Affairs in Canada*.

His visit, Abbott reiterated, "grew out of a profound conviction on the part of the Board that there are defects, some of them serious and fundamental, . . . [in the American] system of . . . Indian administration." The

American investigator wanted to know everything pertaining to the management of Canadian Indians—laws, regulations, expenditures, personnel, departmental methods and policy aims. On his return to Washington, Abbott presented the board with an essentially foregone conclusion: "Canada's Indian policy contains much that is immeasurably superior to our own, much that it is not too late for us to imitate to advantage."[33]

Abbott focused on several aspects of Canadian Indian policy. He especially liked the compactness and conciseness of the rules governing Canadian Indian administration. He noted that he could put all of the laws contained in the Indian Act in his coat pocket, contrasting this to the several thousand pages required to list the Indian laws in the United States. Abbott also praised the nonpartisanship and consistency of Canadian Indian policy, despite changes in Canadian administrations. In addition, he applauded the idea of "closed reservations" that excluded "land grafters," and he especially admired the work of the North West Mounted Police in maintaining law and order on Indian reserves. Abbott also liked the spirit of cooperation between religious denominations and the government, and he pointed out that the respect accorded to Indian agents contrasted sharply with the aura of suspicion that hung over Indian agents in the United States.[34]

In interviewing Canadian Indians, Abbott reported that he had not heard a single word of complaint against the Dominion government. The only complaint came from a group of expatriate Sioux—not about their adopted country, but about the treatment they received in the United States. Abbott then compared the cross-border tribes of the North Peigans, Bloods, and Blackfoot, living on three reserves in southern Alberta, with their cousins across the line, the South Peigans of Montana, commonly called the "Blackfeet." He found the Canadian system superior on virtually all points. The report concluded by recommending the adoption of twelve features of Canadian policy, including the creation of an Indian Act, a system of closed reservations, and stricter liquor laws.[35]

Because of this and other reports, in 1914 and 1917 a movement arose among reformers to codify an American Indian Act. Abbott even asked the DIA for copies of the Canadian legislation to serve as a guide for preparing an American version. These efforts, however, proved abortive. Abbott's recommendations were shelved, although his study reportedly remained in high demand among those who wished to reform American Indian affairs. The only impact of *The Administration of Indian Affairs in Canada* seems to have been a boost to the Canadians' sense of superiority, with domestic newspapers seizing on the report as proof that Canada "showed the best way of managing her Indian people."[36]

During the 1920s Indian reform in the United States did not gain much headway, largely because the commissioner of Indian affairs was the rugged individualist from South Dakota, Charles H. Burke. Nevertheless, the reformers, the popular press, and some legislators continued to pursue and expose shortcomings of the Indian bureau.[37] Finally, in 1928, the Institute for Government Research published its exhaustive study of American Indian managment entitled *The Problem of Indian Administration*, commonly called the Meriam Report, which aided in the passage of the Indian Reorganization Act of 1934.

Even after the passage of the act, American interest in Canadian Indian administration continued.[38] On the eve of World War II, a group of American and Canadian delegates interested in Indian administration gathered at the Royal Ontario Museum in Toronto for a two-week conference on the North American Indians. The papers and speeches of such notables as John Collier reflected the American historical pattern of self-criticism and the search for new solutions. On the other hand, presentations by Canadian officials indicated a general satisfaction with their Indian policy. This historic meeting marked one of the last efforts by Americans to learn from the Canadian experience.[39]

Even though war scuttled the Toronto conference's resolution to conduct future exchanges on common problems in Indian administration, in 1939 a team of American anthropologists from the Columbia University Anthropological Field Laboratory began to study the Blackfeet. These studies provided a wealth of information on Blackfeet tribal culture after some sixty years of reservation life. Unfortunately, although they utilized some historical sources, these reports dealt only tangentially with the relationship between Indian policy and Indian assimilation.[40] Therefore, the current examination resumes the pioneering but largely forgotten work of earlier investigators, refocusing on the Blackfoot Confederacy, a uniquely suitable subject for a comparative study of Indian policy and its implementation on the reservation level.

The three groups of the so-called Blackfoot Confederacy, orignially composed of the Bloods (Kainah), Peigans (Pikuni), and the Blackfoot proper (Siksika), and allied until 1861 with the Gros Ventre, eventually settled on reservations in Montana and Alberta. Some confusion exists about the terms that should be used when referring to these people. Those who came to reside in the United States were called the *Blackfeet*, although they were actually the South Peigans, sometimes spelled "Piegans." In Canada the official term for these Indians is *Blackfoot*, but this term can be applied to the entire confederacy or to the Blackfoot tribe residing in Alberta, from which the confederacy derived its name.[41]

Aside from sharing a common culture and language, the three groups

of the confederacy lived in a similar geographical area of the northwestern plains. Members of this loosely tied confederacy spoke an Algonkian
dialect, which related them to the eastern woodland tribes. The Blackfoot
territory included present-day southern Saskatchewan, Alberta, and northern Montana, although war parties ranged widely, with some raiding as
far as the American Southwest. Like other plains Indians, the Blackfoot
were nomadic and warlike, with their life revolving around the horse
and the buffalo. By the middle of the nineteenth century, these people
reached the zenith of their power.[42] Proud, fierce, and unpredictable,
the Blackfeet became the dreaded enemies of American fur trappers and
Indian neighbors alike.

But even their military prowess was not enough to save the Blackfeet
from the disastrous consequences of contacts with white civilization. Beginning in the late eighteenth century, several bands experienced the devastating impact of smallpox epidemics, which at times reduced their
numbers significantly. A more persistent threat soon came from white
emigrants, who began to arrive in the Oregon country following its usur-
pation from the British in 1848. In the middle of the nineteenth century,
the United States decided to enter into a formal arrangement with local
tribes to allow settlers to enter the northwest. In 1855 the United States
signed a treaty with several tribes, including a few Blackfoot bands, which
left the Indians in possession of about half of Montana. Following this
treaty, Indian signatories returned to their former pursuits, even though
an Indian agent arrived to supervise them and to distribute the promised annuities.[43]

The 1860s marked the beginning of precipitous change for the Blackfoot
Confederacy. South of the forty-ninth parallel, bitter clashes occurred
between Indians and white gold-seekers crossing Blackfoot lands and
between Indians and settlers trickling into Montana territory. A desire to
obtain more Indian lands soon led to calls for more cessions. In 1865,
negotiations moved the southern boundary of the 1855 treaty north to
the Teton River. The U.S. Senate, however, never ratified this treaty
because of a series of sporadic but bloody incidents over the next five
years, referred to collectively as the "Blackfeet War." Three years later,
the government made another attempt to clear the land title, but this 1868
treaty, virtually identical to its predecessor, again remained unratified.[44]

As violence mounted between settlers and the Blackfeet, and as many
Indian raiders slipped across the border into British territory, calls increased
for military action against the hostiles. In January 1870, troops attacked a
peaceful and small pox-afflicted Peigan village on the Marias River. The
resultant indiscriminate killing of the Indians, known as the Baker Massacre, met with a storm of protest in the East, but with general approba-

tion among Montanans. This military action ended forever the Blackfoot threat to the settlement of Montana Territory.[45]

Public outrage at massacres of the Indians, such as the one on the Marias, prompted a change in United States Indian policy in 1870. Humanitarians prevailed on the government to stop fighting the Indians and to try peaceful means of civilization and Christainization to save them from annihilation. For the next dozen years or so, this "Peace Policy" became the watchword of the American Indian administration.

Unfortunately, in Montana, as in other places in the West, this humane policy, anticipated as the final solution to the "Indian problem," fell short of its goal. The policy began to fall apart because of the rapid settlement of the trans-Mississippi West, inadequate funding of civilization programs, and perennial problems in reservation administration. Although the government dispatched civilian agents to the American Blackfeet throughout the 1870s, these officials experienced little success in bringing their charges into the fold of civilization.

Despite the three aborted treaties, the Blackfeet still had no reservation by the early 1870s. In the meantime, the influx of settlers into the unceded area made it imperative for the administration to formalize its relations with this tribe. In 1873, the president ordered the establishment of a large reservation, running across the northern third of Montana, for the Blackfeet, Gros Ventre, Assiniboines, and River Crows. Before this executive-order reservation could be established, however, cattlemen occupying the southwestern range pressured for the removal of the proposed boundary to the Birch Creek and the Marias River, despite the protestations of the Blackfeet and their agent. Thus, by the mid-1870s the range of the American Blackfeet had shrunk considerably, and the process continued for the next half-century.[46]

Although the forty-ninth parallel marked the boundary between the United States and the Dominion of Canada, that boundary did not result, as some have argued, in the arbitrary division of the Blackfoot people.[47] The Blackfoot, along with portions of the Bloods and Peigans, spent most of their time, of their own volition, in the British territory. By the middle of the nineteenth century, the latter group became recognized as North (Canadian) and South (American) Peigans; and the Americans called the South Peigans the Blackfeet. This division of the confederacy became more distinct during the 1870s, although the three Canadian bands continued to move south in pursuit of buffalo, to present themselves to the American Indian agent for rations, and to intermarry with their southern relatives. The separation of the confederacy became somewhat more formal in 1877 with the signing of the "Blackfoot Treaty," or Treaty Number 7, between the Canadians and the Bloods, the North Peigans, and the Blackfoot proper. As one historian put it, these bands chose to become subjects of the Canadian government rather than wards of the United States.[48] If this was a conscious decision on the part of the Blackfeet, only time would tell whether it was a wise one.

In contrast to Indian–white experience in the United States, relationships between native people and white settlers remained relatively peaceful on the British side until the 1860s. To a large measure, this amity resulted from the paternalistic domination of the Canadian West by the Hudson's Bay Company. This trading monopoly depended for its existence on Indians who supplied the company with furs. In 1869, the reign of the company came to an end when it surrendered its vast possessions to the newly formed Dominion of Canada. With the addition of this vast unexplored country, which became the North-West Territories, Canada nearly doubled her previous size. She also became responsible for replacing the presence of the Hudson's Bay Company with an administration situated in Ottawa and virtually isolated from communication with the West by the formidable Canadian Shield. With the transfer of western lands, the native people of the area came under the jurisdiction of the new federal government. The immediate consequence of the Dominion takeover was the short-lived Red River Rebellion by the Metis and the Half-breeds of southern Manitoba, who felt threatened by a change in sovereignty about which they were not consulted.[49]

On the southern plains of what would become the provinces of Alberta and Saskatchewan, the withdrawal of the Hudson's Bay Company brought dire consequences. American whiskey traders invaded this area and found a lucrative market. Whiskey produced spectacular violence among the Indians, with many dying in drunken brawls or of exposure following drinking sprees. The Canadian government proved unable to intervene, since the only law was a small garrison stationed at Winnipeg.[50]

Finally, in 1874, the Dominion dispatched the North West Mounted Police to the territories. Many Canadians believed that the Dominion was prompted to send the newly formed force by its desire to end lawlessness and the exploitation of the Indians as well as by its intention to prepare them for the coming of the railroad and settlement. Others argued that the government sent the now-legendary North West Mounted Police more out of fear that the territories would fall into the hands of the Americans than out of concern for the Indians' welfare.[51]

Whatever the actual motives, news of the arrival of the police did send American whiskey traders scurrying back to the United States. The police erected posts at Fort Walsh and Fort Macleod, in the heart of the Blackfoot country, and they soon established an amiable relationship with their Indian neighbors. Much of the credit for Blackfoot amicability belonged to Crowfoot, the head chief of the Blackfoot tribe, who on numerous occasions expressed to the police the gratitude of his people for saving them from certain destruction. Indeed, three years later, the Indians' confidence in the police and Crowfoot's prestige played an important role in the Blackfoot Confederacy's decision to sign (with two other plains tribes, the Stoneys and the Sarcee) a treaty with the representatives of the Dominion government.[52]

The Blackfoot Treaty was the seventh treaty concluded since the government had initiated the western treaty process in 1871. Treaty 7 provided a common reserve along the Bow River for the Blackfoot, Blood, and Sarcee, while the North Peigans received a separate reserve west of Fort Macleod. Shortly thereafter, however, the Bloods asked for their own reserve on the Belly River. This separation increased to three the number of Blackfoot Confederacy reserves in Canada.

While the Americans signed three agreements with the Blackfeet before 1873, and kept none of them, the Canadians concluded only a single treaty with their segment of the confederacy. This led some Americans to conclude that the Canadians had been more faithful in adhering to their Indian treaties. Evidence indicates, however, that the Blackfoot and other Indian tribes did not understand the significance of the treaty. Father Constantine Scollen, a Catholic missionary with long experience among the plains tribes, explained that they consented "because prior to the treaty they had always been kindly dealt with by authorities and did not wish to offend them." The treaty was thus based on a misunderstanding: government officials failed to convey to the Indians that they were losing their lands forever, while the Indians believed that they were essentially agreeing to a peace treaty.[53]

After treaty making and the assignment of reserves, the Blackfoot, Bloods, and Peigans returned to their former pursuits. But in less than half a decade, the buffalo disappeared, and the Blackfoot world on both sides of the border collapsed. The former scourges of the northwest suddenly became entirely dependent on the Canadian and American governments. What measures the two countries adopted to deal with these people and how successful they were is the subject of this study.

1

Canadian and American
Indian Policy and Administration:
A Historical Overview

Indian administration in Canada and the United States was based on the British colonial system inaugurated in 1763. Indian Departments or administrative districts and special officials responsible to a central administration enabled the system to deal with Indian tribes. Of more lasting significance was the British practice of recognizing and extinguishing aboriginal title to land by treaties, a policy that other European colonizing nations did not adopt. After the War of Independence, Americans embarked on an Indian policy that began to diverge in several areas from that of British North America. This chapter examines where and why this divergence occurred.

Within a half-century after the American Revolution, pressure from land-hungry settlers prompted the removal of the eastern and southern tribes across the Mississippi River. Humanitarian advocates of this policy thought that removal would separate the Indians from avaricious frontier riffraff and buy time for the Indians to become Christianized and civilized. By 1840, however, American settlement had already crossed the Mississippi, and for the remaining fifty years the American West often became a battleground between Indians and newcomers. One consequence of the removal policy was to shift the focus of American Indian administration to the West, where the government tried in vain to regulate Indian–white relations according to the principles established under the British regime and during the early years of the American Republic.[1]

On the other hand, settlement in the British colonies grew at a much slower pace, and consequently Indian–white relations did not become seriously strained. During the revolutionary wars the British managed to retain the loyalty, or at least the neutrality, of most of the eastern tribes; thus, an image of the Canadian Indians as "loyal wards of the Crown"[2] took shape. In turn, the British repaid their Indian allies by ignoring their interests at the Treaty of Paris. After the war of 1812 the crown persisted in its absentmindedness toward the aboriginal population. In the mean-

16

time, the new American government recognized as early as 1791 an obligation to save the Indians from extermination, and subsequently provided appropriations for Indian civilization.[3] The British government did not recognize a similar responsibility until the 1830s.

One chronicler of Canadian Indian administration argues that the sudden concern for the future of the Indians did not grow out of humanitarian considerations, but was the product of one official's self-interest.[4] Faced with the abolition of his office, the head of the Indian department in the United Provinces came up with a new justification for its existence: the civilization of the Indians. Inertia, however, continued to dominate the crown's attitude toward her loyal wards, so much so that a British humanitarian group frequently memorialized the goverment about this subject.[5] Thus, the attitude of somehow not being quite aware of the native people developed early in Canada and persisted until the late twentieth century. This situation was made possible by the slow rate of settlement and the widely scattered Indian population.

In contrast, while by the 1840s the majority of American aboriginal people lived in the trans-Mississippi West, where the rapidly expanding United States soon engulfed them, in Canada a sizable Indian population remained in the eastern, "older provinces," since Canada had not instituted a wholesale removal policy.[6] As far as white observers could tell, Indians in the southern parts of the eastern provinces retained little of their aboriginal life style and could easily be granted all civic privileges and responsibilities. Only those Indians in the northern reaches and those west of Lake Superior, who were still living in the stage of "savagery," had to be protected and guided toward civilization. Consequently, Canada developed a dual Indian policy: some of its provisions applied only to those tribes that reached certain levels of civilization, while other tribes remained exempt until they reached a similarly advanced stage.[7]

The responsibility for administering Indian affairs fell under the jurisdiction of federal bodies in both countries. In the United States, the mandate came from Article I, Section 8, Clause 3 of the Constitution, giving Congress the power to "regulate commerce with foreign nations, and among the several States, and with the Indian tribes." Until 1871, Article II, Section 2, Clause 2, authorizing the president to make treaties with the natives, gave American Indian treaties the attributes of international agreements between sovereign nations. Moreover, the rulings of Chief Justice John Marshall in the 1830s, declaring Indian tribes "domestic dependent nations," reinforced a concept of sovereignty of American Indian tribes as well as the concept of aboriginal title.[8]

From a historical and legal perspective, the thorny issue of Indian sovereignty in Canada is a moot point. The authority to deal with Indian tribes originated from a different source than in the United States. The management of Indian affairs remained an imperial responsibility until 1860, when the crown transferred jurisdiction to the legislatures of the several provinces. Upon the establishment of the Dominion of Canada in 1867 by the British North America Act, Indian affairs returned to a central authority, the Parliament of Canada. Under Section 91, Subsection 24, the government received the power to legislate for "Indians and lands reserved for Indians." This sweeping grant of power encompassed the right of the Dominion to make treaties with the tribes. Canadian courts subsequently interpreted Indian treaties as being similar to contracts for cessions of land; therefore, these treaties did not confer the status of sovereign nations on Canadian Indian tribes.[9]

Consequently, the Canadian government could always freely legislate in matters pertaining to Indians without having its legislation declared *ultra vires*. On the other hand, American administration did not gain such power to legislate unilaterally in Indian affairs until 1871, when Indian "treaties" became "agreements." Legally, however, Indians in both countries occupied the status of minors, or wards, while the federal government assumed the position of a trustee. Releasing the Indians from wardship and ending federal trust responsiblity toward Indians and their land and property became the long-range intention of both governments.

The implementation of Indian policy fell upon special federal departments. During the latter half of the nineteenth century, the American Bureau of Indian Affairs became the target of more criticism than any other federal agency. Even though the Office of Indian Affairs, created in 1832 within the War Department, was transferred to the Department of the Interior in 1849, the question of military-versus-civilian control dogged American Indian administration. The dispute arose from the conviction shared by many that in civilian hands the bureau had turned into a "sink of corruption."[10]

The Bureau of Indian Affairs formed one of several branches of the Department of the Interior. At the head of the BIA was the commissioner of Indian affairs, whose immediate superior, the secretary of the interior, reported to the president. Although the bureau served as the linchpin of Indian administration, at times the secretary and the president played crucial roles. For example, the president had to give his assent to allotment and to the opening of reservations, and he exercised control over trust patents. The secretary issued fee patents and certificates of competency, and served as the source of final appeal against the actions of the commissioner.[11]

In Canada, the Office of Indian Affairs frequently shifted within the adminstrative structure. Before Confederation, various bodies such as the

Office of the Secretary of State, the Crown Lands Department, and the secretary to the governor-general administered Indian affairs through an officer generally called the superintendent general of Indian affairs. In 1873, the Indian branch was placed under the newly created Department of the Interior. Seven years later, the Department of Indian Affairs became a separate office, headed by the minister of the interior who, for the most part, served also as the ex officio superintendent general. During the early years of the Dominion, from 1878 to 1895, Prime Minister John A. Macdonald served as the superintendent general. However, much of the actual work of the department rested on the shoulders of the deputy superintendent general, a career civil-servant position created in 1874. During a general reorganization of the Indian service in 1897, the deputy position was abolished and its responsibilities transferred to the deputy minister of the interior. This system lasted until 1902, when the deputy superintendent resumed his post as the acting head of the Indian department.[12]

The placement of the Indian affairs office under the Interior departments provided a similarity in administration between the two countries. Neither Canadian nor American officials considered the arrangement a conflict of interest, although such a conflict became obvious as the last century drew to a close. The Interior departments could not promote the development of western lands while simultaneously protecting the tribes' rights and interests, especially where reservation lands were concerned. This conflict has continued into the present day.

Despite similarities in administrative structure, Canada adopted one additional feature called the Indian Act, which has no parallel in the United States. Enacted in 1876 as "an Act to amend and consolidate the laws respecting Indians," this single statute consolidated all laws governing Indian affairs in Canada.[13] The Indian Act provided a reasonably short, clear, and comprehensive guide for Indian management; by examining its features, the development of Canadian Indian policy can be readily traced.

In theory, the Indian Act gave officials of the DIA the power to exercise virtually complete control over the personal, political, social, and economic life of native people. Various clauses were aimed at protecting Indian lands and property, while others provided the mechanism for Indian enfranchisement, thus ending their special status. Protection and advancement became the theme of Canadian Indian administration.[14]

One of the act's most significant features was the legal definition of an Indian. Such an individual was any male person of Indian blood belonging to a particular Indian band, any child of such a person, or any woman who had lawfully married such a person. This definition set up in Canada the legal distinction between "status" and "nonstatus" Indians, with the former consisting of native people recognized to be Indians under the terms of the Indian Act, and the latter comprising those who are not considered Indians under the terms of the act, even though they are indeed genetically and culturally Indian. Until 1985, when the law was changed by the passage of Bill C–31, the most conspicuous members of the nonstatus group were Indian women who lost their Indian status upon marrying "non-Indians" (even though the husband might be a full-blood Indian). Together with their children, these women became legally "white," and they gave up tribal rights to reserves. Conversely, status male Indians conferred their status after marriage to their wives, whether white or nonstatus Indian women, as well as to their children.[15]

By contrast, the United States lacked a clear legal definition of who was Indian. Indian women who married white men could continue to reside on the reservation as tribal members. Husbands also had the right to live on the reservation, and more often than not, they gained through their wives access to tribal property. As a result, on many American Indian reservations these "squaw men" proved to be a disruptive element, causing headaches for many Indian agents. In Canada, because of the legal definition of "Indian," this situation never arose.[16]

One of the reasons many Americans believed that Canadians had better success in Indian affairs stemmed from the Dominion's hiring system for the Indian sevice. In the United States, graft, corruption, and incompetence became synonymous with the Indian bureau. This situation arose largely because personnel from the commissioner downward received their positions as rewards for political service. The pork-barrel approach to Indian administration often brought into office rapacious individuals who, as a rule, had no experience in dealing with Indians. The results were predictably disastrous. Ironically, even if these political appointees proved to be competent they could be dismissed summarily when the other political party won the federal election. Moreover, if the Indian agent carried out his duties too well he often met with disapproval from the local white population, and could be hounded out of office on trumped-up charges of corruption.

The extent of the public's distrust of the BIA manifested itself in 1869 in the creation of the Board of Indian Commissioners. This body consisted of philanthropic individuals who served without compensation; they supervised the purchase of Indian supplies and, if needed, they investigated all aspects of Indian policy. The board remained active until 1933, and no other federal department was monitored by a similar, permanent, and independent committee.[17]

Groups such as the Indian Rights Association as well as many of the higher federal officials, including comissioners Francis E. Leupp and Robert G. Valentine, were devoted to the protection of what they conceived to be the interests of native Americans, and they realized that a system of political appointments harmed the Indian service. The solution rested in either returning the BIA to the War Department, a move that humanitarians rejected, or in abolishing political appointments, a move opposed by vested interests. Despite opposition from the latter, in 1891 some positions in the Indian service, including those of physicians, superintendents, matrons, and teachers, were placed under civil service regulations. Two years later, the government began to replace politically appointed agents with Indian school superintendents who, by then, fell under the Civil Service Act. But these changes came slowly, and cries against the "spoils system" continued. As late as 1897, for example, a bill proposed the abolition of the office of the commissioner of Indian affairs and its replacement with the nonpartisan Board of Indian Commissioners.[18]

In addition, finding and retaining qualified personnel in the American Indian service proved to be a challenge for several reasons. Salaries remained low, commencing in 1912 with the commissioner's pay of five thousand dollars annually. Frustration and disenchantment among the employees also led to a rapid turnover in office. It was estimated that during a single year some four thousand out of six thousand employees would resign, transfer, or receive discharges. However, the last two options proved to be no solution to staffing problems, since the perennially short-handed Indian service often simply shuffled around incompetent employees. In turn, staffing problems spawned management difficulties, especially after the turn of the century.[19]

For example, during the five-year period between 1905 and 1910 the American government enacted more Indian legislation than during the same previous period, but the staff size at the headquarters in Washington did not keep pace. In 1902, the BIA handled 77,000 incoming letters with 132 employees; nine years later, a staff of 227 handled 209,000 letters. Not only Washington employees but reservation personnel were inundated with a sea of regulations "giving instructions on this, that and the other thing." Someone calculated that from 7 July 1913 to 8 July 1914 there were 122 circulars issued, arriving at the rate of one every three days. In the ten year period after the BIA had last compiled its rules and regulations, some 900 new circulars arrived.[20] Small wonder that during this period Americans began to consider a version of the Canadian Indian Act as the only sane solution to their administrative problems.

Most critics agreed that the American Indian administration was most in need of better personnel management. The key was, as Frederick Abbott put it, "permanency of appointments, fixedness of policy, [and] selection based on merit." The Canadians appeared to possess all three. Abbott went on to contrast the management of the Canadian Indian department's personnel to the situation in the United States.

> The Indian agent appointed by any party in Canada, in accordance with well established written law, will continue to hold his position indefinitely regardless of changes in party in control provided he refrains from political activity in elections and does his task honestly and well. . . . In Canada there is no muck-raking of men in the Indian service, and there are no "sleuths" connected with the Indian Department to dog the trails of agents and other employes [sic] every time a breath of criticism or suspicion is borne to the ears of the headquarters service. There, employes [sic] are treated with dignity and respect and are presumed to be honest until the contrary is shown. . . . When a superintendent is found incompetent he is almost invariably dropped from service and not transferred elsewhere as happens too often in this country. . . . In short, every subordinate Indian field official in Canada is treated as a man and not a suspicious character who needs watching. Having no hope under such system of hounding men out of the service without sufficient cause, outside influences seldom make charges against Indian Service employes [sic] without first having something besides suspicion, or pretense of suspicion, upon which to base their charges. The result is a spirit of loyalty and an esprit de corps in the Canadian Indian Service which have no counterpart in the Indian Service in the United States.[21]

This rather rosy picture of Canadian Indian administration had some basis in fact, but it must have seemed especially attractive to the Americans in light of the dismal conditions in their Indian service. Compared to political involvements in the United States, Canadian politics played a minor role in staffing the Indian department. For example, the post of the deputy superintendent general was held between 1874 and 1893 by a career civil servant. When the Liberal party won the election of 1896, and the new minister of the interior Clifford Sifton reorganized the department and evicted Conservative party appointees, his actions were unusual rather than routine.[22]

For some Canadians, the Indian service turned into a family tradition. Frederick Abbott noted with amazement how many department officials served from fifteen to thirty-five years, with most rising through the ranks from clerks to high positions and acquiring, in the process, knowledge of an Indian language. For example, Lawrence G. Vankoughnet served for some twenty years, from 1874 to 1893, as the deputy superintendent general. When Duncan Campbell Scott assumed the post in 1913, he had already served some thirty-five years in the department, beginning as a seventeen-year-old copy clerk and rising to the position of superintendent of Indian education. He continued to head the department until 1931. In contrast, the average tenure of the American commissioner of Indian affairs between 1833 and 1933 was three years; John Collier's twelve-year term in office (from 1933 to 1945) was unprecedented.[23]

While blatantly political appointments to the Indian service remained the trademark of American Indian administration, in Ottawa the Indian department tried—not always successfully—to ensure a basic competency in its appointees. As civil servants, these individuals held their positions at the pleasure of the government, and they could not be dismissed except for good and sufficient reasons. Certain activities of the agents were sure to bring displeasure from headquarters. For instance, between 1896 and 1898, among a total of sixty-seven persons who left the Indian department in the North West Territories, seventeen were dismissed by the department—the majority for taking part in politics and the rest for drunkenness, incompetence, and neglect of duty. A Touchwood Hills agency clerk found himself transferred rather than elevated when he lobbied for his appointment as agent based on his loyalty to the Liberal party. Those individuals who tried to lobby members of Parliament for an increase in their salaries or to obtain better positions were often told that their action would be considered as proof that their case did not stand on its own merits.[24]

Ironically, while the largest problems of the American Indian service proved to be corruption, incompetence, and rapid turnover, the Canadian system fell victim to inertia. New solutions, the hallmark of American Indian administration, stood little chance in the Canadian Indian department. Not only Americans but Canadians as well had noticed the conservative nature of the Dominion's Indian administration. Canadian officials, however, took pride in this lack of innovation, pointing out that the Canadian Indian policy had developed over a century and a half and did not admit easily new ideas. As D. C. Scott told his American audience: "It is an immense advantage for men coming newly into our Indian service to find this policy and law so well defined; it curbs them and very soon their initial vagaries are quieted and they come into the old stream of administration and begin to see some wisdom in it." Some two years later, he reiterated, "The keynote of our policy is caution and prudence."[25]

While curbing the enthusiasm of newcomers may have seemed a laudable idea to Scott, in the long run this approach bred an attitude in which the preservation of administrative routine became the sole concern of officials. Senior staff trained junior members in the same conservative vein in which they had been instructed. Moreover, due to the long tenures of employees, the Canadian Indian service at headquarters was becoming geriatric by the turn of the century. In 1898, calls went out for hiring and training younger clerks when officials suddenly realized that the supply of senior clerks to fill vacancies would dry up unless new appointments were made. In addition, many of the heads of the Indian department, including John A. Macdonald, deputy superintendents Vankoughnet and D. C. Scott, and ministers of the interior Clifford Sifton and Edgar L. Dewdney, were conservative in their attitudes toward Indian affairs. Under their leadership, routine administration rather than original solutions became the trademark of the Canadian Indian department.[26]

Part of the reason for fossilization in the DIA stemmed from the Canadians' lack of interest in the activities of the Indian service. In the United States, the Indian wars riveted public attention for most of the nineteenth century. After the wars ended, nearly a quarter of a million Indians occupied some 72 million acres of valuable land on some 200 reservations. In Canada, the Indians were not only pacified virtually without bloodshed, but only about 100,000 of them lived scattered on some 1,500 reserves encompassing some 5 million acres. These differences may explain why the questions asked about Indian matters in the House of Commons were generally mundane in character, while congressional debates proved much livelier.[27]

Americans began to question not only what made America's Indian policy different from Canada's; they also began to ask whether Americans had an Indian policy in the first place. Many Americans believed that indeed their government had no policy.[28] The reformers complained that "while Canada has had a fixed Indian policy, . . . the Indian policy in the U.S. has been vacillating, changing with each new administration and almost from year to year." They pointed to the frequent changes in BIA personnel as the key to the problem. For example, Senator Henry Dawes wrote that in the last six years there had been four different commissioners of Indian affairs, each with his own policy and his own convictions about the best method to administer Indian affairs. One administration, Dawes claimed, changed the policy of the Indian bureau three times in four years. This situation restricted each administration to the pursuit of a plan which it felt could be completed within four years, since its successor could not be relied upon to fulfill it.[29]

For the BIA the solution appeared simple, since the problem obviously was "not so much which is the best plan as that it shall be a continuous one." When addressing American audiences, most Canadian officials stressed the importance of a definite policy and scheme of administration that was well grounded. For them, consistency in policy and management was the great advantage that Canadians had over their American counterparts.[30]

In general objectives, the Indian policies of the two countries were identical. D. C. Scott put it succinctly, declaring in 1912: "The happiest future for the Indian race is absorption into the general population, and this is the object of the policy of our government." During his tenure, Scott did not deviate from his conviction that Canadian Indians must be assimilated.[31]

Scott was not alone in his beliefs. Well into the twentieth century, Canadians and Americans shared with their western European contemporaries a belief in the superiority of the white race, but this belief was also accompanied by a sense of duty toward the "less favored races." Philanthropic and humanitarian groups and religious denominations became the most active advocates of this responsibility. Spiritual and physical uplift, consisting of the evangelical, medical, and educational work of domestic and foreign missions, spread "Christian civilization" to the four corners of the world. Conversion to Christianity, especially to the Protestant version, became regarded by contemporaries as the indispensable element in being civilized. In North America, Christian missionaries played a historic role in Indian–white relations, serving as teachers, physicians, and administrators as well as evangelists. By consensus, these groups and individuals insisted that the Indian had to be civilized, enfranchised, and absorbed into Anglo-American society.[32]

A few dissenters voiced their opposition to attempts, as one put it, to "de-Indianize" Indians. In 1891, in *The Canadian Indian*, an anonymous writer calling himself "Fair Play" posed this question: "Would it not be pleasanter, and even safer for us to have living in our midst a contented, well-to-do, self-respecting community of Indians rather than a set of dependent, dissatisfied, half-educated, and half Anglicized paupers?"[33]

These words proved only too prophetic because the well-intentioned assimilationists could not fathom the chasm between themselves, the products of centuries of Western civilization, and the tribal people that humanitarians tried to lift up to their own "civilized" economic and sociocultural level. Consequently, the process of Indian civilization and assimilation turned into a slow and frustrating process. Most contemporaries, however, could not imagine any alternative for the Indians, especially since native people in both countries were already regarded as a "vanishing" race. In the United States, the policy of segregating Indians on reservations came under attack largely because many critics believed that it transformed the natives into museum pieces instead of allowing natural selection to take place. For the humanitarians, releasing Indians from federal supervision became the primary aim.[34]

Americans tried various legislative measures to speed up enfranchisement and emancipation of the native people from government control. By contrast, Canadians followed an orderly and systematic process of enfranchisement that appealed to Americans. The Indian Act provided for a graduated system of training natives in a municipal system of government. In addition, unlike Americans who tried to do away with many Indian tribal organizations, Canadians considered tribal councils useful for teaching the Indians self-government. As deputy superintendent Scott pointed out, even Indians who were still considered "savage," such as the Blackfoot, Bloods, and Peigans, were guided toward eventual self-government through the utilization of their tribal councils.[35]

In both countries, the grant of franchise usually meant the end of the Indians' legal status as government wards. But between 1885 and 1895, Indians living in the eastern provinces of Canada received voting rights without losing their status.[36] Since granting the Indians citizenship and franchise rights was considered the only solution to the "Indian problem," the means employed toward this end received considerable attention.

Canadians formulated Indian franchise legislation as early as 1857. Individuals desiring emancipation would receive citizenship by applying to the band council or, as later amended, to the superintendent general. But this process of voluntary Indian enfranchisement proved to be slow. Between 1884 and 1904 only two bands applied to be released from wardship, and only 250 individuals were enfranchised between 1857 and 1920. Not until 1920 did Canada take up more aggressive measures, and in a move similar to the American "forced fee patenting," enfranchisement boards were established to ferret out qualified Indians who refused to abandon their tribal status. Some members of Parliament, however, became alarmed at the arbitrary nature of this measure, and the department abandoned the system two years later.[37]

Americans also considered enfranchisement as the final step in the assimilation of their native population. The major difference between the two approaches centered on the means employed and the speed of implementation. Some Canadian scholars pointed out that the Dominion government's mistakes in Indian management stemmed from the belief that Indians could be assimilated in a short period of time. Ironically, American observers thought that the Canadians exercised a far greater restraint and patience with Indians than legislators in the United States. These Americans believed that due to the conservative nature of Canadian administration, the Dominion managed to avoid many of the costly problems which resulted from hastily drawn American legislation.[38]

Many of these difficulties stemmed from the Americans' very efforts to find solutions. The period under study here straddles two major phases of American Indian policy. The seventeen years between 1870 and 1887 are generally referred to as the "reservation period." Although reservations existed before and after this time, this phase was distinctive because Indians were segregated on reservations, issued rations, and subject to agents who endeavored to exercise complete control over them.[39] Reservations tried to keep the Indians away from settlements, while the government and religious bodies took care of their physical and spiritual needs. Later, during the "allotment period," from 1887 to about 1934, the United States passed legislation to terminate its responsibility for Indian tribes by breaking up communally held reservations, forcing individual Indians to take up their lands in severalty, granting franchise, and ending Indian wardship.

The landmark legislation enabling the government to pursue this policy was the Dawes Severalty Act, or the Allotment Act, of 1887. In a society that worshiped private property and self-reliance, communally held reservations were an anomaly. Communalism was thought to be the cause of the Indians' distressing lack of interest in bettering themselves. Convinced that the mere possession of private property would have a civilizing influence, proponents of the Dawes Act hoped to make the Indians "more intelligently selfish."[40] The answer to the "Indian problem," these advocates argued, was in treating the Indians not as a group but as individuals.

In a nutshell, the Dawes Act generally provided for the allotment of 160 acres of reservation land for each head of family. The government would hold title to the land in trust for the Indian allottee for twenty-five years, during which time the land could not be sold or mortgaged. Surplus lands remaining after the division of the lands among tribal members were sold to the public. Having received his trust patent, the Indian owner would be granted citizenship.

The government passed the Allotment Act as a unilateral decision without the tribes' consent, because since 1871 the government had possessed the legal right to legislate for the Indians by fiat. However, reasons for the act went beyond the simplistic belief that private property provided the basis of civilization. Some proponents of the legislation feared that unless Indians held their lands in fee simple, the government would be powerless to protect the reservations in the face of popular pressure to open such valuable real estate to settlement. Reformers knew that in the view of many Americans, the Indians were guilty of possessing too much land.[41]

Advocates of allotment expected that twenty-five years would be sufficient time for Indians to learn the value of private property and to become self-supporting. Even before the trust period expired, however, demands arose for more quickly releasing Indians and their lands from the "shackles of wardship." At the Lake Mohonk conference, reformers declared their advocacy of a "vanishing policy" that would repeal all Indian legislation, abolish the BIA, and force Indians to shoulder their civic responsibility. Since the Dawes Act conferred citizenship on Indians who did not have full title to their lands, the Burke Act of 1906 amended the law so that only Indians who held fee patents could be citizens. Unfortunately, the Burke Act also contained Indian "competency" provisions that had disastrous consequences.[42]

The Burke Act gave the secretary of the interior the authority to issue fee patents, before the trust period expired, to allottees who asked for them and could satisfy the secretary that they were competent to manage their own affairs. In 1913, secretary Franklin Lane, convinced that thousands of Indians preferred wardship to standing on their own feet, decided to establish "competency commissions" to identify competent Indians. After examining the Indians, the commissions would issue fee patents to those judged qualified, regardless of whether they wanted to receive the unrestricted title.[43]

Since the legislation never defined what constituted competency, the commissioners established their own criteria, such as the fact of an Indian's short hair or the ability to sign his own name. In many instances, commissioners never bothered to inspect the allottees, relying on third-party testimony. If an Indian refused to accept his fee patent, the government sent it to him by mail, and issued notification to local tax collectors that the property was taxable. By 1920, when competency commissions had ended, some twenty thousand fee patents had been issued, covering a million acres of reservation land. Most of these lands eventually passed out of Indian possession because the novice land proprietors were not prepared to cope with the intricacies of real estate ownership.[44]

Even the establishment of competency commissions did not satisfy some Americans. Clamor continued for the faster release of Indians—or more accurately, their real estate. Officials noticed early that 90 percent of the patents issued went to individuals of one-half or less Indian blood. The commissioner of Indian affairs drew this conclusion:

> While it is true that the fact of being a mixed blood does not of itself constitute or prove competency, yet it is undoubtedly true that the

mixed blood, both by reason of his inherited capacities, and because of his somewhat more advanced home environment, is, as a rule, better able to care for his property without supervision than is the full blood.[45]

This idea of correlating white blood with competency unfortunately proved too tantalizing a coincidence to be ignored, and it became a new justification for the withdrawal of federal protection from many Indians.

Four years after the establishment of competency commissions came a "new declaration of policy" as the next step in individualizing the Indians. The most important provision in this six-step measure was the "blood-quantum" criteria for Indian competency. The measure provided that all able-bodied adult Indians of less than one-half Indian blood would be given complete control over their property. Patents in fee would be issued to all adult Indians of one-half or more Indian blood who were found to be competent. Pleased with this ingenious solution, the commissioner decided in 1919 to extend the blood-quantum provision to include those of one-half or less Indian blood. Orders went out to the superintendents to submit names of qualified Indians, which resulted in the immediate creation of 4,500 tax-paying citizens.[46]

As a result of the "declaration of policy" between 1917 and 1920, the bureau issued some 17,176 fee patents, nearly double the number issued during the previous ten years. Occasionally, officials acknowledged that in the haste to dispose of Indian real estate, grave errors occurred; but intellectually, the majority of reformers could not concede that the policy had deprived the Indians of a land base, making them dependent on local communities rather than on the federal government. By the time the Indian Reorganization Act reversed the policy in 1934, Indian country had shrunk from 138 million to 48 million acres.[47]

In many respects, the Dawes Act and its adjunct legislation provided the most conspicious difference between American and Canadian Indian policies, although it should not be inferred that Canada rejected reservation allotment entirely. Indeed, the allotment system in Canada provides a perfect example of why, in comparison to the American approach, her Indian policy had been called conservative. The passage of the Dawes Act piqued the interest of Canadian officials who, in 1889, offered a cautious comment on their neighbor's solution. The deputy superintendent noted that if Indians are to successfully amalgamated with the white population, "they must be gradually and carefully prepared; and if . . . our neighbors are going from one extreme to the other, and freely enfranchising Indians, without the necessry preparation, the result will be anxiously looked for—for, if successful, the Indian problem will be more readily solved."[48]

Canadians also believed that private landownership provided the key to Indian assimilation. In the same report, the deputy superintendent remarked that the work of subdividing reserves had begun: "The tribal or communist system is assailed in every possible way, and every effort made to implant a spirit of individual responsibility instead." Unlike the situation in the United States, however, breaking up tribal holdings in Canada did not become an obsessive pursuit. High officials in the Canadian Indian department even voiced what some American counterparts dared not express: "It seems better to keep [the Indians] together, for the purpose of training them for mergence with the whites, than to disperse them unprotected among communities where they could not hold their own and would speedily be down-trodden and debauched."[49]

Nevertheless, allotment became a feature of Canadian Indian administration. In fact, the Dominion adopted a reserve allotment policy as early as 1869. This system, however, differed radically from the Dawes Act. When Frederick Abbott praised the "closed reserve" system adopted in Canada, he erred in stating that Canadian reserves were not allotted. Under the Indian Act of 1869, on advice from the superintendent general, the governor-general could issue letters of patent to any Indian located on a particular piece of land "who from the degree of civilization to which he has attained, and the character of integrity and sobriety which he bears, appears to be a safe and suitable person for becoming a proprietor of land."[50]

The Canadian allotment system first began to operate on several reserves in southern Ontario, but with disappointing results. Even though Ontario Indians were judged sufficiently civilized to be able to see the wisdom of private landownership, the superintendent complained in 1889 that some bands opposed allotment, fearing that the individualized lands would be subject to taxation and that the government would sell the remainder of the reserve.[51] This was precisely what happened to many allotted reservations in the United States.

In Canada, however, such fears were groundless because legislation specifically prohibited the sale of reserves, whether or not they were allotted, without the consent of the band. Moreover, the "locatee" could sell his land only to an Indian of the same band,[52] and never to non-Indians. These provisions avoided the staggering loss of American Indian fee lands to tax sales and to white speculators. In addition, under the provision of the Indian Advancement Act of 1884, petitioners for enfranchisement first had to demonstrate their competence *before* they received location tickets.[53]

The Americans pursued a reverse policy by first issuing trust patents and then fee patents as a means of bringing about enfranchisement.

Enfranchisement and its relation to private landownership, then, formed a major policy difference between the two countries. Americans first allotted lands, sold the surplus, and then forced many Indians to accept fee patents, which automatically enfranchised them. The Indian owner could sell his land to whomever he wished, and the property was subject to taxation. In Canada, on the other hand, reserve lands could not be sold without the band's consent; location tickets did not grant the Indians power to sell their land to outsiders; and enfranchisement came first, followed by the division of tribal property among individuals. In 1917, the superintendent general commented that enfranchisements led to the need to divide some reserves, stating that 213 location tickets were issued that year for a total of 2,111 tickets. In contrast, Americans issued 2,203 fee patents in 1917 alone, a total of 12,097 in the ten-year period since the establishment of the Burke Act.[54]

This system of Indian land tenure in Canada reflected the generally conservative nature of Canadian Indian policy. In an allusion to the American decision to let the Indians learn by adversity, D. C. Scott told his audience:

> Although we exercise our guardianship over the Indians to a very late stage of their development, . . . they are well able to support themselves when we finally let them go. We do not cut them adrift to sink or swim, but wait until we are quite certain that they are qualified to conduct their affairs independently.

To some Canadians such caution appeared detrimental, and they urged a speedier release of Indians from supervision by the department.[55] But such sentiments never gained prominence. Paternalism among department officials and apathy on the part of the general population combined to dominate Canadian Indian affairs at a time when prolific legislative activity occurred south of the border.

The conservative nature of Canadian Indian legislation reflected the general tenor of the entire Canadian political system. The British North America Act created a strongly centralized federal system, and mainly as a reaction to the excesses of American-style democracy. Canadians firmly believed in government from the top down rather than from the grass roots. In the United States, Indian policy had to conform, in many ways, to the wishes of the electorate, especially the aggressive frontier population. Canada's interior minister even told the president of the United States that America's Indian problem stemmed not from the inability to control Indians, but from the failure to control white men.[56]

In Canada, the government in power always controlled Indian policy. According to D. C. Scott, this system accounted for the difference between the formulation of Dominion and American Indian legislation; the House of Commons originated all legislation, and no Indian measure could be brought up by private members unless they were also members of the government. The government had to father all amendments to the Indian Act or special provisions for Indians. This format, Scott pointed out, provided a valuable safeguard against hasty Indian legislation.[57]

Legislative process in the United States led to a situation that could not have arisen in the Dominion. In at least one instance, the commissioner of Indian affairs was caught unaware that a certain Indian bill had been introduced in Congress. In addition, western senators enjoyed substantial influence in the formulation of Indian policy, a situation that had no equivalent in the Canadian experience.[58]

Not only the legislative process, but the entire history of Canadian westward expansion departed at several points from the American situation. Most significantly, the Canadian West experienced a slower rate of settlement and economic growth than the United States. When the Hudson's Bay Company transferred its vast possessions to the Dominion in 1870, Canada acquired a territory that was still in its fur-trade stage. The only settlements were those of the Metis and the Half-breeds of southern Manitoba. Large-scale immigration did not enter the prairies until early in the twentieth century; the transcontinental railway that spanned the American West in 1869 did not cross the Canadian prairies until 1885. Some have designated the years between 1870 and 1930 as the beginning and the end of the Canadian West, calculating a five-year lag in economic growth between Montana, Alberta, and Saskatchewan.[59]

After Confederation, the Dominion government continued to rely on Indian policy adopted by the provinces of Canada in 1830. Its tenets resembled American Indian policy in the 1870s, emphasizing the settlement of nomadic Indians on reserves and their eventual transformation into civilized and Christianized British subjects.[60] The transplantation of this program to the prairie West indicated a general satisfaction in Canada with her system of Indian management. Thus, Canada brought to the North West Territories a conviction that her Indian policy followed the correct path. Neither the public nor the officials experienced the sense of failure and frustrated impatience so pervasive among Americans.

However, the first Canadian entrance into the North West Territories proved to be a disaster. Apprehension over changes in administration from the Hudson's Bay Company to the Dominion, and the failure of the latter to quiet the fears of the mixed-blood population, led to the short-lived Red River Rebellion in 1869. Although promising to deal with complaints, the government waited another fifteen years and had to fight the North West Rebellion before realizing that the problems did not go away.

Full-blood as well as mixed-blood Indians felt uneasy about their future. The withdrawal of the Hudson's Bay Company, the establishment of the Dominion, the influx of American whiskey traders into southern Alberta, the disturbances of the Red River Rebellion, and activities of Dominion surveyors all unsettled the Indians, who began to demand that the government make secure their livelihood and lands before settlers arrived. Consequently, between 1871 and 1887 the government concluded seven "numbered treaties" with the Indians of the North West Territories that established a basis for Indian Policy on the prairies.[61]

The first two Canadian treaties signed in 1871 came at the time when Americans were demoting their Indian treaties to the status of "agreements." Although the terms of the Canadian prairie treaties varied, they generally represented formal land cessions in return for reserves, agricultural implements, annual money payments, and sundry supplies. Many of the generous terms in the treaties were inserted at the insistence of the Indians, who wanted to ensure their survival, and were not the product of the governement's largess.[62]

A considerable body of mythology about the Indian treaties developed in Canada and in the United States. The most common myth is that the Americans always violated treaties, finally abolishing them altogether, while in Canada treaties remained in full force and were scrupulously observed. In fact, the Canadian government not only delayed the implementation of western treaties until the early 1880s, but in subsequent years it violated many of the treaties' terms. Indeed, the Crees participated in the 1885 North West Rebellion largely because the government had failed to live up to its treaty promises.[63]

Yet since the government took steps to extinguish aboriginal title, to dispatch the North West Mounted Police, and to survey the land well in advance of settlement, the Dominion avoided bloody, head-on clashes between Indians and newcomers. Moreover, those settlers who arrived in the territories brought with them a tradition of respect for "Queen's law" and a deference to authority, traits that many Americans are proud to note were absent from their frontier population. Conversely, the main problem of the Canadian settlers was that the government in Ottawa paid little attention to their needs and aspirations.[64]

Ottawa paid equally scanty attention to the needs of the Indians. Prime Minister John A. Macdonald, the consummate conservative who headed the DIA for some twenty years, did not pursue an innovative Indian policy in the territories. He preferred to let his deputy superintendent, L. G. Vankoughnet, dictate the direction of Indian policy. Vankoughnet's administration ran largely toward creating greater economy in the Indian service. The most immediate result brought great suffering to plains tribes left unprovided for after the disappearance of the buffalo. Under Clifford Sifton, the minister of the interior between 1896 and 1904, administrative economy rather than practical considerations of local needs continued to guide Indian policy.[65] Indeed, reorganization of the Indian service in Manitoba and the North West Territories in 1897—in the name of economy—became the only notable change in Indian administration since the creation of Canada.

The first serious effort to solve the "Indian problem" in western Canada came after 1904, when Frank Oliver became the new minister of the interior and the Dominion embarked on a promotion of prairie settlement. Two policies issued from the department: to bring about quicker Indian assimilation and to reduce Indian reserves for the benefit of the expected settlers. Assimilation consisted of suppressing "savage" customs and improving Indian education, while the latter policy pressured Indians to consent to the cessions of portions of their reserves. When D. C. Scott became head of the Indian department in 1913, his office received increased funding to bring about Indian assimilation, but Scott's policy resulted in the further segregation of Indians from the remainder of Canadian society.[66]

In sum, even though the United States and Canada adopted a policy of trying to end the Indians' protected status and introduce them into the economic, social and political mainstream, the Dominion, in comparison to the Americans, proceeded at a much slower pace. But caution created its own problems. In fact, protection and advancement, the principles of Canadian Indian administration, proved to be a contradiction. To make the Indians advance, protection had to be reduced; but given the historical development of Dominion's Indian administration, officials were reluctant to take this step. At the end of the second decade of the twentieth century, as Americans clamored for even quicker withdrawal of their federal government from Indian affairs, Canadian officals warned that a greater discretion must be exercised against premature enfranchisement, declaring that "as yet instances of Indian capacity to manage even his personal affairs are rare."[67]

Here lay the dilemmas faced by both countries. Americans opted for the speedy withdrawal of guardianship as the means toward instilling self-reliance in Indians. The result was the disastrous loss of native real estate and the further impoverishment, rather than the independence, of the aboriginal population. Canadians, on the other hand, opted for supervision—in fact, an increase in supervision—in the belief that they were training their wards for independence, while actually allowing them no independence at all.[68] How these philosophies worked out in the management of the Blackfeet reservations is the subject of the discussion that follows.

2

Administering the Reservations

While formulating the general principles of Indian policy was relatively easy, implementing them on reservations proved to be another matter because even the simplest, well-intended plans hatched in Washington or Ottawa sooner or later collided with the environmental and cultural realities of reservation life. In 1880, a Canadian official expressed confidence that day by day the management of Indians in the North West Territories would "be perfected and adapted to the growing exigencies and wants of the native population;"[1] but with each passing year, Indian administration in the United States and Canada failed to meet the needs of reservation Indians. This situation resulted not only from an unrealistic Indian policy, but also from personnel problems and an anachronistic administrative system.

"Upon the qualities of the superintendent and his subordinates depends the success of Indian administration," remarked one American authority on Indian affairs,[2] and many Canadians would have heartily agreed with his assessment. Yet such sentiments concealed the paradoxical position of Indian service employees. The field workers—individuals who worked on the reservations—assumed all the responsibility for implementing Indian department policies, yet they had virtually no say in their formulation. This lack of communication between the field service and headquarters, or the inside service—those Indian department officials in Washington or Ottawa—created a problem endemic to Indian administration in both countries.

In the United States, especially, those individuals who denounced Indian agents for corruption or incompetence seldom had any idea of the realities of everyday life at an Indian agency. The agent and his family, as well as other employees, often lived in trying conditions, and were not only underpaid and understaffed but poorly housed with access to few of life's amenities. As a rule, the Indian agent and agency employees constituted a world largely unto themselves. Often isolated from other whites or at odds with white neighbors, the agency could turn into a place rife with petty jealousies, incompetence, despotism, drunkenness, and graft—while simultaneously expressing dedication and genuine concern for the Indians' welfare.[3] Surrounded by charges whose behavior could range from uncooperative to downright dangerous, the Indian agent's duty was to carry out the policies of his government, even if the enforcement of rules and regulations proved to be at best, ill advised or, at worst, suicidal. In sum, the agent was expected to transform almost single-handedly a people's entire culture—while showing annual savings in agency expenditures.

Although American "reservation policy" had been officially inaugurated in 1870, ten years later this plan still had not made a noticeable impact upon the American branch of the Blackfoot Confederacy. The South Peigans shared the 26-million-acre Great Northern Reservation with the Gros Ventre and the River Crows, and by 1880 these tribes showed virtually no progress toward becoming "civilized." Indian agents provided only tenuous supervision, which consisted of handing out treaty issue and admonishing the tribes to end their raids upon each other. The Blackfeet agent reported in 1880 that he could not offer any accurate census of his Indians because he could not persuade all of the bands to come to the agency at one time. He estimated that there were 7,500 Indians scattered in their winter camps located some two to three hundred miles from the agency.[4]

The three groups of the Blackfoot Confederacy resided for most of the year in British territory, but they crossed to the American side to hunt buffalo and to raid horses from their tribal enemies as well as American settlers. The conclusion of Treaty 7 made no impact upon the lives of the Indians because the Canadian government was not anxious to finance the measures necessary to turn the nomads into sedentary agriculturalists. Only the sudden disappearance of the buffalo forced the Blackfoot confederates to settle on their respective reserves. As one authority noted, the Blackfeet remained buffalo Indians until there were no more buffalo.[5]

When the Dominion acquired the North West Territories, the presence of the aboriginal population was not of uppermost concern to the government. In order to save expenditures, the government preferred to let the Indians fend for themselves in areas not threatened with immediate settlement. For a number of years, officials expected to follow a policy of "gradualism." Under this plan, the Indians would continue to live by hunting while slowly being introduced to farming. This system would allow the Indians to be weaned from the nomadic life without placing on the government the entire burden for their support.[6] This plan unfortunately backfired, and two years after the conclusion of the Blackfoot Treaty, several thousand Indians were starving in Ottawa.

The disappearance of the Blackfoot food source helped in precipitating the first instance of simultaneous failure by the Indian administrations in both countries. The American failure was perhaps more serious because the United States, unlike Canada, already had in place officials to administer relief. In contrast, in Canada, there were almost no local Indian department personnel; the North West Mounted Police was the only organization available to disburse assistance.

Several reasons existed for such conditions in the North West Territories. When the government established a ministry of the interior in 1873, its head, David Mills, knew next to nothing about the Indian groups or their locations throughout this vast area. To look after the Indians, the government created two Boards of Indian Commissioners, one for British Columbia and one for Manitoba. Three years later, four superintendencies replaced these boards. The largest, the North West Superintendency, covered Treaties 4, 6, and 7—an area of some 206,000 square miles. The government envisioned that eventually one or two agents in each superintendency would be able to issue annuities, to teach farming, and to exert moral influence over the Indians.[7] If anything, this plan indicated the general ignorance of officials regarding the manpower and financial commitment necessary to administer Indian affairs in the West.

Part of the problem centered in Ottawa, where the deputy superintendent Vankoughnet held the reins of power. To Vankoughnet, Indian affairs was primarily a matter of administrative exactness, and like most Victorian civil servants, he was obsessed with detail and control. Since the highest official of the department did not believe in flexibility or local initiative in policy matters, the government responded to the needs of North West Indian administration with glacial speed.[8] In the meantime, the needs of the western Indians became desperate.

By the mid-1870s, warnings circulated in Canada about the possible extinction of the buffalo, and at about the same time, that probability was brought to the attention of the American authorities. Despite these warnings from local officials, however, neither government prepared contingency measures. Furthermore, the influx of some two thousand Sioux in 1877 further aggravated the Canadian situation. The newcomers not only put a strain on limited food source; they also raised fears of an intertribal war between Canadian and American Indians over the diminishing food supply. In Montana, the situation grew equally grim because the American government had been issuing only part rations to the South Peigans, forcing them to supplement their food by hunting.[9] Those Blackfoot who remained on the Canadian side, however, did not even have the inadequate government supplies to fall back on when hunting failed.

Nothing but bad luck dogged the Canadian Indians after signing Treaty 7. The Blackfoot Treaty assigned one square mile of land to each five people, giving to the Blackfoot, Bloods, and the Sarcee a strip of land four hundred by two hundred miles along the Bow river, a country more suited to hunting than to farming.[10] Subsequently, the Bloods requested a separate reserve, while the North Peigans received their reserve on the Old Man River, but by the spring of 1879 Canadian Indians were in desperate straits. Not only had the buffalo nearly vanished, but other game also had begun to disappear.

Father Constantine Scollen, an Oblate missionary who had known the Blackfoot for sixteen years, described the dreadful situation among the Blackfoot in a scathing eleven-page letter to the assistant commissioner of the North West Mounted Police at Fort Walsh:

> I [have] seen a Blackfoot brave withdraw from his lodge that he might not listen to his crying children when he had not meat to give them!
> . . . Many sustained life by eating the flesh of poisoned wolves, some have lived on dogs, and I have known others to live several days on nothing else but old bones which they gathered and broke up, wherewith to make a kind of soup.[11]

By summer only the Blackfoot remained on Canadian territory; the Bloods and Peigans had left for Montana to hunt the scattered buffalo, while starvation also stalked the Gros Ventres, the Stoneys, and the Sarcee. Powerless to help, officials in Winnipeg could only issue ammunition to the Indians and encourage them to move south to follow the retreating buffalo.[12]

Under these conditions, the Canadian government set out to establish an administrative system for the native people of the territories. The first step was to appoint an Indian commissioner of the North West territories, but the situation there became so tense that several Hudson's Bay Company men, experienced in dealing with Indians, rejected government offers to assume the new post. Finally, Macdonald managed to persuade Edgar L. Dewdney, a member of Parliament from British Columbia and an engineer by training, to accept the position. Macdonald expressed his faith in Dewdney's abilities to rectify the situation in the territories by stating that Dewdney possessed experience with Indians in British Columbia. After all, Macdonald stated, "Indians are all alike."[13]

Upon Dewdney's shoulders fell the responsibility of appeasing discontented Indians, for overseeing Indian agencies in Treaties 4, 6, and

7, and for looking after the Manitoba and Keewatin superintendencies, an area stretching from the western boundary of Ontario to the Rocky Mountains.[14] To prevent a recurrence of starvation and to provide for the future subsistence of the Indians, the government instructed Dewdney to encourage them "by every possible means to engage in the agricultural cultivation of the soil and the raising of cattle." Dewdney was to oversee the establishment and operation of fifteen farming agencies supervised by farming instructors, with four for the Blackfoot nation located near Fort Macleod; in addition, he was charged with making provisions for the distribution of cattle among the bands. The government warned Dewdney to exercise the "strictest possible economy"[15] in carrying out his instructions. This letter thus established the basis of Canadian Indian policy in the North West Territories, whose principal objective was to make the Indians self-supporting. Significantly, this decision came about not as the result of prolonged agitation for better treatment of the Indians, but rather as an almost instant solution to a crisis.

Unfortunately, the appointment of an Indian commissioner did not end the crisis. Dewdney met with the discouraged Indians at Blackfoot Crossing, and issued emergency supplies that were exhausted by September. He then issued additional supplies to enable the Indians to pursue buffalo across the border, "thus making a saving," as Dewdney explained later, "of two years rations to the government." Dewdney's action met with the complete approval of the parsimonious DIA. The deputy superintendent justified the measure by stating that if these Indians were forced to stay on the reserves "we should be compelled to feed them and get nothing in return."[16]

Chief Crowfoot and his Blackfoot band had no choice but to cross the "medicine line" to join other Canadian and American Indians in their search for the dwindling buffalo. As if survival were not precarious enough, whiskey traders reappeared and the chiefs, including Crowfoot, watched helplessly as discipline in the camps deteriorated.[17]

Canadian Indians who were surviving in Montana on the last of the buffalo and by killing cattle had realized by 1881 that the buffalo were gone. Starving and sick, they began to return to Canada, traveling largely on foot, having lost their ponies to raiders and whiskey traders. It is estimated that between 1879 and 1881 at least a thousand Canadian Blackfeet died.[18] With the disappearance of the buffalo, the entire confederacy became dependent on the largess of the Canadian and American governments. Tragically for the Indians, this dependence coincided with one of the government's periodic efforts in encouraging austerity in the Indian service, which made the job of Indian agents in both countries extremely difficult.

Until 1880, since the Indians of Treaty 7 had no agent assigned to them, the North West Mounted Police issued treaty payments. In that year, following a barrage of reports of the wretched conditions in Treaty 7, the government sent out its first Indian agent, Norman T. Macleod, the brother of Colonel James F. Macleod, the commissioner of the police. Most of the Blackfoot bands had not yet returned from Montana, but by the spring of 1881 the population swelled within ten days from 750 to 1,500. While battling attempts in Ottawa to reduce the already thinning rations, Norman Macleod devoted most of his time to securing food for the nearly 7,000 Indians who ultimately descended on Treaty 7.[19]

Meanwhile, Indian administration in the United States also failed to deal with the rapidly unfolding crisis. Even though Indian agents had been assigned since 1855 to those Peigans remaining on American soil, their presence proved to be of little help to the starving natives. While Indian agents unquestionably played an important role in the success or failure of Indian policy, often they as well as the Indians became victims of circumstances beyond their control. The experience of "Major" John Young, the man who served as Blackfeet agent during the transition period from hunting to a sedentary existence, epitomized many of the problems faced by American Indian agents. Indeed, his administration could serve as a case study of the gap between the theory and the reality of Indian reservation administration in the United States.

Young took over in 1876, remaining at the agency for eight years, an unusual length of service for an Indian bureau official, especially a Blackfeet agent. Young, apparently infirm and elderly, was appointed by the Methodist Episcopal church during the waning days of the "Peace Policy." Evidently, congeniality, tact, and tolerance were not his strong points. Whatever his personal shortcomings, however, he should not be held solely responsible for the tragedy that befell the Peigans in the year 1883–84.[20] For eight years, the agent corresponded with Washington officials about the need to provide the Blackfeet with sufficient sustenance, but officials never indicated that they paid the slightest attention to his field reports. As a result, some six hundred Blackfeet starved, and the career of agent Young ended with his reputation forever tainted by charges of corruption and incompetence.

On 15 December 1876, Young arrived at the agency at Badger Creek, some 90 miles from the telegraph and post office at Fort Shaw, and 140 miles from Fort Benton. He was either accompanied or later joined by his two daughters, who became agency school teachers, and by his son, who worked as a part-time clerk. The Young family did not find welcoming accommodations. The agent wrote to the commissioner that the agency buildings were in unfinished condition, devoid of any amenities of civilization, and that agency employees and their wives and children "had to go to the *bush* through the snow for the natural necessities."[21] Consequently, Young's first official duty seems to have been to build a latrine. However, the agent was not wasting time that he should have devoted to the Indians. His charges—except the very young, the sick, and the very old—were away on a buffalo hunt. Two years later, Young still had not met all of the Peigans. They lived scattered over the large reservation, many of them hunting outside its boundaries. When inquiries came about the number of Indians at his agency, Young responded that he estimated their number at 7,500; he explained that no accurate census was possible since some bands never came to the agency.[22]

Even though the American public and Indian bureau officials expected Indian agents to impart the principles of civilization to the "savages," many agents, including Young, were forced to devote most of their time to more basic concerns such as keeping the Indians alive. Even though the bureau issued rations of bacon, beef, flour, rice, hard bread, sugar, and coffee at the Blackfeet agency, the buffalo remained the mainstay of the Blackfeet diet because these rations were inadequate. Young was aware that by the late 1870s the Indians had begun to experience difficulty in preparing sufficient stores of buffalo meat, and in his annual estimate for the year 1879–80 he asked the bureau to purchase all of the supplies he requested since the Blackfeet soon would be dependent on these rations.[23] But the bureau ignored his requests.

In fact, the correspondence between the agent and the BIA reveals the breadth of the communication gap between field workers and headquarters. On 14 January 1880, for instance, Young received a letter asking why his Indians were not confined to the reservation. This inquiry came after Young had spent the past three years in explaining that inadequate rations made the Blackfeet partly dependent on hunting off the reservation. Young explained that if the Blackfeet were confined to the reservation the government would have to provide more funds, and with the present appropriations he could not feed the entire camp for more than two months.[24]

In June, the commissioner asked Young to report on rumors of unrest at the agency. The commissioner had obviously ignored Young's reports, filed in April and May, about the increasingly tense situation at the agency. Young explained that the army had forcibly removed the Blackfeet to the reservation, where they were confined for the first time. Needless to say, the Indians did not like it. Young warriors who had never experienced any restraint complained the loudest. The agent had to contend with their sulky manners, insubordinate language, and insolent demands for rations. "Knowing but one person responsible for their management,"

Young explained, "they not unnaturally connected me with their forced removal, and its attendant troubles and losses." Young thought that increasing the rations would improve their disposition immensely.[25]

In addition to the perennial running battle with the distant bureaucracy, Young confronted local problems as well. His situation was typical of that faced by many other American Indian agents who found themselves under fire from a rapacious local population. Young's trouble began in 1881, when Montana cattlemen, through their territorial representative Martin Maginnis, agitated for the permanent confinement of the Blackfeet to their reservation.[26] Although under the treaty of 1855, the Blackfeet possessed the right to hunt on the ceded territory for ninety-nine years, by the early 1880s they began to clash with the cattlemen who invaded the area. To feed themselves, many Peigans were forced to kill cattle roaming over the former buffalo range, and these killings infuriated the ranchers who, in turn, blamed the agent for handing out inadequate rations. The misfortune of the Blackfeet provided a justification for the removal of agent Young and the reduction of the reservation.

In April 1883, the grand jury of Choteau County investigated Indian cattle depredations, and concluded that "the greater part of these depredations [were] chargeable directly to the incompetency of Major John Young." Ample testimony convinced the jury that nearly all of the Indians were starving, with their allowances consisting of only ten ounces of meat per week. The jury charged that the agent had willfully misrepresented reservation conditions to Washington, and Young was accused of "keeping a harem of young Indian girls." The jurors concluded that nothing "would tend more to the peace of this country, the safety of property, and welfare and happiness of these Indians, than his removal at once."[27]

Young was understandably outraged by these charges, which he labeled as gross libel—except for those findings concerning insufficient rations. Young demanded an independent investigation of his conduct to clear his reputation, and he explained the reasons for the jury's findings: "I [had] aroused the animosity of the Cattle Association by my opposition to the Bill for taking the better part of this reservation from the Indians under my care." Young contended that since this association dominated the grand jury, he was hardly surprised that it desired his removal.[28]

Young correctly suspected selfish motives behind these attacks, for in June a delegation from Washington, headed by Martin Maginnis, arrived to investigate the northern reservations and to negotiate for their reduction. The delegation visited the Blackfeet reservation in September. After a brief stay, its members concluded that the Blackfeet were in a wretched condition and their future was almost hopeless, but they exonerated agent

Young. Moreover, the delegation urged that the Department of the Interior and Congress take urgent measures to help the Peigans. It pointed out that the Peigans were quite willing to part with a portion of the reservation in exchange for supplies, implements, houses, and cattle.[29] This dismal situation ultimately paved the way for the breakup of the Great Northern Reservation in 1888.

In the summer of 1883, Young received an inkling of what lay ahead for him and "his" Indians. Rations of flour and bacon, five hundred head of stock cattle, and forty-five beef steers arrived at the agency, amounting to supplies that would keep the Indians from starving for only a short time. After the first of July, local newspapers reported, the Blackfeet would have "absolutely nothing to eat." Newspapers noted that for some reason the government would not provide supplies on time, and because of this terrible blunder, three thousand starving Indians would be turned loose in the countryside.[30]

Shortly after the visit from the Maginnis delegation, agent Young tendered his resignation, effective upon the arrival of his successor. Ironically, this decision confined Young to the reservation during the winter of 1883–84, which became known among the Blackfeet as the "starvation winter." Paltry rations began to run out in the fall, and for most of the winter the agent flooded the commissioner, the army, and local merchants with requests for supplies. While Young was appealing for help, government auditors perused his accounts, taking exceptions to such issues as eight pounds of oatmeal until proper vouchers were presented.[31]

In fact, during Young's eight years as agent, the bulk of correspondence from Washington castigated him for improperly filled vouchers, while reports of starving Blackfeet and Young's frantic efforts to alleviate their suffering received only sporadic attention. Admittedly, accounting was not Young's strong suit, but some of the accounting practices established by the BIA were unrealistic. For example "Circular 26" required each Indian family head to receive an explanation of each issue and to sign a receipt. The overworked agency clerk replied with a seven-page letter explaining why he could not comply with these regulations: "The signing of a Voucher (three times) by an Indian while apparently a very simple thing, is practically not so simple." The clerk stated that none of the Peigans could read or write, and given 752 heads of families, it would have been impossible to complete the issue in one day. Moreover, all agency employees would be required to act as issuers and witnesses.[32]

Although Young became the villain to many observers, the blame for the misfortune of the Blackfeet should have been placed on the shoulders of E. John Ellis, the chairman of the House Subcommittee on Indian Affairs. For a year, he callously refused to release already approved appropriations, despite pleas from the Indian Rights Association.[33] The bureau was equally guilty of extreme negligence when it ignored reports from the agent, the military, and the Indian Rights Association and did nothing to release the funds. Clearly, bureaucratic incompetence at the highest levels was responsible for the Blackfeet starvation.

After Young's departure, conditions on the reservation remained serious. The new agent, R. N. Allen, assumed his office in April 1884, walking into a disaster in progress. He wrote to the commissioner that conditions at the agency were "exceedingly unpleasant." He insisted that Congress must quickly increase appropriations for the Blackfeet, "else the consequences will be such as should make the people of this nation blush with shame."[34]

By July, Allen began killing the agency herd to provide food for the Indians. "You may rest assured," he wrote defiantly to the commander at Fort Shaw, "that I will not be governed by regulations in this matter, but by the exigencies of the time." By August, stories of the starving condition of the Blackfeet reached the commissioner, who sent agent Allen a telegram "asking for the facts." Allen did not mince words: "In May and June there were times when they stripped the trees and ate the inner bark to keep their souls and bodies together and all the time they were begging for food. Does that look as though they were in a starving condition?"[35] Although Congress approved increased appropriations for the following year, the new agent found his position so frustrating that he resigned after two years. Allen's resignation ushered in a pattern of short tenures for a bevy of succeeding Blackfeet agents.

While the Blackfeet of Montana starved during the winter of 1883–84 because of government inattention, north of the line the Canadian government followed a virtually identical path that ended in the Riel Rebellion a year later. At first, the entire responsibility for Treaty 7 Indians fell on Norman Macleod, while farming instructors served as acting agents at the Peigan and Blood reserves. These men were overworked and underpaid. The Blood agent was paid thirty-five dollars a month, and supervised 3,146 Indians with a staff of six men, one interpreter, and one cook.[36] When Macleod resigned in 1882, Cecil E. Denny, an ex-Mountie, replaced Macleod, and the area was divided into two sections. William B. Pocklington, another former policeman, became subagent at the Blackfoot reserve.

In addition to appointing agents, the government also hired farming instructors to teach agriculture to the Indians. Ottawa expected these men to persuade young Indians and mixed-bloods to learn to break up land; to sow, reap, and thresh; and to build houses, care for livestock, and use farm implements. As soon as the instructors arrived in Treaty 7, they were asked to select a site for the future model farms, to begin to break up land, and to build residences for themselves and barns and stalls for cattle and horses.[37]

Since the number of qualified white candidates in the North West Territories was negligible, Indian department personnel came from eastern provinces, especially Ontario. In 1879, Minister of the Interior J. C. Dennis asked Ontario's members of Parliament to submit the names of young men qualified to become farming instructors in the territories.

While perfectly logical to Ottawa, the plan contained fatal flaws when applied to the North West Territories. Agents and farming instructors were put in charge of far too large an area to be able to carry out their duties effectively. No successful farmer would leave Ontario to work for low pay, living in isolation from whites and among Indians who were, for all intents and purposes, still "savages." Consequently, these positions attracted men who hoped to improve their situation in the West, men who were often failures back home.[39] Small wonder that the gap between the expectations of the Indian department and the reality of reserve life proved considerable, generating frustrations and bickering over reserve administration.

Prior to the arrival of C. E. Denny, turmoil wracked the Blackfoot. Not only did the deparmtent issue paltry rations, but agency employees demonstrated little tact in dealing with people who had lost everything but their pride. As winter approached, continuous parsimony and the suspicion that they were being cheated of their rations kept the Blackfoot agitated, and incidents of Indian insubordination mounted. Black Soldiers, a Blackfoot warrior society, walked around the agency, threatening employees and taking pot shots at them; and an attempt to arrest one Blackfoot nearly caused a war.[40]

Reports of the tense situation prompted commissioner Dewdney to investigate. He replaced the staff with the two ex-policemen, Denny and Pocklington. Denny immediately took steps to remedy the situation by increasing rations and persuading the Indians to plant gardens and build houses to replace their worn-out teepees.[41] Looking after Indians in Treaty 7 would have been easier if Denny had not been forced to contend with the Indian department bureaucracy. For two years, the agency administration experienced periodic bouts with chaos, as Denny struggled with his superior, Indian inspector Thomas P. Wadsworth. Wadsworth's appointment as the inspector of Indian agencies was his first appointment in the civil service,[42] and his management style immediately clashed with Denny's. Wadsworth insisted on administration by the book, while Denny opted for a more casual approach, partly as a result of his inclination and partly because of his experience with Blackfoot people who were genuinely fond of the ex-policeman.

Official correspondence attributed differences between Denny and Wadsworth to a clash over prerogatives. The conflict originated in a dispute over who would issue orders to the farming instructors. When Wadsworth gave one of the instructors control over the Indians of Blackfoot Crossing, Denny complained that the new appointee had never seen an Indian before his arrival, and that the Blackfoot were not the easiest Indians to manage.[43]

Denny warned that the constant changes in personnel upset the Indians, and if the department persisted in forcing upon him a young and inexperienced staff, trouble would result. Wadsworth responded with a litany of complaints of his own, stating that "the man to be agent in this treaty should be calm, sober in spirit, far-seeing man, of business training and methodical habits, strictly temperate, and good morals—not one of the above qualities has Mr. Denny." Denny's alleged intemperance particularly outraged Wadsworth's Victorian sensibilities; he complained that the liquor on Denny's breath could knock down a horse.[44]

While the two officials sparred, Vankoughnet implemented his policy of greater economy in Ottawa. In November 1883, a telegram from headquarters instructed the agents in Treaty 7 to dispense with the services of all farm hands except farming instructors, ration issuers, interpreters, and cooks. Denny joined the chorus of protest from the staff of other agencies. Staff reductions played havoc with reservation administration, Denny complained; he had no interpreter at the Peigan reserve, while more staff was allowed for the Blackfoot reserve than for the Blood's, even though the latter was a much larger reserve. The necessity to take on both Wadsworth and Vankoughnet proved to be the last straw for Denny, and he handed in his resignation.[45]

At first glance, Canadian Indian administration would appear to have been more responsive than the American to complaints of this type. For example, Canadian Indian agents could appeal to the commissioner's office, situated in Regina, while American agents had to wait until Washington decided to act. In reality, however, the Canadian administrative hierarchy worked far less efficiently because the headquarters, or more specifically, its acting head, refused to allow any substantial authority to devolve to the reserve level.

Indeed, general secretiveness shrouded the proceedings of the Canadian Indian service. For instance, in 1884 Vankoughnet issued a stringent order to department employees stating that they could not discuss any departmental business with outsiders unless specifically authorized by the head. The following year, the order was reissued with the threat that those allowing "leaks" to the press would be summarily dismissed. This memorandum resurfaced periodically thereafter in various forms.[46]

Thus, in Canada the Indian department worked in isolation from public scrutiny, which would have been unthinkable in the United States. But secretiveness did not ensure trouble-free Indian administration. Part of the reason stemmed from the relationship between the top three officials.

Commissioner Dewdney remained subordinate to the "insiders" in Ottawa, namely, to the officious Vankoughnet. Their superior was John A. Macdonald, and the two men served the prime minister with blind loyalty. When disagreement arose between the commissioner and the deputy superintendent, each man appealed to Macdonald over the head of the other, while both refrained from criticizing the policies of the Macdonald government. This unwillingness to attack the root of the problem led to a situation in which the government, despite reports to the contrary, could pursue a penny-pinching policy that ignited the Riel Rebellion.[47]

Even though Vankoughnet visited several reserves in the North West Territories in 1883, his ability to fathom the difficulties involved in transforming plains warriors into British farmers proved to be beyond his understanding. After his return to Ottawa, Vankoughnet wrote to Denny instructing him to cease the "irrational custom" of giving Indians feasts and presents whenever officials visited them. Now that the treaties were concluded, Vankoughnet maintained, such extravagance was not necessary. In reply, Dewdney defended the practice, insisting that gifts symbolized an age-old custom of goodwill between white men and the Indians. He told Vankoughnet, "The expense to the Government that is entailed through the gift of these presents is trivial when compared with the good feeling they tend to engender."[48]

Nevertheless, Vankoughnet insisted on economy, and his disregard for reports from his field officials contributed to the second Riel uprising. Two months before the outbreak, Dewdney sent a long memorandum to Macdonald, complaining about the deputy superintendent's inflexibility in policy matters. "It cannot be denied," Dewdney acknowledged, "that general policy as regards Indian affairs should emanate from the Government itself, but owing to the distances of the seat of Government and the field of operation it becomes imperative that the details of such policy [should] be carried out by a responsible head in the country." Once officials got to know the Indians, Dewdney wrote, many "have had to change entirely the ideas first formed and act in some instances directly opposite the course first laid out." The deputy superintendent, Dewdney continued, had no idea of the rapid changes taking place in the North West Territories and his decisions could easily lead to trouble. Dewdney explained that he would follow general regulations, but would leave the final decisions up to individual agents. He was convinced that things would run more smoothly if Macdonald did not "bind too tightly the hands of the agents or the inspectors."[49]

Fortunately for the Canadian government, the Blackfoot Confederacy, the most powerful group of western Indians, rejected Cree overtures to join them in a general Indian uprising; but it took considerable effort on the part of the Blood, Peigan, and Blackfoot chiefs to restrain their young men. The situation was especially trying for Crowfoot, since Poundmaker, his adopted son and Cree chief, joined the rebels. In an effort to forestall trouble from the confederacy, Dewdney, at Crowfoot's request, reappointed Cecil Denny as Indian agent in Treaty 7. Denny was authorized to increase rations for the three bands, and this act removed some of the most immediate causes of complaint. Nevertheless, even after the rebellion was suppressed, rumors circulated for much of the summer about an imminent uprising of the Blackfoot nation.[50]

After the rebellion, a blistering attack in Parliament on Indian administration under the Conservatives presented one of the rare instances of public scrutiny of the Indian department. Charges of mismanagement in the western agencies sounded identical to those hurled at the Indian bureau in the United States. In Canada, however, the shock of the revolt was more profound because Canadians believed that they managed the Indians much better than the Americans.

The Liberal party charged the Conservatives with causing the rebellion by appointing officials who were dishonest, careless, and immoral. The Liberals claimed that the government had broken faith with the Indians and violated the treaties; it had issued spoiled rations while refusing to investigate complaints; and for the last six years, it had pursued a policy of submission by starvation. One opposition critic declared, "Not only have the Indians . . . been robbed, defrauded and swindled, frozen to death and starved to death, but we at the same time expected them to be quiet, peaceful, submissive, faithful and loyal subjects of the Queen."[51]

Prime Minister Macdonald was absent during the question period, and his party made a lame defense of its Indian policy. The Liberal party carried the day, pointing out the callous attitude of the prime minister in repeating his past statements. Macdonald had allegedly stated that the issuance of bad rations could not be considered a fraud on the Indians "because they have no right to that food. They are simply living on the benevolence and charity of the Canadian Parliament, and as the old adage says, beggars should not be choosers."[52]

In spite of the flurry of denunciations in Parliament, the government weathered the episode without losing an election. While the rebellion forced some action to be taken to deal with the problem of the mixed-bloods, resulting in the establishment of the Half-Breed Commission, the

Indian administration soon resumed its former direction. By the following year, even settlers had forgotten about the Indians and the Metis. As
the nineteenth century drew to a close, the Indian department became,
as one historian put it, more and more insulated from reality in its concern for bureaucratic efficiency and economy.[53]

Across the border in Montana, and some ten years after the mass starvation of the Blackfeet, Washington officials displayed no more sensitivity to the needs of the Indians than their Canadian counterparts.
Policymakers essentially followed their own path, regardless of reports
from the agencies. Not all Indian agents accepted this situation, however. "Major" George Steell, who served as Blackfeet agent from 1890 to
1893 and from 1895 to 1897, was one of these men. He had a long association with the Blackfeet as a trader, had married an Indian woman, and
was an upstanding Republican. The Blackfeet called him "Sleeping Thun-
der" because of the volatile temper that dwelled under his calm exterior.
Steell's original appointment received the support of notable personages,
but he also became the target of political machinations that ended his
first term as agent.[54]

In 1892, when the bureau called upon Steell to account by whose authority he had exhausted rations intended for the entire year, Steell replied
acidly that the government's decision to reduce rations had been ill-advised
because if the Indians were half-starving they could not be expected to
work. Steell grew particularly infuriated by the propensity of officials to
disregard his reports. At one time, Steell accompanied his annual estimate of expenditures with these words: "It seems to me that my judgement as to what these Indians require should receive proper consideration,
otherwise I see no reason why the Department should not prepare the
estimate instead of having me do so."[55] Of course, the bureau ignored
Steell's outbursts, and the infuriated agent resigned.

Steell's replacement, Captain L. W. Cooke, approached his work like
an army commander, only to be reminded repeatedly that he was not in
charge. When the bureau returned his estimate of agency expenditures
marked "exhorbitant [sic]," Cooke fumed that during thirty years of preparing estimates for the army, no one had ever called him "exhorbitant!"
[sic] Cooke continued to pester the bureau, demanding not only increased
expenditures for the Indians, but also decent accommodations for government employees. He wrote to the bureau at one point: "This place
[the agency] defies my powers of description. The illustrations appear-
ing in the *Century Magazine* three or four years ago of a Siberian prison
and stockade fittingly portray the situation."[56] Not surprisingly, Cooke
lasted only two years at his position.

Not only did the agents skirmish with the Indian office; they also grappled with miscellaneous aggravations that accompanied the job. Most employees' incomes were far too low for the area they had to live in, ranging in 1895 from 1,200 dollars per year for a clerk to 360 dollars for an assistant farmer. Small wonder that some employees supplemented their income by other means, most of them illegal. One agent reported that he had to discharge a blacksmith and a carpenter, each earning 900 dollars annually, when he discovered they were working for white settlers and using government supplies. A few years later, an agency farmer decided to go into the cattle business, using cattle illegally purchased from the Indians.[57]

Often, steps taken against employees made the agent a target of revenge. In 1909, agent Clarence A. Churchill tangled with two agency physicians who were not only drunks, but also brutal to their patients. The two started a petition against the agent among the white citizens of Browning, the agency town, accusing him of improper advances toward the wife of one of the men. Thank God, the agent wrote, he was leaving the agency anyway.[58]

The administration of Indian reserves in the North West Territories was also affected by the gap between local needs and federal policy. To make matters worse, the Canadian government believed that no problems existed. Two years after the short-lived Riel rebellion, the government declared that the nature of the business transacted by the Indian department had changed materially, and during the past three years, various troublesome questions and complications had been largely solved and "the principal work of the Department is of a routine description."[59]

The only significant change in Canadian Indian administration came in 1897 with the reorganization of the Indian service in the North West Territories. Clifford Sifton, the new minister of the interior, pressed for the change in order to reverse what he perceived as the extravagance of the previous Tory administration. In the Indian department, budget cuts were aimed at Indian administration in the territories, since these expenditures consumed three-quarters of the total budget, even though western Indians comprised only one-quarter of the total Indian population.[60]

In the name of efficiency and economy, the department moved the office of the commissioner of Indian affairs for the North West Territories from Regina to Winnipeg, and reduced its staff and workload drastically. The department believed that these changes would in no way interfere with the administration of Indian affiars because the commissioner had no powers beyond those delegated by Ottawa. Ottawa officials thought that the western office represented merely a duplication of work. After reorganization, all routine business of agency and Indian superintendencies would be handled in Ottawa. Ottawa officials explained archly that they "should not be subject to the judgement of an outside office as to what matters should be worthy of attention by the Department."[61]

To avoid the problem of withdrawing all close supervision, the government changed the commisioner's office to an inspectorate, and revamped the system of reserve inspections. The North West Territories were divided into three districts—Battleford, Qu'Appelle, and Calgary—with each under one inspector. The Calgary district included the three Blackfoot reserves under inspector T. P. Wadsworth, agent Denny's old nemesis. Changes also included the dismissal of agency clerks as well as a decrease in salaries that the department considered "unnecessarily high," but which produced an annual saving of 27,000 dollars.[62]

Although officials assured the government that the commissioner had not been "denuded" of his powers, the changes were disastrous. The commissioner occupied an important position because he was the closest high official to whom agents could turn for advice in situations requiring immediate attention. This post became especially significant in Indian administration because officials in Ottawa showed little understanding of the everyday needs of reserve administration. For example, the deputy superintendent informed the agents and the commissioner in 1895 that he found their inquiries annoying. The deputy wrote that once the department policy had been plainly enunciated, agents should appeal to him only as the last resort. If the department was to retain influence on the reserves, he said, "it ought to be kept out of the Indians' sight as much as possible, for . . . familiarity . . . tends to breed contempt, and these constant appeals to the Department weaken its authority."[63]

Without doubt, administration of all of the Blackfoot reserves suffered from the reduction in staff and in salaries. Despite assurance that inspectors would provide the necessary local supervision, the inspections proved woefully inadequate. Belatedly, the department admitted that Treaty 7 had not been properly inspected. The Blood reserve had no inspection for two years and four months, the Blackfoot had none for three years, and no one visited the Peigans for two and a half years; but the department considered as desirable an inspection every six months.[64]

Meanwhile, western field officials protested loudly against the centralization brought about by the changes made in 1897. Jason McKenna, the assistant Indian commissioner, asked the department to restore the commissioner's former autonomy, which "relieved the headquarters of a mass of work that he was in a better position to deal with owing to local knowledge; and in doing so, left the Department more time for the consideration and decision of large questions of policy." "It is a grave mistake," McKenna continued, "to suppose that Indians have progressed so far that local control can be lessened and shortly dispensed with entirely."

Such, he insisted, had been the problem in the United States, where he thought western reservations suffered from "undue centralization" in Washington. McKenna urged the Canadians to learn from the mistakes of their neighbors.[65]

Complaints such as those of the assistant commissioner created a brief flurry of investigations into the effectiveness of the reorganization. D. C. Scott, then the chief accountant, assured the deputy superintendent that the changes had not affected the primary goal of the department—to make the Indians self-supporting. Replying to McKenna's call for more power at local levels, Scott stated that the headquarters "should not be subject to the judgement of an outside office as to what matters should be worthy of the attention of the Department." "I hope," Scott concluded, "in a few years to know that Ottawa has been established as the point from which all action is taken, and to which all officers report."[66]

Despite assurances from headquarters, the new commissioner at Winnipeg, David Laird, a man with long experience in government service, felt "denuded" of authority. He harangued the department for not allowing field officials to inform him about the instructions they received from headquarters. Some agents, claiming they were acting upon headquarters' wishes, refused to answer the commissioner's inquiries about agency matters. As far as Laird was concerned, chaos reigned in the Indian administration of the territories.[67]

Ironically, some American officials became aware of the evils of centralization and made periodic attempts to decentralize. In 1911, commissioner Robert G. Valentine proposed a "Denver Plan," placing the head office of field service in Denver. One chief supervisor would oversee eight subdivisions. Valentine hoped that this reorganization would move bureau services closer to the sites in need. This effort failed, however, because it infringed on the prerogative of the secretary of the interior. Had it been implemented, this system would have gone a long way toward remedying some of the problems entailed in administering western Indian affairs from Washington. Years later, the Meriam Report singled out excessive centralization as a major obstacle to efficiency.[68]

In the meantime, Washington persisted in shackling its field-service employees with rules and regulations. Many of the newly educated Indians complained about the situation. One Blackfeet spokesman said:

A man tied with red tape that required the approval and permission of a $900 clerk 2,700 miles away to write up the authority, could not succeed. A man who has no feeling for the welfare of the charges given him cannot expect to succeed. . . . Waiting for authority, seeds, and tools, and getting them after the season of their use is passed will make a failure of any man in charge of Blackfeet. Some men have failed entirely because of the failure of the Indian Bureau to permit him to do what ought to be done or to exercise his own judgement.[69]

However, in one aspect of Indian administration, Americans proved again more adventurous than Canadians. Prompted by calls for the termination of Indian wardship, some Americans toyed with the idea of allowing Indians a voice in their own government as a way of teaching them civic responsibility. In 1916, a bill was proposed "granting Indians the right to select agents and superintendents." Unfortunately, the bill was narrowly defeated, as was a similar proposal for the recall of superintendents by an Indian band.[70]

Had these proposals carried, the American Indians would have regained significant powers of self-government. However, the implications of giving the Indians veto powers over bureau appointees alarmed many bureaucrats. Canadian officials reacted in an identical fashion to a similar proposal. Despite declarations that the department supported Indian self-government, the minister of the interior, in 1899, resolutely turned down the idea that Indians should have a voice in their own management.[71]

By the turn of the century the centralization of Indian management at headquarters had won the day in both Canada and the United States. This development was partly the result of the introduction into government of new management methods practiced by "modern" businesses. Centralization was deemed to produce uniformity, which, in turn, created efficiency. Unfortunately for reservation administration, this equation proved to be fallacious. Basically, centralization resulted from the fear of bureaucrats, in one part of the service, that they would be eclipsed by another branch. Efforts to do away with the commissioner's office stemmed as much from the desire to save money as from apprehension that the office might act independently of Ottawa. Even while advocating decentralization of the Indian office, American experts on management were aware of the potential jealousies and conflicts between various parts of the service.[72] Clearly, despite all protestations to the contrary, considerations other than efficiency played a role in the administration of Indian affairs.

Such a system produced problems, most of them visible in the day-to-day administration of reservations. Unquestionably, many Indian agents in both countries were incompetent and avaricious.[73] Others proved to have good intentions, but became harried and frustrated by the system they served. Still, there were dedicated men like William B. Pocklington, who served the Bloods from 1884 to 1892. After a visit in 1891 to the reserve, the editor of *The Macleod Gazette* wrote: "Everything that conscientious, hard working men can do is being done to civilize these Indians, and if they don't ultimately succeed, the government must look for fault in their own system, not in the men they employ to carry it out."[74] At the Blackfoot reserve, John H. Gooderham and George H. Gooderham, father and son, chalked up a record fifty-five years of service in the Indian department, most of it with the Blackfoot. On the American side, agents such as George Steell and the much maligned John Young and Arthur E. McFatridge did their best in difficult circumstances.

Despite all well-intended efforts, neither country found the perfect answer to the problem of Indian administration. Canadians managing Indian reserves experienced problems different from those encountered by the Americans. Political appointments of agents did not become as controversial in Canada as in the United States because the Canadians exercised more control over the process. In addition, Canadian Indian department employees enjoyed longer tenure than the American Indian service personnel. Unfortunately, longer tenure also produced inflexibility at the top levels of administration, which proved to be as injurious to the management of Indian reserves as the American custom of revolving door administration.

The largest problem, however, was not personnel, but the system of decision-making. Directives issued from headquarters generally had little relevance to the needs of the Indians or of the field service employees. Both Indian offices essentially shackled their field workers by allowing them to make only perfunctory decisions at the local level. The centralization of power in distant offices all but ensured the failure of most of the plans conceived there. Ironically, although a closer study would reveal that Canada had a firmly centralized Indian administration, Americans persisted in seeing the Canadian administration as more flexible and responsive to local needs.[75]

An inspection in 1919 of the American Blackfeet agency found it to be in a "run-down and neglected condition," and revealed that the tribe had made no progress for several years. The investigators blamed faulty agency administration for the situation. "There had been nine superintendents during a period of thirteen years," the observers pointed out, "and there had been no continuity of purpose or control, the place seemed to have been forgotten by the Indian bureau."[76] The administrative system also failed the Bloods north of the border, who, at about the same time, found themselves in similar conditions. Yet both countries expected their ill-designed administrative systems to bear the responsibility for turning the Indians into self-supporting, educated, Christianized, and civilized individuals. Small wonder that the results were not encouraging, even after forty years of effort.

3

The Search for
Self-Support and the
Development of Dependency

Acquiring western lands, settling the area, and bringing the plains under the plow formed integral parts of the history of the development of the United States and Canada. Native people already occupying the West were forced to accommodate their life style to the new circumstances in order to survive. In light of changing conditions in the Far West, the primary concern of Indian administration in both countries became to teach ex–buffalo hunters an alternate means of self-support; yet, in retrospect, few would argue that under the policies of the respective governments Indian reservations in Canada and the United States became integrated successfully into the general economy.

Some scholars explain the reason for this failure in terms of an exploitive relationship between a mother country and her colonies. In this colonial paradigm, the original possessors of land and its resources became irrelevant because generally they lacked the capital, education, and skills to develop their resources. As a result, inhabitants of such "colonial" enclaves as reservations fell prey to unemployment, underemployment, and poverty with their attendant social problems.[1] Many Indian reservations in Canada and the United States clearly illustrate this pattern of economic and social maladjustment.

The roots of Indian dependency[2] can be traced to the period after the native populations first became entirely dependent upon white society for self-support. An examination of the development of the Blackfoot Confederacy's dependency reveals that a combination of factors—geography and climate as well as profound cultural differences and ill-advised and poorly executed policy—prevented the development of a viable Blackfeet economy.

Teaching the Indians to subsist by "civilized pursuits"—namely, agriculture, and, to a lesser degree, stock raising—became the linchpin of Indian policy in Canada and the United States. Farming was regarded as a civilizing occupation because it required a settled life style, and taught discipline through steady labor, patience, perseverance, and self-reliance. Advocates of the agricultural policy believed that farming would not only provide the native population with its livelihood—and thereby free the nation of the economic burden of feeding and supporting them—but it could facilitate Indian civilization as well. Pursuit of this agrarian ideal continued to dominate the activities of the respective Indian offices well into the twentieth century.[3]

Unfortunately, those who advocated agriculture as the only occupation for the natives gave little attention to the possibility that it might not be suitable for all of them. The Blackfoot Confederacy proved to be one of these tribes. Nomadic warriors and buffalo hunters such as the Blackfeet had no agricultural tradition, and consequently they did not find farming appealing. Their most basic objection was against turning Mother Earth "wrong side up."[4] This perception revealed the cultural chasm between the policymakers and the Indians. Teaching plains tribes farming would involve the transformation of their entire worldview, and not merely instructing them in when and how to plant seeds. However, officials ignored not only these powerful cultural obstacles, but also the geographic or climatic realities of northwestern Indian reservations. This combination of cultural and environmental factors, combined with a bungling administration, almost guaranteed the failure of Indian self-support.

At the core of the repeated failures of Indian economic development lay the inability of most officials to understand that long-term, massive expenditures would be necessary in order to make the Indians eventually self-supporting. On the contrary, the goal of all American and Canadian administrations became the reduction of Indian service expenditures. Indian service officials struggled with an irresolvable dilemma. On one hand, officials agreed that the Indians must receive help if they were to become farmers. On the other hand, officials believed that aid must be withdrawn as soon as possible if the Indians were not to become too dependent on the government. Caught in the middle, the Indians lost out in this struggle between budget and ideology.

The intention of transforming the Blackfeet into farmers had been present since the first official contact between them and the American government. The Treaty of 1855 provided for an expenditure of funds to teach the Indians "agricultural and mechanical pursuits." Subsequent treaties, such as the Treaty of 1868, also encouraged the Blackfeet to farm by promising to supply them with implements, seeds, and the services of farming instructors. Although officials tried as early as 1855 to establish a farm at Sun River for the Blackfeet, this early attempt in convincing the Indians to become farmers proved to be a failure.[5]

The Canadians did not make similar efforts to induce the Blackfeet to take up agriculture until twenty years after the Americans' attempts. In the Treaty of 1877, the government pledged livestock, agricultural implements, and seeds to help the Blackfeet begin farming.[6] As previously discussed, however, Canadians expected the Indians to be weaned gradually from hunting and to turn to the cultivation of soil. Unfortunately, with the sudden demise of the buffalo, officials faced the question of what to do with prairie Indians sooner than Ottawa expected.

Provisions in the American and Canadian treaties with the confederacy reflected the belief that government aid to tribes should be of limited duration. For example, the Treaty of 1855 guaranteed the Blackfeet a period of ten years during which they would receive agricultural instructions. The unratified Treaty of 1865 included an annual payment of fifty thousand dollars for twenty years, for the purchase of stock and agricultural implements. Three years later, provisions in the new treaty indicated the belief of officials that the Blackfeet could become self-supporting in a short period of time. For example, the treaty commissioners optimistically promised the Blackfeet who settled on the reservation rations of one pound of meat and flour per day for four years, "provided the Indians [could] not furnish their own subsistence at an earlier date."[7]

The Canadians proved to be even more naive than the Americans about the ability of the plains Indians to feed themselves. Under the terms of Treaty 7, the Blackfeet received two thousand dollars annually for ammunition, which was commutable to other goods. The treaty also stipulated that payments of farming implements, seeds, and cattle would be issued "once and for all, for the encouragement of the practice of agriculture among the Indians."[8] Thus, even the most optimistic officials realized that while the Indians learned to support themselves the government would have to provide them with food rations, clothing, and other necessities of life. The question remained how long this practice should continue.

The issuance of government rations provided a corollary to the reservation system. Originally conceived as a temporary measure, rations became a symbol of the dependent status of Indians. Tending to confuse cause with effect, officials in both countries attributed the lack of Indian economic progress to the gratuitous issuance of rations. Officials feared—not unjustifiably, in some instances—that the ration system only exacerbated the Indians' dependence. However, when rations were reduced to eliminate this problem, most Indians found themselves in an economically precarious situation. They were off the ration rolls, and therefore in theory, they were self-supporting; but in reality, most were barely able to maintain their existence, let alone make progress. In perusing the shortened ration rolls, both governments responded by generally cutting aid, thus establishing a perpetual and deepening cycle of poverty.

Questions about how to encourage Indians to become self-supporting became a frequent topic of discussion among American officials. Not surprisingly, the Indian ration system in Canada was an aspect of Canadian Indian administration that interested Frederick Abbott, the American emissary. In his report to the Board of Indian Commissioners, Abbott wrote that Canadian Indians earned, by their own efforts, more than two dollars for each one dollar earned by American Indians. From agricultural products alone, Canadian Indians received sixteen dollars per capita, compared to only thirteen dollars received by Indians in the United States. A hundred thousand Indians in Canada made almost as much in wages as three times that number of American Indians.[9] Using these statistics, Abbott concluded that Canadians managed to make their Indians work for their own support with much greater success than Americans.

Abbott stressed that the Canadians had not rejected the ration system entirely, but administered it more efficiently. Canadian officials worried as much as their American counterparts about the demoralizing influence of free rations on Indian incentive; yet, Abbott wrote, the Canadians had not starved their Indians because of some theoretical opposition to the ration system. Indeed, the Dominion had exercised more patience than the United States in changing former buffalo hunters into self-supporting farmers. In fact, those who were old and needy received regular rations. At the Blood reserve, Abbott noted that a system of getting the Indians to give up rations voluntarily worked admirably, and he found the Canadian system of teaching Indians self-reliance superior to similar attempts by his countrymen.[10]

Assuring the public of a continuous reduction in expenditures for Indian support became the basic theme in the annual reports of the American commissioner of Indian affairs and of the Canadian deputy superintendent. A desire to prove that Indians were steadily advancing into economic independence dominated the reports to such an extent that rarely, if ever, did these officials admit that the Indians had not done as well as the reports indicated. For example, in 1883, Lawrence Vankoughnet reported on the great advancement of Indians in the North West Territories toward self-support, an advance that prompted him to close several model farms established for the instruction of the Indians and to cut down food rations[11]—actions which, in turn, caused some of the Indian bands to join the Riel Rebellion. Annual departmental reports often revealed a striking disparity between the reservation conditions described in the agents' returns and the optimistic tone used by their superiors. Frequently, it became obvious that either officials never read any of the field returns or the agents' eagerness to report what their superiors wanted to hear colored their reports. Many agents saw no other choice if they wanted to retain their positions.

Indian agents in both countries lived under constant pressure to reduce expenditures as a proof of the Indians' progress. A circular sent out in 1878 to the agent for the South Peigans stated plainly that "the practical test of improvement at your Agency will be the decrease in the quantity of supplies which the Government will be called upon to furnish your Indians."[12] Eight years after the "starvation winter," the bureau reiterated its position in no less strident tones:

> The one great object this department has now in view, is the civilization of the Indian, and to enable him to support himself by agriculture as soon as possible. I therefore expect and will require all Indian Agents and Agency employes [*sic*] who wish to be retained in the service, to use every means . . . to instruct, encourage and assist the Indians to this end . . . Nothing less than a very great improvement over former years will be satisfactory, as the law requiring all able bodied male Indians to perform service on their reservation for themselves and their tribe, to entitle them to subsistence. [This law] will now be applied to the fullest extent possible, that an increase in production and a decrease in estimates for the purchase of subsistence may at once result.

The agent was instructed to inform the Indians that he spoke in earnest when he told them that they must support themselves and that "the time has come when they must do so or starve."[13] As usual, these instructions demonstrated little understanding of the economic problems of reservation life. Although the agent could write the most distressing accounts of crop failures and livestock, his superiors refused to acknowledge that their policy was unrealistic.

In an effort to make the Indians independent of government aid, Canadian officials considered themselves far ahead of the Americans. In 1904, the deputy superintendent compared his country's efforts with those of America. He stated that since the beginning the department had laid down the rule that all Indians must become self-supporting and that no gratuitous issue would be made to the able-bodied. This official maintained that Americans did not adopt a similar rule until 1900.[14] Some thirty years later, an American student of Indian policy accepted this view, pointing out that the idea of Indian self-support pervaded not only the Indian Act, but the entire Canadian Indian policy. He argued that for decades Canadians had disabused Indians of the idea that they would be gratuitously supported; the Canadian concern over "pauperizing relief" prompted the government to extend help only in dire emergency, and then only as a temporary measure.[15]

Such statements are misleading, however, because both countries adhered to the principle of Indian self-support as a matter of policy. Canada was anxious to make the Indians self-reliant because she wished to avoid, above all, the financial burden. Even when the policy of "gradualism" failed, the government believed that support would be only a temporary measure. Most officials expected the Blackfeet and other plains Indians to be able to take care of themselves within a relatively short period of time.[16] Given such expectations, Canadians arrived early at the decision to force Indians to fend for themselves. The view that rations were a temporary evil rather than an integral part of the plan to make Indians self-sufficient retarded the establishment of a firm economic basis.

Americans, on the other hand, did provide some rations for the Blackfeet, but the Indians had to continue to hunt in order to survive. Ironically, the government decided to reduce rations to force the Blackfeet to support themselves at a time when they were least able to do so. An investigation by the Indian Rights Association confirmed that support was withdrawn before the Blackfeet were given any opportunity to learn "civilized pursuits."[17] Following the "starvation winter," American officials accepted rationing, albeit inadequate, as a necessity until the Blackfeet could earn their own living. In the long run, their terrible experience made the Blackfeet cling tenaciously to the ration system, and efforts to abolish it met with stiff opposition.

When the Blackfeet had not become self-supporting after years of rationing, officials decided that the ration system encouraged Indians to prefer idleness to working for their livelihood. While it is true that many Blackfeet came to see rations as their inalienable right, blaming the ration system for the failure of the self-support policy oversimplified a complex situation.

Given contemporary attitudes toward self-reliance and the distrust of the dependent poor, it is not surprising that officials in both nations tended to see rations as evil. Self-reliance and the agrarian ideal permeated the Indian service as well as popular sentiment. American Indian police even wore uniforms with one of the buttons bearing a picture of an Indian behind a plow, emblazoned with the motto "God helps those who help themselves." The Americans considered this admonition seriously. In 1875, they passed a law requiring able-bodied Indians to perform labor in exchange for rations, but some reservations were exempted from these provisions.[18]

The Blackfeet received such an exemption in 1878, upon the recommendation of agent Young, who explained that the Indians were still too intractable to be made to work, with the warriors considering work fit only for women. Ironically, at times it was underemployment, not opposition to work, that became a problem, since Indians usually had no opportunity to work anywhere else except around the agency. In 1884, following the "starvation winter," the agent reported that the Blackfeet wanted to work for extra rations, but he had so many applicants he could not find continuous employment for all of them.[19]

Despite the feeling in Washington that the ration system only pauperized the Indians, most agents complained that rations were hardly sufficient to keep the Indians from starving. Agents such as George Steell found particularly annoying Washington's tendency to assume that it knew best what the Indians needed.[20]

As the century drew to a close, American officials feverishly sought ways in which to make all Indians self-supporting before government obligations toward them expired. The ration system came under attack by officials and philanthropists as the major cause of Indian dependence. In 1900, the commissioner called the ration system an obstacle to self-support. In 1901, the Board of Indian Commissioners concurred and reiterated its previous recommendation that the bureau cease the issuance of rations to able-bodied Indians who refused to work for them. In 1904, the bureau flatly declared that the Indians must be given the responsibility for working or starving.[21]

The Blackfeet ration system seemed especially odious to many Americans because some 2,100 individuals received rations in 1901.[22] Around the turn of the century, the bureau began to reduce Blackfeet rations issued under the terms of a land cession agreement made in 1895. Rumors that Washington might cut the rations alarmed the Blackfeet because rations ensured a dependable, if not exactly bountiful, food supply.

Prompted by his charges, the agent inquired why rations had been reduced. Washington gave a curt explanation: "It is the concensus [sic] of opinion of those, who by study and experience are in a position to know, that the ration system is demoralizing and one of the principal barriers to the progress and civilization of the Indians." Annoyed officials reminded the agent that the tribe had already used up two of the nine annual payments under the 1895 cession, pointing out that the Blackfeet showed no evidence of progress. Washington feared that if the Blackfeet continued at the present rate, when the nine years expired their money would be spent and they would be no closer to taking care of themselves.[23]

One agent, James H. Monteath, took the bureau's admonitions seriously, and in 1901 he dropped 776 mixed-bloods from the ration roll. Such energetic steps pleased the commissioner, who repeated his view of the situation: "The able-bodied must understand *now* that the time is rapidly approaching when if they don't work they don't eat." The full-bloods were given a year to get used to the idea that in a year's time they must go to work either on or off the reservation. Such draconian measures prompted the Blackfeet to request that a delegation be allowed to go to Washington to discuss the proposed ration reduction.[24]

In the meantime, agent Monteath forged ahead with further reductions. A hundred able-bodied Indians found employment working on an irrigation ditch, which left only eight hundred on the roll. Monteath commented, somewhat laconically: "The striking off from the ration roll is going to cause some suffering and hardship. It is very doubtful if the suffering will be any greater than that endured by the white pioneers of this Western country." By 1903 only 550 Blackfeet received rations, and the agent advised the bureau not to press for further reduction for fear that the Indians might begin killing cattle.[25]

While the agent's actions succeeded in culling the rolls, the measure failed to make Indians self-supporting. A new agent, J. Z. Dare, arrived in 1905 to find the Blackfeet in sad shape. The only work they could obtain came from seasonal Indian bureau projects, such as fencing the reservation and digging irrigation canals. "The amount received for this labor is not sufficient to supply [their] wants during the year," the agent told the commissioner. The agent even requested his counterpart on the Blood reserve in Canada to refrain from issuing more than two passes per month to those Bloods who wished to visit their South Peigan relatives. Dare explained that his Indians were not receiving rations, and since all winter they had no employment to speak of, they were naturally very poor and had trouble obtaining enough food.[26]

The Blackfeet did not readily accept the new order. In 1909, they made another effort to send a delegation to Washington to have rations restored to those over forty-five years of age and to have farm implements and wagons issued without having to work for them in return. They also asked that the irrigation project on the reservation managed by the Reclamation Service be stopped, and that irrigation funds be divided among them.[27] Even though the Blackfeet made these demands in earnest, annuities supplied to them under the terms of the 1895 agreement came to an end in 1907. Many Indians were left without a regular ration system, dependent on whatever work they could find or on their relatives.

Six years later, the Blackfeet still had failed to become self-supporting, and quite by accident, a discouraging picture emerged of the situation on the reservation. When the commissioner learned that a Blackfeet delegation to Washington had complained that the Indians were starving, he ordered an inquiry. The complaint turned out to be the result of a mistranslation, but a report of the Blackfeet superintendent revealed a bleak situation on the reservation. The superintendent denied that the Indians were starving, but he stated that "many of the Indians are poor and needy, and a number of the able bodied have experienced some difficulty in keeping the wolf from the door." His ration roll stood at six hundred, far more than in the past three years; and the rains of the previous summer had ruined the hay crop, the principal source of Blackfeet income. The superintendent, however, laid the blame for most of the economic distress on Blackfeet "improvidence," and he indicated that the whole tribe would have jumped at the chance to be put on the ration roll if he had not practiced vigilance. He sent to the bureau samples of seven requests for rations, coming from people who were perfectly able to take care of themselves.[28]

Despite assurances that the Blackfeet were not actually starving, the tribal economy stood on a precarious footing. From 1911 to 1915 many Blackfeet found work in constructing irrigation ditches, but this employment, even when combined with selling hay and raising cattle, did not make the majority of Indians economically secure. In previous times of need, such as in 1883 and 1895, the Blackfeet had ceded their lands to provide necessities for themselves; by the second decade of this century, officials once again found the answer in the Indians' lands, this time in allotting the reservation and throwing open the surplus.

Ironically, while the advocates of allotment policy believed that their plan would finally force the Indians to become independent, allotment actually doomed the opportunity of most allotted tribes to establish a viable economic system. For the tribes, including the Blackfeet, lacked the capital to develop individual holdings. "Notwithstanding the large individual land holdings," one superintendent wrote, "many of them [the Blackfeet] are very poor having neither workteams, harness, farming implements, seeds or any means of getting them, and it is impossible for them to get started farming their allotments without some assistance." Cattle raising also offered no solution because cattle were unevenly distributed, leaving some Indians with large herds while others had none. A reimbursable fund of ninety thousand dollars established to buy cattle for the Blackfeet provided only about two heads per person, scarcely enough to get them started in the cattle business.[29] Still most officials believed that the sale of surplus reservation lands would provide the capital necessary to solve the economic stalemate.

Despite claims that Canadians aimed their entire policy toward making Indians independent, they wrestled as much as the Americans with the question of how to make the Indians self-supporting. The Indian department periodically reminded the agents: "It may be stated, as first principle, that it is the policy of the Department to promote self-support among the Indians and not provide gratuitous assistance to those who can provide for themselves."[30] This eagerness to see Indians standing on their own economic feet resulted partly from the awareness that the Dominion would have to bear a large financial burden if it simply rationed the Indians, as the United States seemed to be doing.

In 1884 the department not only reduced rations, but made it policy that able-bodied Indians should work for them. Canadian native people did not accept this policy quietly. At the Battle River reserve in Saskatchewan, the Indians assaulted a farming instructor when he refused to issue rations to able-bodied Indians unless they worked for them. The Bloods also threatened trouble if their rations were reduced. Yet even if the Indians were willing to work, this did not guarantee their advancement. The Blood agent said in 1885 that "many of those who, year after year, have worked steadily, find themselves no better off, pecuniarily, than when they first started."[31]

The Canadian Indian department also adopted the attitude that if the Indians did not work they would not eat, and attempts were made to keep rations to a bare minimum. Appropriations for the territories amounted to a mere 24,000 dollars in 1890. In 1891, daily rations on the Blood reserve consisted of 1.3 pounds of beef and .44 pounds of flour. That year, the department announced a further 30 percent reduction in expenditures for Manitoba, and in the North West Territories they were cut from 278 dollars to 195 dollars per head.[32] A year later, in 1892, the entire expenditures on Indians became the subject of one of the rare debates in Parliament on Indian policy.

The occasion was the question of funding the North West Mounted Police, but the debate expanded to include the cost of feeding, clothing, and supervising the Indians. One speaker, Member of Parliament David Mills, argued that Canada was in no position to continue to support the Indians. Members of the opposition suggested bluntly that the government was interfering with the natural survival of the fittest by supporting the Indians. In turn, the government argued that it had a duty to support the Indians and maintained that, all obstacles considered, the Indians were making remarkable progress.[33] Although, in the end, the government rejected arguments to throw the western tribes upon their own resources, it continued to seek ways to cut the expenditures of the Indian department.

One such move involved the reorganization of the western Indian service in 1897. Critics of the plan claimed that the reorganization led to inefficiency and to an actual increase in Indians receiving rations. Chief accountant D. C. Scott had to defend these changes in 1904. He justified the reorganization by arguing that the department and the commissioner's office in Winnipeg had succumbed to inertia and therefore had to be revamped. Scott urged new efforts to improve the entire Indian ration system in Treaties 7, 4, and 6, claiming that more stringent steps must be taken with those Indians who did not apply themselves to agricultural pursuits or toward making themselves self-supporting. Scott charged that Indian agents in the three treaty areas expended little effort to compel their charges to work, for most agents found it easier to ask the department for more rations.[34]

Despite Scott's charges, not all Indian agents neglected their duties. One of them, William Morris Graham, built a reputation on getting Indians to work for their living. Graham began his career as an agency clerk at Moose Mountain reserve in 1885. He rose quickly through the ranks to become Indian agent at the Cree agency of Qu'Appelle, Saskatchewan, thanks to his "peculiar ability in leading Indians to become self-supporting." In 1901, shortly after assuming his new position, Graham proposed a plan guaranteed to make the new generation of Indians independent farmers.

The plan involved placing graduates of Indian schools in segregated farming settlements. Graham established the first settlement, called File Hills, at the Qu'Appelle agency. The File Hills colony as well as the entire agency became a resounding economic success: the Indians were self-supporting and the ration system was abolished. Graham's experiment welcomed many visitors including the governer-general of Canada and Frederick Abbott, who found the idea praiseworthy.[35] In Treaty 7, it was agent J. A. Markle who took steps to make the Indians self-supporting. Markle served as agent to the Blackfoot, and his energy in reducing ration rolls endeared him to the Indian department.

Soon after his arrival at the Blackfoot agency in 1900, Markle set out to end the "degrading influence of the ration house." Since the conclusion of Treaty 7, he stated, the Blackfoot believed that the government had a duty to supply all of their food as well as other rations. The Blackfoot even refused to accept the issue of cattle because Crowfoot told them that if they did, the government would cut their rations and they would be expected to support themselves.[36] To the Indians, then, the questions of rations involved the very nature of treaty promises and went beyond their aversion toward work.

Two years after his arrival, Markle informed the department that he expected to end the issuance of rations to the Blackfoot much sooner than he had planned. Markle cut the daily rations to .80 pounds of beef, .41 pounds of flour, and less than half a pound of beans and peas. His unilateral action pleased Ottawa so much that it decided to "force" this system upon other reserves in the territories. As a result, the issue of beef, flour, and bacon in Treaties 7 and 4 was decreased dramatically; and D. C. Scott predicted that if such decreases continued, no issue of beef would be needed for fiscal year 1908–9.[37]

On the Blood reserve, the agent was instructed to reduce his estimates of 1.25 pounds of beef and .75 pounds of flour to Markle's level. Those Indians who worked would be able to supplement their diet; those who did not were not entitled to more, and the aged did not require as much sustenance anyway—or so the officials told the agent, who was to explain to the Indians that the Dominion had no obligation to feed them and that those who were capable of work would not be fed indefinitely after they had been given reasonable assistance.[38]

Throughout the 1900s, the Canadian government used the stick-and-carrot approach to get Indians off ration rolls. Beef rations were cut, and beans were substituted in the name of greater economy and dietary variety. When the Blood agent expressed apprehension that the reduction would prompt the Indians to kill their cattle, the department advised him to offer a reward of twenty dollars to those who would inform on the culprits.[39]

At the same time, however, the department also tried more constructive means to get the Indians off ration rolls. On the Blood and Blackfoot reserve Frederick Abbott observed a system that combined rations and simultaneously encouraged the Indians to work. Indians who raised cattle were required to turn them over to the agency slaughterhouse, where they were given a credit voucher for the value of their steers, amounting to a maximum of one pound of beef per day. Abbott stated that such measures helped the government to realize substantial savings and forced the Indians to contribute to their own support.[40]

But even the combination of austerity and self-help measures had not made Indians self-supporting. By 1910, Markle's work-or-starve approach resulted in continuous poverty among the Blackfoot.[41] That year, the department found a simple solution to Blackfoot economic woes that proved popular south of the border—a sale of some 120,000 acres of the reserve. The Blackfoot agreed to the sale on the condition that each individual would be guaranteed food and clothing as well as livestock, houses, and farming implements as long as he or she lived.

The Peigans also won a measure of economic security by selling a part of their reserve. Only the Bloods resisted the blandishments of prosperity, despite all official efforts to get them to part with a portion of their land. Although the agent for the Bloods reported in 1915 that teaching Indians to work was the greatest problem,[42] the Bloods managed by the late teens to establish a fairly prosperous cattle economy. Unfortunately, this prosperity evaporated during the last years of the Great War, as a combination of severe weather and mismanagement by officials set the Bloods back almost to their condition in 1883.

A similar situation developed across the line on the Blackfeet reservation. A drought and severe winters between 1918 and 1920 plagued the budding cattle business. A member of the Board of Indian Commissioners who visited the agency gave a grim summation of the Blackfeet economy and a bleak prediction for their future. If prompt mesures were not taken, he predicted great suffering among the Indians and the possible extinction of their herds. As if these natural disasters were not enough, allotment of the reservation and the subsequent erosion of the land base further undermined the ability of the Blackfeet to establish and maintain a viable economy. By 1920 the Blackfeet were once again destitute, with some two-thirds of them dependent on rations.[43]

During the forty years under study here, both governments wished to be relieved from the burden of feeding their Indians, not only because the ration system was costly but because it prevented the Indians from acquiring one of the essentials of civilization—self-support and economic independence. One American official best expressed this attitude when he declared labor to be the foundation of civilization, and changing Indians from consumers to producers as the objective of his government's policy. Canadian officials voiced the same sentiments.[44] Still, some observers such as Abbott perceived a difference between the two governments in their attitude toward Indian self-support and the ration system.

Evidence indicates, however, that the two governments followed a similar path. Once native people were confined on reservations, they received some form of rations since, as one wit put it, it was cheaper to feed them than to fight them. However, despite numerous declarations during the last quarter of the nineteenth century, only after 1900 did the Americans make serious efforts to abolish the ration system as an obstacle to self-support. Unfortunately, Washington withdrew rations before the Indians could become self-supporting. Thus, when disaster struck the Blackfeet in the late teens they had no resources to fall back on, and rations again became the solution.

Canadian officials, on the other hand, frequently stated that their entire Indian policy revolved around making native peoples self-supporting. In reality, however, inducing the Indians to work depended more on their agent's inclination than on the wishes of Ottawa's bureaucrats. In most instances, agents found it simpler to issue rations than to force the Indians to work. By the turn of the century, the department had noticed that a pall of inertia had settled over the reserves; and it was not until after individuals such as Graham and Markle took the initiative that officials began to attack the ration system. By then, alas, the Indians had become discouraged with the repeated failures of various economic schemes and so dependent on rations that their withdrawal plunged many of them deeper into poverty.

The principal reasons for the Blackfoot Confederacy becoming once again dependent on rations after forty years of life on their reservations stemmed from two failures: the failure of the two countries to establish a stable economic system on these and other Indian reservations,[45] and the failure to convince many native people to accept the cultural values necessary to support such a system. These failures did not result from a lack of effort. On the contrary, considerable energy and expenditures were devoted toward turning the Indians into independent farmers and inculcating in them the values of Western civilization.

4

The Failure of
Reservation Economies

The development of agriculture on Indian reservations became the primary, yet largely elusive, objective of Indian service officials in both countries. American officials never doubted the wisdom of this policy; for example, in 1911 the commissioner of Indian affairs had declared that while not all Indians could or should become farmers, farming offered the best opportunity available to the majority. At the end of the second decade of the twentieth century, the commissioner still continued to insist that "agriculture is the basis of prosperity among the whites, and is even more essential to Indian welfare."[1] Canadians also believed that plains Indians must become farmers, and the instructions issued to commissioner Dewdney plainly stated this intention.

Despite these avowed declarations, western Indians made a poor showing in agriculture for several reasons: the lack of adequate funding, poor administration by inexperienced or incompetent agents and farming instructors, an unsuitable climate, and resistance from the Indians. A history of failed farming efforts on the reserves of the Blackfoot Confederacy illustrates vividly the problems of turning plains Indians into self-supporting farmers.

Two years after John Young assumed office as the agent of the South Peigans, he gave the agricultural potential of the reservation a pessimistic evaluation. "In Montana," he stated, "agriculture can only be carried on by means of irrigation. . . . Stock raising is at the present the leading occupation of the white settlers of the Territory and the Indians are better adopted to that pursuit than to any other." Thus far, he had induced only three Blackfeet to take up farming, an occupation that was foreign to them, as Young pointed out.[2]

Reports on the Blackfeet future in agriculture were not uniformly discouraging, however. Most agents agreed with the view that in order to survive the Indians must become farmers, whether willing or not. Consequently, many reports on Blackfeet economic progress revealed a curious juxtaposition of pessimism about the current state of affairs with optimism regarding the future. Even Young concluded his annual report of 1881 with the prediction that, given the proper encouragement in agriculture, the Blackfeet could become self-supporting in a few years.[3]

Even the most outspoken agents felt compelled to follow the official policy of turning the Blackfeet into farmers, despite the knowledge that the endeavor would most likely result in failure. The peppery George Steell expressed his dilemma when he wrote in 1890: "Under the best circumstances, I do not consider that this is farming country. . . . Still, it is necessary that the Indian be encouraged towards raising what he can and take [his] chances."[4] Steell, in turn, became one of a number of agents who pleaded for the issuance of cattle to the Blackfeet, believing that ranching could prove to be successful in the northern climate. Yet attitudes of agents toward farming continued to seesaw. In the 1890s, for instance, agent L. W. Cooke insisted that the Blackfeet could make progress in agriculture only if they were taught how to use irrigation. When Cooke departed, his successor, George Steell, declared that the reservation was unequivocally grazing country. The next three agents concurred, yet their successor insisted that the Blackfeet should be "induced" to cultivate land.[5] Since none stayed on the reservation long enough to implement any system, the Blackfeet economy remained rudderless.

Sustaining progress toward economic self-support became especially difficult because the BIA did not seem to realize that agriculture required a great capital outlay, especially during its initial stages. Shortages of basic supplies such as farming implements frustrated many agents as well as the Indians. When one agent ordered twenty-five mowers and rakes and received only fifteen, he observed caustically that the BIA could not expect four hundred families to make do.[6]

The lack of competent instructors further aggravated the problem. Throughout the nineteenth century, farming instructors were routinely appointed to American reservations on the basis of their political proclivities rather than their agricultural experience. Moreover, their duties usually included tasks other than teaching Indians to farm. Farming instructors worked as ration issuers, clerks, handymen, and assistants to the agent or superintendent. Although the Indian bureau made appropriations in 1885 to hire "practical" farmers, the efforts to actually teach Indians to farm did not make any headway until the first decade of the twentieth century, when the BIA declared a "new era" in educating the Indians in the latest farming methods.[7] The sudden interest came as a result of the realization that the Indians had to be taught agriculture before the federal government terminated its supervision.

By contrast, in Canada the farming instructor was more akin to an Indian agent. This development grew partly from the policy in the late 1870s of placing several reserves in the West under one agent, while a farm instructor managed affairs at an individual agency. He could be called upon to perform the duties of a physician, judge and jury, ration issuer, or house builder, as well as farmer.[8] These varied demands on the farming instructors in both countries did not leave them with much time to teach agriculture to the Indians.

The American government made its first serious efforts to provide the Blackfeet with systematic farming instructions after they had been confined to the reservation for nearly thirty years. In 1910, a circular from the BIA instructed the agent to hire expert farmers, divide the reservation into districts, and place one demonstration farm in each district under the management of a farmer.[9] In this approach Americans duplicated, most likely unwittingly, the system long in vogue on Canadian reserves of employing farming instructors to operate government farms.

Despite these plans, funding of the projects remained a problem. In 1911, agent Arthur E. McFatridge declared that the "new departure" for the Blackfeet, funded by ten thousand dollars from a reimbursable fund, was far too small an appropriation, and he urged its tripling or even quadrupling. Yet the plan appeared to work, since the farm instructors reported a respectable yield of crops of alfalfa, oats, sugar beets, and potatoes from the demonstration farms. These signs of success, however, had not changed the agent's mind. McFatridge declared the reservation suitable for forage, but not for market crops, and urged the production of hay for the cattle industry.[10]

The BIA had other plans for the Blackfeet. When Indians ceded a portion of the reservation in 1895, the agreement described the reservation as "wholly unfit for agriculture" and pledged that the land would never be allotted without the Indians' consent. Twelve years later, passage of the Blackfeet Allotment Act broke that promise. The act gave to individual Indians forty acres of irrigable land and 280 acres of pasture, or to those who preferred, 320 acres of grazing lands; and provided for the building of an irrigation system on the reservation.[11] It appeared that the Blackfeet would finally be forced to consider agriculture as their only means of support. Unfortunately, efforts to irrigate the reservation became one of the most spectacular failures of the agricultural policy.

Attempts to irrigate the reservation had already begun in the early 1880s. Ironically, the BIA's irrigation scheme resulted in the tribe's starvation during 1883–84, when the subcommittee on Indian appropriations refused to release funds for rations, claiming that since the Blackfeet already received 100,000 dollars for irrigation they should be able to feed themselves.[12] Nevertheless, in the long run, irrigation brought some unanticipated benefits to the Blackfeet.

In the late 1890s, agent Steell began the construction of irrigation ditches, even though he knew that the Indians demonstrated little interest in farming. Steell found a perfect justification for the project: ditch construction provided employment and income for the Indians. Steell told the commissioner that this construction work "would cause greater advancement than anything that could be done for these people in the way of farming." Subsequent agents soon found themselves in a situation where even though they found the ditches useless for farming, they felt compelled to continue the work since it provided the Blackfeet with virtually their only employment. Ironically, many Blackfeet came to prefer work on the irrigation projects over the slow and uncertain business of farming, because ditchdigging provided instant cash income.[13]

A few intrepid agents, however, revealed the truth about the irrigation scheme. In 1900, James H. Monteath called the projects "monuments of misdirected energy, being utterly impracticable."[14] He charged that poor planning and the Indians' stubborn resistance to farming had created the debacle. An area irrigated by the Cut Bank Canal was located ten miles northwest of the agency, while those whom the ditch was intended to serve lived ten to thirty-five miles south of the agency. Moreover, inducing the Blackfeet to take up irrigated lands also proved to be difficult. The agent reported that there "is a disinclination, amounting almost to prejudice, among the Indians in regard to taking up land upon the line of this canal." He managed to persuade twenty-five men to promise to settle on twenty-five-acre plots, but when spring came only seven of them arrived, and their combined cultivated area amounted to less than fifty acres.[15]

Even in locations where irrigation was practicable and the Indians wanted to utilize it, a conflict over water developed between settlers and the Indians. For example, in 1904 a protracted struggle ensued between the Blackfeet and the Conrad Investment Company over the latter's diversion dam on Birch Creek, located upstream from the reservation. While Indians claimed half the water, the company appropriated the entire flow. Not until 1908 did the court issue an injunction against the company.[16] The bureau was not unaware of the problems surrounding Blackfeet irrigation. The commissioner announced in 1906 that the Cut Bank project had cost seventeen thousand dollars, but the Blackfeet had not utilized it because the reclaimed area was not suitable for agriculture. Nevertheless, the commissioner concluded, the result would be worth the effort.[17] What result he had in mind was not clear, but during the next several years the entire purpose of the irrigation project became suspect.

Montanans had long regarded the Blackfeet reservation as a prime piece of real estate. In 1906, for example, newspapers called the reservation the best watered land in Montana, and indicated obliquely that the Indian bureau's irrigation system would be useful to the settlers once the reservation was opened to entry.[18] Ten years later, congressional committees conducting hearings on the opening of the reservation began to question the irrigation scheme. Witnesses testified that in 1907 the Blackfeet Allotment Bill had not only been passed without the consent of the Indians, but under that act anyone could use the canals constructed supposedly for the benefit of the Indians. Moreover, the Blackfeet would be saddled with paying for the cost of the construction.[19]

That the irrigation enthusiasts had painted themselves into a corner became obvious when a Senate committee inquired more deeply into the Blackfeet project. When asked whether in ten or twenty years the Indians would need the irrigated lands that the bureau proposed to open to settlement, the assistant commissioner replied that he did not think so because the Blackfeet raised stock. When asked then why the government had spent one million dollars on the project, the assistant commissioner announced that the project was a mistake, but considering the amount expended it would have to be completed. Conservative estimates predicted that the entire project would cost 3.5 million dollars.[20]

Given such reasoning, the bureau continued to pour funds into the irrigation of alloted lands that the Blackfeet did not want and did not utilize. Agent McFatridge plainly informed the commissioner that "the large systems of irrigation [were] beyond the comprehension of these Indians," and he urged instead the creation of small-scale, more manageable projects. To add insult to injury, the majority of the Blackfeet chose grazing over agricultural allotments, while the officials tried to devise "the best plan by which to induce" the Blackfeet to select lands that could be cultivated. The BIA even sent instructions to the allotting agents to persuade families who selected grazing allotments to exchange them for farm lands, but the effort ended without noticeable success.[21]

In the meantime, the Blackfeet agricultural effort continued to limp along until 1917, when the BIA mounted an all-out drive to aid the war effort by increasing agricultural output on Indian reservations. A circular urged superintendents to impress on Indians their patriotic duty to cultivate every acre of their reservations. The commissioner hoped that the momentum gained during the war would carry into the future. He was pleased to report that cultivated acreage on reservations had increased by 31.6 percent over the previous year, and announced the leasing of additional reservation lands on liberal terms.[22] Unfortunately, hopes of accelerating Blackfeet agricultural production were not realized.

During this time, Canadian officials showed no less determination than their American counterparts to turn the Blackfoot, Peigans, and Bloods into farmers. The government made its decision at a time when little was known about the agricultural potential of the North West Territories. By the mid-1880s, the only industry in what would become southern Alberta was cattle raising, and herds from Montana frequently grazed on Canadian prairies. Although farmers took up lands along the new Canadian Pacific Railway during a wet cycle in the West, drought and early frosts in 1883–84 drove many of them away. During the blizzards of 1886–87 the Canadian cattle business suffered a blow, although not as severe as in the United States. From 1880 to 1891 more than a million settlers fled the Canadian West, defeated by frost, blight, and inadequate technology,[23] but the Canadian Indians could not leave.

In the meantime, officials in Ottawa remained optimistic about the eventual success of the Indians in agriculture. The plains tribes began to farm for the first time in 1882, and the deputy superintendent general reported that the Bloods, some 3,500 strong, raised 200,000 pounds of potatoes, as well as turnips, oats, and barley. The Blackfoot also tilled the soil for the first time, and the Peigans appeared to be doing especially well. Their agent had already predicted two years earlier that they would be the first of the southern plains Indians to become self-supporting.[24]

The following year, the government continued to paint a rosy picture of industrious Indians well on their way to self-support. The Blackfoot Confederacy, the "most warlike Indians in the Dominion," settled down to peaceable pursuits, with nearly every family living in a house and tending a farm or a garden. Still, there were disturbing reports that the agricultural success of the Bloods and Blackfoot had resulted largely from the efforts of the farming instructors.[25] But even this chimerical success of Indian farming did not reappear in succeeding years. In fact, the future of Indians in agriculture grew more bleak.

In part, the failure of Canadian Indian farming could be attributed to the usual problems in administration. Eastern farming instructors were ignorant of the climate and the prairie soil, and frequent turnover in staff also caused problems. Reductions in expenditures by the department had not helped either. By 1883 the department began to phase out model farms on the reservations because, ironically, these operations proved too expensive for the department to maintain,[26] and by the end of that decade, Indians judged sufficiently advanced were told to make their own land rollers, harnesses, fork handles, and hay rakes. The department expected that after two or three good seasons it would be relieved of all major expenditures for Indian support.[27]

In the long run, economizing proved to be ill advised. A new agent at the Blood reserve complained that those Indians who were willing to work could not do so because they had been allowed but one instructor to oversee Indian farms that stretched for fifty miles. The department also failed to provide the Bloods with an adequate number of wagons and implements.[28] Moreover, at about this time the weather conspired to deal a blow to the novice farmers.

During the early 1890s, drought and early spring and fall frosts turned farming into a frustrating experience for the Indians. In his memoirs, agent Cecil Denny recalled that between 1892 and 1905 the Indians raised barely enough seed crop. Throughout the 1890s, reports of the failure of crops on the western reserves flooded the department. Coming upon the heels of predictions of impending Indian self-support, such news baffled the officials. As a result, the department was confused about what direction it should follow. For example, in 1896 the deputy superintendent wrote that for several years he had recognized that the future of the Blackfoot Confederacy did not lie in farming. The same year, a memorandum from a dissatisfied assistant commissioner noted that Indians in the territories were not farming, and it reiterated the policy of the department to make the Indians contribute toward their own maintenance.[29]

Given the conflicting directions from the DIA, some agents decided to ignore Ottawa completely. At the Peigan reserve, where the Indians demonstrated the most willingness to take up agriculture, the frustrated agent told officials:

> For about fifteen years a large outlay has been annually made in labour and seed while fruitlessly attempting to grow grain here. While the preparation of the ground was a wholesome—though discouraging—occupation for the Indians, the seed grain was literally thrown away, and it is . . . the intention of the agency to make no further efforts in that direction, but to concentrate all possible attention on cattle raising.

In the same year, the Blood agent also declared that his reserve was quite unsuitable for farming.[30]

Despite such reports, the policies of the department continued to vacillate. In 1899, Ottawa declared that more stress would be placed on stock raising and the careful cultivation of limited areas. Two years later, officials announced that they had abandoned the cultivation of grains in Treaty 7 because of an unsuitable climate. The agrarian ideal died hard, however, and by the mid-1900s Ottawa returned to its original intention of turning the plains Indians into farmers.[31]

To encourage Indians to take up farming, the department turned to mechanized agriculture. From the Blood tribal funds, the department purchased in 1907 a steam plow to break a strip two miles long and a mile wide. Fifteen Bloods received eighty-acre plots as their individual farms. A similar experiment took place on the Peigan reserve.[32] This move resulted partly from the agents' complaint that the Indians could not break the tough prairie sod with plows pulled by their ponies, and partly from a desire to make the Indians farm by whatever means.

These measures, however, provoked an outcry from neighboring white farmers, who protested the department's use of heavy farm machinery on behalf of the Indians while offering white farmers no such help. One writer complained that these Indians should use horses and walking plows like everyone else. The officials felt compelled to calm the irate settlers by admitting that perhaps they were moving a bit too fast in introducing mechanization on the reserves, but after spending a fortune on rations, the government hoped that these measures would ultimately reduce the cost of feeding the Indians.[33]

Yet not even mechanization could ensure the success of Indian agriculture. In 1910, crop failure stood at 90 percent after a year-long drought in southern Alberta. Not surprisingly, the Indians were reported to have lost interest once again in farming. While the Bloods enjoyed some success with farming, the situation became serious at the Blackfoot reserve, where inhabitants, according to one authority, slid into a "catatonic stupor." The Blackfoot owned some ponies and a few head of cattle, but they did not farm. Most of their livelihood came from selling hay, working on neighboring ranches, and selling coal from a coal seam near the Bow River.[34]

The outbreak of World War I sparked a temporary economic rally for Canadian as well as American Indians. In the Canadian West, some reserves became part of the Greater Production campaign, a brainchild of the intrepid W. M. Graham, who conceived the plan to put idle reserve lands into production to aid the British Empire's war effort. The government liked the concept and appointed Graham as a commissioner for the campaign in Manitoba, Saskatchewan, and Alberta. In addition, provisions were made for the leasing of reserves to white settlers at liberal terms. In a nutshell, the government confiscated the reserves and took over their agricultural operations. On the Blackfoot reserve, for instance, the government operated a three-thousand-acre farm in addition to leasing large blocks to non-Indians. The Blood reserve also became part of the Greater Production scheme, with the establishment of a sizable government farm and the lease of fifty grazing sections to outside cattlemen. Unfortunately, the campaign turned out to cost the government more than it earned.[35] Even worse, some charged the campaign with causing considerable harm to the Bloods' economic development.

Meanwhile, efforts to irrigate Indian reserves proved as disappointing in Canada as in the United States, but for opposite reasons. While something of an irrigation frenzy seized the western United States and the Indian bureau by the turn of the century, Canadian officials showed little interest in irrigation projects in the prairie West or on Indian reserves. The reasons were twofold: Canadians had little experience with irrigation, and the slow involvement of federal government in western reclamation reflected the generally retarded development of the prairies.[36]

The three reserves of the Blackfoot Confederacy occupied an area of the North West Territories called the Palliser Triangle. Without irrigation, this fertile but semiarid land was suitable only for cattle raising. Although Mormon settlers built small-scale irrigation projects, such as those operated by the community of Cardston just outside the southern boundary of the Blood reserve, settlers in the territories had a difficult time in persuading the Canadian government to support irrigation projects. Not until the early 1890s, after a disastrous drought in southern Alberta, did Ottawa begin to consider an irrigation policy patterned after the American example. The return of a wet cycle, however, weakened federal commitment to the project.[37]

The first attempt to provide irrigation on the southern Alberta reserves occurred in 1893 at the Blackfoot agency. Two years later, the government declared its intention to extend the practice to the rest of Treaty 7, but the project failed because the DIA, much like the rest of the Department of the Interior, was largely ignorant of irrigation techniques. Therefore, in 1894 the Indian department dispatched its chief inspector of surveys to attend the Irrigation Congress held in Denver to gather information "in the matter of irrigating Indian reserves."[38]

Canadians also showed less awareness than Americans of the need to protect Indian water rights. In the United States, litigation to protect these rights occurred early and frequently. In 1907, President Theodore Roosevelt even vetoed the opening of the Blackfeet reservation, largely in order to protect the Indians' rights. In the Canadian West, litigation over water during the same period was rare, largely because of the existence of the North West Irrigation Act of 1894, which abolished riparian rights.[39] While Ottawa saw no need to protect Indian water rights, some Indian agents viewed these rights as critical to the success of Indian agriculture.

As early as 1894, agent R. N. Wilson recognized the need to protect the water supply for the Blackfoot and Blood reserves, but the department did nothing until the issue arose on the Blood reserve ten years later. In 1905, agent Wilson requested a survey of the reserve, with the objective of constructing a twenty- or thirty-mile-long canal from the Belly River. He notified the department of the need to protect the Indians' water rights, since the Mormons had begun to construct two canals to irrigate their newly acquire lands bordering on the reserve.[40]

For the next year the government dragged its feet, while the agent and the surveyor sparred over the snail's pace of the survey. The chief surveyor urged officials to hasten the project, fearing that all available water would be appropriated before the survey was completed and the papers filed. Unfortunately, five days before the chief surveyor's letter reached officials, the water commissioner of the North West Territories informed the department that the Bloods' water had already been claimed.[41]

In response, the department decided to abandon the irrigation project rather than fight for the rights of the Indians. When informed of this decision, the agent protested vociferously, stating that the project was of immense importance to the Bloods, and he accused the department of grossly neglecting them.[42] In reply, agent Wilson received a reprimand from Ottawa: "The Department, while willing to have your opinion as to the benefit to be derived from the proposed irrigation scheme, will decide as to whether it is of immense importance to the future of the Blood Indians."[43]

Wilson, by then in a combative mood, stuck to his guns and demanded justice for the Bloods. In the end, it was the local officials, namely the intrepid inspector J. A. Markle, who contributed to the scuttling of the Blood irrigation project. Markle estimated that the scheme would cost 300,000 dollars, and he expressed doubt that Parliament would vote to "enrich" these Indians when they could pay for it themselves, he argued, by surrendering the southern portion of their reserves. Thereupon, the government dropped the project, which was not revived until 1914.[44]

The Bloods were not the only band that lost out due to departmental inertia. The Blackfoot, who had possessed a haphazard irrigation system since the 1890s, received an inspection from the provincial commissioner of irrigation in 1912. He informed the department that the ditches were in disrepair, and that according to the water license, he had the right to cancel the permit for water use. He asked whether the department would repair the canals or preferred to lose its license. On the recommendation of the agent and the inspector, who stated that the area had eight out of ten wet seasons, the department relinquished its permit after deciding that a considerable amount of funds would be necessary to restore the ditches.[45] Three years later, the West entered a drought cycle that lasted for five years.

Once agriculture had failed, the only alternative for the Indian economy appeared to be the cattle industry. Unfortunately, both governments regarded cattle raising as a second choice; consequently, this endeavor received even less financial support than agriculture. Nevertheless, already in 1881 the South Peigan agency kept a cattle herd of some six hundred head that bore the "ID" (Indian Department) brand. The main purpose of this herd was to provide the Indians with beef, rather than serving as the nucleus of a reservation cattle industry. Even though agency herders were supposed to look after the cattle, the herd dispersed and disappeared during the next few years because of neglect.[46]

Still, cattle were issued to the Blackfeet under the terms of the several treaties with the tribe. For instance, a land cession agreement in 1887 stipulated the purchase of cows and bulls. Yet officials had misgivings about giving cattle to the Indians because they feared that a pastoral economy would have less civilizing influence than agriculture. A member of the Board of Indian Commissioners assured these doubters that ranching "can be pursued by [the Indians] not as nomads, but from settled homes."[47] The first delivery of cattle under the terms of the Treaty of 1887 took place three years later. Not all Indians received cattle, however, since the agent was instructed to distribute them only to "deserving Indians," prompting him to reply that according to the treaty all were deserving. The agent further complained that those Indians who were already "fixed up" received cattle, while the poor were issued only clothing. Subsequent agents urged the BIA to issue more cattle, pointing out that some families received no cattle while others killed theirs for food because of the shortage of rations.[48]

By butchering the cattle clandestinely, the Blackfeet broke the bureau's injunction against the unauthorized killing, selling, or bartering of issue cattle. The intention of the government was to build the Indian herd to a viable size, but the orders failed to take into account reservation realities. No Indian bureau circular could prevent hungry stock owners from butchering a cow. Moreover, many Blackfeet still regarded horses as the only measure of wealth and status, and they often bartered away cattle to their more perspicacious tribal members or to non-Indians living both on and off the reservation.[49] Despite such obstacles, the cattle industry slowly gained acceptance among the Blackfeet. The land cession of 1895 gave the Blackfeet more funds for the purchase of livestock, and this money provided the embryo for the Blackfeet cattle industry, an industry that experienced a roller-coaster existence.[50]

Cattle soon became embroiled in reservation politics. Many agents rightly suspected that the issue of cattle to the Blackfeet served as a signal to non-Indians to go into the cattle business. "I have been flooded with requests for participation in the coming cattle issue," the Blackfeet agent complained in 1903. Some requests came from people who were not even remotely connected with the Blackfeet and had never lived on the reservation.[51] While these people had acquired "ID" cattle through clandestine trade, others were willing to marry into the tribe to benefit from departmental cattle issued to an Indian wife and to take advantage of grazing privileges on the usually well-grassed reservation. "Straight" cattle, which the newcomers owned personally, mingled with BIA cattle, and soon it became impossible to separate the progeny. Since "straight" cattle could be sold without permission, these cattlemen made a handsome profit with little investment.

The bureau considered the matter serious enough that it issued a circular instructing agents to remove from the reservation white men who married into the tribe and violated the trading ban.[52] As one would suspect, these regulations were widely evaded. Moreover, the ill-gotten gains were not confined to scheming white men. The ever-increasing mixed-blood population proved more aware of the value of cattle than their full-blood brothers. Indeed, in 1903 agents were already complaining that of the twenty thousand head of Indian cattle, only five thousand were owned by full-bloods, who comprised two-thirds of the population. At least 90 percent of the full-bloods sold their cattle as soon as they could because they considered horses more valuable.[53] Such maldistribution contributed to the continuous economic malaise of the Blackfeet. Contrary to the old days, the poor members could not acquire wealth through raiding, and officials considered them too improvident to merit more than a perfunctory handout. As a result, a class of the permanently poor became entrenched on the reservation.

Still, the demands of the cattle industry provided the Blackfeet with one important, if unreliable, source of income—the leasing of grazing lands or the sale of hay. Leasing reservation pasture to cattlemen, miners, and farmers formed a part of the government's policy to "encourage the development and utilization of all our general resources."[54] However, grazing leases proved to be a tiresome proposition to administer and virtually impossible to enforce for the full benefit of the Indians. The Blackfeet lost thousands of dollars annually to lease violators and to reservation trespassers. Outsiders tried various ways of evading grazing fees. One enterprising individual sold his herd to a Blackfeet tribal member for a nominal sum in exchange for having the Indian graze the stock gratis on the reservation, while the settler remained the real owner.[55]

In 1914, the government did an about-face and declared that it would pay more attention to stock raising on Indian reservations by reestablishing tribal herds, to be administered by bureau officials. In 1915, the bureau purchased for the Blackfeet reservation 1,800 head of cattle, which increased to some 4,300 by 1917. That year, an inspector observed that while the herd was a success as a tribal investment, it failed in providing an object lesson in cattle raising to the full-bloods, who regarded the cattle as if they belonged to someone else. On the positive side, many of these Indians earned income by selling hay for the cattle.[56]

While the government decided to encourage the cattle business, it also pursued a policy of allotment that contradicted this proposition. Ironically, the much maligned agent McFatridge pointed out the paradoxical situation: just as the cattle industry began to enjoy some success, the Blackfeet were told to abandon it because allotment rendered their holdings too small to support viable-sized herds. To ease the hardship of another transition from a cattle to a farming economy, McFatridge urged the BIA to retain a portion of the reservation as a common grazing land for ten years. The agent considered the bureau's attitude toward the Blackfeet reservation as especially misguided, and he urged officials to investigate the whole proposal.[57] Despite these pleas, the allotment of the reservation proceeded.

In 1917 a member of the Board of Indian Commissioners visiting the Blackfeet reservation commented on the "atmosphere of optimism" that pervaded it, and expressed hope that just as cotton had solved the economic problems of the Pimas and the Papagos, selling hay for cattle would save the Blackfeet. During the next two years, however, these fond hopes evaporated. A drought that lasted two years reduced the hay crop to nothing, leaving the Blackfeet in a "deplorable state."[58] During World War I increased beef prices led to the sale of cattle, and by the end of 1920 the cattle business on the Blackfeet reservation was shattered. An observer warned that if prompt measures were not taken, there would be great suffering and loss of life among the people as well as the possibility of extinction of their herds. In order to forestall this disaster, rations were again issued to the Blackfeet. By 1920, then, the Blackfeet had again reached an economic nadir, a situation calling for drastic measures and resulting in another issue of rations. In 1921, an energetic and enthusiastic agent, Frank C. Campbell, arrived to institute another program of Blackfeet economic recovery, a "Five Years' Plan" aimed especially at the full-bloods.[59]

North of the line, Canadian officials also regarded raising cattle as a less acceptable occupation than farming for the Blackfoot bands. At first glance, the terms of Treaty 7 seemed to indicate that Canadians wanted the Blackfoot Confederacy to become cattlemen. For instance, the treaty promised the issuance of between two and four head of cattle to each Indian, depending on the size of the family. For those who desired to cultivate the soil, the treaty also provided implements instead of stock. However, the treaty stressed that the cattle issue was for the purpose of encouraging *agriculture* among the Blackfoot bands.

For a number of years, the Bloods, Blackfoot, and Peigans did not show any more interest in cattle raising than in agriculture. When the first herd arrived in 1877, Commissioner Dewdney discovered that the Blackfoot refused to have anything to do with the cattle. Chief Crowfoot expressed fear that the herd would be killed by his young men and that the Blackfoot would get no more help from the government.[60] In the meantime, the oprhaned herd was left in the hands of the North West Mounted Police. In 1883, agent C. E. Denny reported that the herd had not done as well as expected. Since the Indians did not want the cattle, he decided to break up the herd, sell some cattle, and disperse the rest among the reserves. Denny advised the department not to issue anything else in lieu of the cattle.[61] Indeed, the department made no effort to restock the reserves until the 1890s, despite the general boom of the cattle industry nearby.

In the meantime, the government experimented on the western reserves with "mixed farming," or the combination of agriculture and stock raising. At two agencies, the department introduced on an experimental basis herds of cattle intended eventually to provide beef for the Indians, and thus relieve the department of the cost of purchasing beef cattle for rations. On other reserves, the government tried to make Indians look after dairy cattle.[62]

Throughout the 1880s, the Indian department concentrated on making the Indians farm while the cattle industry expanded around them. Virtually the only cattle that most Indians came into contact with were the oxen which the department tried to teach the Indians to use for farm work. Local officials noted that this effort was not successful.[63] After 1884, only the Peigans kept a herd, which by 1888 totaled eighty-eight head. In 1891, the Indian inspector commented that this herd had enjoyed a good increase, providing proof that "cattle-raising is a safe and profitable industry when properly managed."[64]

In 1891, the need to diversify Indian economy was brought to the attention of the government. Commissioner Hayter Reed urged the distribution of more cattle to the Indians to establish herds on all reserves. The western Indians, Reed pointed out, could not make a living without adding cattle to their economy. He also reported that Indians in Treaty 7 had largely abandoned their early opposition to cattle. Reed stressed that the department could not make a wiser investment in the long run than to purchase cattle for Indians.[65]

Reports of the repeated failures of agriculture as well as continued Indian rationing compelled the government to consider Reed's suggestions. Officials in Ottawa began to instruct field officials to issue cattle to Treaty 7 Indians, pointing out that even if they did not care for the stock it still could be turned into beef. Among the Blackfoot bands, the North Peigans were the first to accept cattle. Not only did they already have a small herd, but they were willing to accept more stock. In 1891, an inspector wrote to Ottawa that the Peigans were so anxious to obtain cattle that they went to the American side to trade their ponies for heifers.[66]

By the close of the century, the Indian department finally became aware that cattle raising had assumed an important position in the North West Territories. Yet some officials remained tentative about the purpose of issuing cattle to the Indians. Many continued to treat cattle as a buffer against harvest failure, permitting the Indians to fall back on selling their stock.[67]

Despite the lack of commitment on the part of the DIA, cattle raising took hold on two of the three reserves. An inspection of the Blackfoot reserve prompted the comment that Chief Crowfoot had prejudiced his people against cattle. One inspector lamented, "If they could be induced to look after their cattle one-half as well as they do their miserable horses, it would mean success." But the other two bands proved to be more receptive. While the Blackfoot had only 397 head, the Peigans raised 775 and the Bloods 1,454. Considering that the Blood cattle industry had begun only five years earlier,[68] the tribe had made creditable progress. In 1901 the department noted, with some surprise, that in Treaty 7 the "farming Indians" now depended almost entirely on cattle, while the Bloods had made the best showing, with nearly 3,000 head owned by 176 individuals.[69]

Much like the South Peigans, the Canadian Blackfeet did not remain unsupervised in their enterprise. Regulations regarding cattle were especially stringent because officials maintained that the Blackfeet would make progress only under the watchful eye of the department. Some officials even rejected the idea of the Indians trading ponies for cattle because, as one official explained, "the Indians are liable to think they should control the cattle when they paid for them." The DIA also forbade the Indians to sell or trade cattle without permission. Moreover, Indians were forbidden to place their personal brand on the cattle. Some agents recognized that the restrictions with which the department hedged the cattle business discouraged Indians' interest in the occupation. For example, in 1914 the agent of the Bloods memorialized Ottawa that the Indians should be encouraged to look after their livestock instead of having agency employees do so.[70]

Grazing lands on the reserve provided Canadian and American Blackfeet with income not only from their cattle, but also from leasing these lands to white cattlemen. By the turn of the century the cattle business was well established on the western reserves, although the Canadian Indian department sometimes refused to accept cattle raising as a viable economic alternative for the Indians. Ironically, the department saw no objection to allowing others to profit by using Indian grazing lands. In 1903, a lease on the blood reserve for seven thousand head went for five thousand dollars annually for ten years, while another company leased pasture on the Blackfoot reserve for ten years at two thousand dollars per annum.[71]

Local officials considered the department's lease system ill advised, and proposed that when the Bloods' lease ended the department should not renew it, but should establish a tribal herd for the benefit of the Bloods. One inspector wrote that ranching was as good, safe, and legitimate a business as anyone could wish, and the Bloods owned the best grazing lands in Alberta. The inspector asked, pointedly: "If other people can afford to pay thousands of dollars for the privilege of running cattle [on the reserve] and to make an immense profit, why should not we be able to do so [?]"[72] Yet even with the half-hearted support of the department, the Bloods developed by the midteens a fairly prosperous economy based on agriculture and livestock. After the outbreak of World War I, however, the Bloods suffered a serious setback due to the ill-advised actions of the DIA.

The plight of the Bloods was exposed in a lengthy memorandum by R.N. Wilson, ex-Mountie and ex–Indian agent of the Peigans and Bloods. In 1921, Wilson wrote "Our Betrayed Wards," an exposé of the rise and fall of the Blood cattle industry. Wilson pointed out that a 1918 amendment to the Indian Act had enabled the government to expropriate reserves for wartime production without the consent of the occupants. The department had gained, in effect, the free use of Indian lands, which previously they had refused to surrender or lease. This new legislation, Wilson asserted, meant a "raw deal" for the Indians.[73]

Wilson also charged that officials from the prime minister on down had mismanaged the Greater Production campaign on the Blood reserve. This process began, Wilson charged, in 1917 when the prime minister, as head of the Indian department, allowed "reservation exploitation in the interest of covetous white men." Wilson cast W. M. Graham as the principal villain, accusing him of causing massive losses of Indian cattle during the winter of 1919–20. The main objective behind the callousness of department officials, Wilson stated, was to cripple the economy of the Bloods so that their land could be taken away from them under the pretext that they did not need it for their cattle.[74]

In his effort to obtain an explanation, Wilson encountered only stonewalling from officials, which dragged on for several years. However, no explanation would have helped the Bloods. By 1920 they were back on rations, with their economy having turned full circle back to the destitution of forty years earlier. The Blackfoot also suffered losses of cattle during 1919–20, as a result of the combined shock of bad weather and the bunglings of commissioner Graham. Thanks only to the efforts of their agent, G. H. Gooderham, Blackfoot cattle losses were not as devastating as those among the Bloods and Stoneys.[76]

By the end of nearly a half-century of reservation life, the Blackfoot Confederacy in neither country had been able to establish a viable economy. All bands experienced numerous ups and downs under the farming policy. The discouraging results were due partly to the reluctance of the Blackfeet to farm, and were aggravated by inadequate systems of instructions, funding, and poorly executed programs such as irrigation. Cattle raising was more successful, but its administration created unequal distribution of wealth, thereby giving rise to a group of permanently poor Blackfeet. To be sure, even this occupation had its pitfalls, since it was subject to the vagaries of weather and uninformed administrative decisions.

The lack of funding to finance long-term development of the reservations aggravated the Indians' economic conditions because few projects were carried to completion before the Indian office terminated aid. Ironically, most of the farming and ranching efforts in the United States, and to a lesser extent in Canada, were financed from the sale of reservation lands; this policy reduced the Indians' land base and further removed the possibility of a self-sustaining reservation economy. Tragically, neither the officials nor the public saw the hidden pitfalls of the Indian land policy of the two countries.

Edgar Dewdney and wife, Regina, 1885. Glenbow Archives, Calgary.

Magnus Begg, Blackfoot agent, 1885. Glenbow Archives, Calgary.

William B. Pocklington, Blood agent, with Indian chiefs, 1886. Glenbow Archives, Calgary.

Agent George Steell and South
Peigan cheifs and headmen,
Montana. Seated left to right:
Four Horns, Little Bear,
Running Crane, Little Dog,
Little Plume. Standing left to
right: White Calf, George
Steell, Tail Feathers Coming
Over the Hill, White Grass,
Joseph Kipp, Indian trader,
1891. Eleventh Census,
Indians Taxed and Not Taxed.

Frederick H. Abbott. *The Red
Man*, 1913.

Above left. "Uncivilized" Blackfeet family, in summer camp. Montana, 1891. Eleventh Census, Indians Taxed and Not Taxed.

Opposite left. David Little Axe and family, Blackfoot reserve, Canada, 1890s. Glenbow Archives, Calgary.

Above. "Civilized" Blackfeet family, cutting potatoes for seed. Montana, 1891. Eleventh Census, Indians Taxed and Not Taxed.

Indian log cabin, Blackfeet reservation, Montana. This house is in better shape than the average Indian dwelling on the reservation. *The Red Man*, 1915.

Mixed-bloods, Blackfeet reservation, Montana, 1890. Eleventh Census, Indians Taxed and Not Taxed.

Blackfoot Indians at agency office. Agent J. H. Gooderham is seated in front of window, 1918. Glenbow Archives, Calgary.

Blackfeet council, Montana, 1890. Eleventh Census, Indians Taxed and Not Taxed.

Anglican missionaries and Blood parishioners, ca. 12885. Third left in the rear is the Reverend Samuel Trivett; fourth and sixth have been tentatively identified as the Reverend J. W. Tims and the Reverend George Mckay. Glenbow Archives, Calgary.

St. John's home, North Camp mission, Blackfoot reserve, ca. 1896. Glenbow Archives, Calgary.

Two of the first pupils at Blackfoot Anglican School, ca. 1886. Glenbow Archives, Calgary.

The Reverend Samuel Trivett, ca. 1880s. Glenbow Archives, Calgary.

THE BLACKFOOT LANGUAGE AND SYLLABARIUM

SYLLABARIUM:—

HYMN "JESU, LOVER OF MY SOUL"

	A	E	I	O

ASPIRATES ETC.

DIPH. VOWEL I
DIPH. VOWEL O
INTERMEDIATE S
ASPIRATE H
GUTTURAL KH
FULL STOP .

P

T

K

M

N

S

Y

W

JESU LOVER OF MY SOUL
LET ME TO THY BOSOM FLY
WHILE THE NEARER WATERS ROLL
WHILE THE TEMPEST STILL IS HIGH
HIDE ME O MY SAVIOUR HIDE
TILL THE STORM OF LIFE BE PAST
SAFE INTO THE HAVEN GUIDE
O RECEIVE MY SOUL AT LAST.

TSISAS KITAKOMIMOKI
KAKASKSAWAKAMOKSI
KITAKOMIMAU NOTAKKI
NITSITAPIPIKS KSESTOWA
AYO NINNA KSISSAKIT
NAKSTAIKIHTOYIS ANOM
SPOMOKIT NAKITOTOS
ISSOHTSIK KOKOWAYI.

Above left. Blackfeet Indians visiting their children in the Carlisle Indian School, Pennsylvania. *The Red Man*, 1913.

Opposite left. North Camp school, Blackfoot reserve. The teacher is Hugh Baker, left rear; the Reverend Tims is rear right, 1892. Glenbow Archives, Calgary.

Above. Blackfoot language and syllabics, taught by the Reverend Stocken. Glenbow Archives, Calgary.

William Upham, Blackfeet Indian, harvesting a field of oats. Blackfeet reservation, Montana, 1914. *The Red Man*, 1914.

Priests, sisters, and Blackfoot children at St. Joseph's Catholic residential school, Blackfoot Crossing, 1900. Glenbow Archives, Calgary.

Dog Child, North West Mounted Police, scout and wife, Blackfoot
Indians, ca. 1890s. Glenbow Archives, Calgary.

Indian policeman, Blackfoot reservation, Montana, 1890. Eleventh Census, Indians Taxed and Not Taxed.

Steam engine and its Indian operators, Blood reserve, 1915. Glenbow Archives, Calgary.

The Reverend S. Middleton and patriotic Blood Indians, ca. 1917. Glenbow Archives, Calgary.

Harvest on the Blood reserve, 1920. Fifteen binders hitched to three "Oil Pull" tractors harvesting a 2,500-acre field. Glenbow Archives, Calgary.

Preparation for Sun Dance lodge, Blackfoot reserve, 1905–6. Glenbow Archives, Calgary.

North West Mounted Police officers and Blood Indian scouts, Fort Macleod, ca. 1880. Middle row, first left, identified as Cecil Denny. Glenbow Archives, Calgary.

Sun Dance camp, Blackfoot Crossing, 1920s. Glenbow Archives, Calgary.

5

Land Policy

The lack of adequate land base provided one reason why many reservation Indians in the United States failed to reach economic self-sufficiency. Although the reduction of Indian real estate began with the arrival of the first Europeans, the trend grew most precipitous toward the end of the nineteenth century, as the American government accelerated the reduction of lands reserved for Indians "in perpetuity" by numerous treaties. This repeated diminution of reservations left the Indians not only with a shrunken land base, but often in possession of lands poorly suited for agriculture. Ironically, the situation arose at a point when most officials considered agriculture the backbone of Indian economy.

The periodic expropriation of lands belonging to the American Indians gave rise to the truism in the United States that the American government had broken every Indian treaty. By contrast, many observers believed that the Canadian government respected and protected lands promised to the Indians by treaties. For this reason, it is argued, Canadians managed to avoid a major cause of Indian dissatisfaction, thus escaping the Indian wars that plagued the American West. In turn, the Dominion acquired a reputation for fair treatment of the Indians, especially where aboriginal lands were involved.

On the other hand, officials of the American Indian service, along with the general population, shared the view that all government-held lands—including the public domain and Indian reservations—should be released to private ownership as quickly as possible. In addressing the annual meeting of the Indian Rights Association in 1889, commissioner Thomas J. Morgan flatly stated that the days of the Indian reservations were numbered, and it was not in his power to rescue them. "It is idle to expect, and folly to hope," he told his audience, "that a handful of ignorant, helpless savages, occupying vast regions of territory which they do not cultivate, can resist the tidal wave of population which is speeding from the Atlantic to the Pacific."[1] Morgan's views summed up the attitude of many later Indian commissioners.

American Indians were divested of their lands in two ways: by surrendering a portion of their reservations, and after 1887, by allotment. The first move involved some form of tribal consent, even if it was gained by duress or by fraud. The second approach required no tribal consent, only congressional legislation. By contrast, until after the turn of the century, the Canadian government could obtain reserve lands only with the Indians' consent. During the midteens, the government amended the Indian Act, empowering the governor-general-in-council to ask for the relinquishment of reserve lands situated near a town with a population of at least eight thousand inhabitants.[2] This amendment, however, did not result in the wholesale legislative expropriation of Indian lands.

Some scholars maintain that after the turn of the century the Canadian government yielded to the wishes of the electorate and began to orchestrate a reduction in Indian lands.[3] Undeniably, the government did seek to reduce some western reserves, but the pressure from the public and special interests to reduce Indian lands played a less significant role in Canada than in the United States. Actually, it was the Dominion government's desire to speed up settlement of the North West Territories that prompted the move to reduce reserves. Consequently, Canadian Indian policy remained controlled and reflected more the interest—or the lack of it—of government officials in western development. In contrast, the history of Blackfeet reservation reductions in the United States clearly illustrates the decisive influence of public pressure on federal American Indian policy.

The pressure to reduce the Great Northern Reservation, set aside by executive order in 1873, began soon after its establishment. In 1874, the president restored the area between the Sun and the Marias rivers to the public domain upon the urging of the Montana territorial delegate, but over the protests of the Indians and their agent.[4] Nearly a decade later, complaints reached Washington about Indian depredations on cattle herds trespassing on the reservation. The cattlemen demanded the confinement of the still nomadic Blackfeet to their reservation, and the exclusion of "British Indians" from American territory. Washington warned agent Young to keep his charges on the reservation; the commissioner warned, "In the present temper of the settlers, a slight provocation might precipitate a conflict between them and the Indians, the results of which would be deplorable."[5]

But the presence of the Blackfeet, on or off the reservation, continued to annoy many Montanans. Agent Young, who spent much of his time fending off criticism of his administration, felt certain that the complaints came from the Choteau County Stock Association. These people, he fumed, wanted the government to "take a slice off the reservation, and thus increase the stock ranges."[6]

Young's fears proved to be well founded. Martin Maginnis, Montana's territorial delegate, spearheaded the attack by introducing in 1882 a bill for further reduction of the large reservation. Young appealed directly to Maginnis to withdraw the bill in the name of justice, humanity, and the sake of the Indians' future. He argued that the reduction would leave the Blackfeet the mountainous portion of the reservation and virtually no agricultural land. The existing reservation, Young wrote, was none too large for their needs.[7] Maginnis, however, ignored Young's pleas. He announced the creation of a commission to visit the various Montana agencies in order to, as he put it, "assign the Indians there to comfortable quarters, and at the same time give the country the benefit of lands which are now practically worthless to mànkind because of the Indian ownership of them."[8]

When the commission arrived at the Blackfeet agency in December 1883, the commissioners took for granted that the Indians would cede the lands—the question was what their terms would be. They found a sad state of affairs at the agency, with the Indians starving and desperate. The situation made the cession, with its promise of food and supplies, seem like a humanitarian gesture.[9]

The Blackfeet were receptive to the offers, since most were anxious to secure some form of aid. At the prompting of the mixed-bloods, various Blackfeet speakers asked the government to pay between two and three million dollars for their lands, an offer the government representatives rejected. The commissioners retorted that no money would be handed out, but that the government would help the Indians work for their living, since, as one of the commissioners put it, "it is by work that the white man has got [sic] rich."[10]

When the commission departed, agitation mounted among local Montanans for the reduction of the reservation. The governor assured the secretary of the interior that although Indians in Montana Territory possessed an enormous amount of land, they were so poor that they "would be only too glad to exchange lands almost worthless to them for some of the comforts and necessities of life." The governor, like many others, mixed equal parts of avarice and benevolence in pressing for the expropriation of Indian lands.[11]

Pressures to reduce the reservation culminated in February 1887 with the arrival of a new commission. Because of the extreme cold and deep snow, many Blackfeet failed to arrive at the cession hearings, and consequently, the proposal passed with a bare majority. This agreement received the approval of other tribes sharing the reservation, and split the area into three separate agencies. The Blackfeet retained some forty-five square miles of land, and seventeen million acres were opened to settlement. The Blackfeet received 125,000 dollars per annum for the next ten years.[12]

The breakup of the reservation resulted from the demands of the settlers as well as the Indians' desire to avoid another winter of starvation. The cession essentially paid for Blackfeet subsistence throughout the next decade. However, even before the terms of this surrender expired, public sentiment began to favor a further reduction of the reservation. This time, the push came not from cattlemen or settlers, but from prospectors. Rumors that the western portion of the reservation, called the "St. Mary's Strip," contained valuable minerals prompted calls in the early 1890s to open the area. The news that a scheme was afoot to relieve them of more land alarmed the Blackfeet.[13]

Pressured by constituents, Congress approved negotiations for the St. Mary's Strip, even though there was only sketchy evidence of the existence of minerals. A meeting of a Blackfeet council voted twenty-nine to three in favor of opening the area to mineral entry, a vote that undoubtedly stemmed from the awareness that it would be fruitless to resist the demands of the American public. Even the Blackfeet agent, an ex–army officer, admitted that if a "gold rush" occurred, he would be powerless to stop it.[14]

The final agreement for ceding the mineral strip was signed in September 1895. George Bird Grinnell, a prominent ethnologist who served as a commissioner, thought for a while that the rest of the Blackfeet might reject the proposal. In the end, the commissioners secured 190 out of a total of 330 votes. The Blackfeet ceded 800,000 acres for 1.5 million dollars, but the opening was delayed for another year. In the meantime, agents fended off requests from and clandestine entries by impatient prospectors. One agent wrote anxious letters to the commissioner, pointing out that he could not keep "sooners" out of the mountains with his police force of eighteen men. Ironically, when the area was finally opened in 1898, the prospectors were disappointed. No gold, only copper and other less valuable minerals were discovered. The agent predicted that the whole "rush" would soon be abandoned.[15]

In the twenty-five years following the establishment of the Blackfeet reservation, the government yielded three times to public pressure to reduce the reservation. But the largest "land grab" still lay in the future. Some five years after the St. Mary's cession, there again arose rumors that the Blackfeet would be asked to give up lands north of Cut Bank Creek and Milk River. The commissioner instructed the agent to quiet the Indians' fears by stressing that no cession was being considered at that time. He wrote that "when such negotiations come to be proposed, if at all, the Indians are not in any way compelled to agree to any cession, unless they wish to and upon such terms as are perfectly satisfactory to them."[16]

Such reassurances, however, ran contrary to the spirit of the times. Calls for the reduction of the reservation, whether through cessions or allotment, increased around the turn of the century, and neither the existence of treaties nor Indian opposition carried much weight in Congress. For example, in 1902 Senator Joseph L. Rawlins of Utah introduced a bill for the sale of a portion of the Uintah reservation. When he finally learned of the bill, Commissioner W. A. Jones stressed that he did not believe the Indians should hold large tracts of land, but he did think it would be necessary to obtain the Utes' consent to the cession. The annoyed senator asked why the commissioner simply did not take the lands. Rawlins put it bluntly: "We have theoretically proceeded upon the idea of obtaining the consent of the Indians, which is usually a farce."[17]

For the Blackfeet, the agreement of 1895 also proved to be a farce. According to article 5, the Blackfeet were assured that no allotments in severalty would be made for the duration of the agreement. After the agreement expired, lands were to be held in common until the majority of adult males requested allotment in writing.[18] In 1907, the government violated this agreement when it imposed the allotment policy on the Blackfeet and legislated the opening of the reservation without the tribe's consent.

These reductions of the Blackfeet reservation took place before the turn of the century, and they came as a result of agitation from settlers and prospectors for more land, coupled with the desire of the Indians to secure a guaranteed livelihood. After 1900, reservations in Montana became subject to the General Allotment Act, which did not require consent from the Indians. Under the allotment system, vast amounts of Indian real estate, in Montana and elsewhere, found its way into the hands of non-Indians. The consequences for Indian economic well-being were disastrous.

During this period, some Americans came to believe that the Canadians had made no arbitrary moves to deprive their native people of their lands, and that the Dominion adopted a generally wiser Indian land policy. The reality, however, was not so clear cut. Although the Canadians rejected the American version of resevation allotment, Ottawa adopted a policy of reducing reserves soon after the turn of the century, especially on the prairies where the government wanted to encourage settlement.

The reason for the delay in Canadian reserve reduction stemmed not only from the generally slower development of the prairie, but also from the attitudes of government officials toward western settlement. Once the government had ensured orderly prairie development by providing land surveys and granting land to the railroads, western administration became a matter of routine. When questions arose about opening the Indian reserves, ministers such as Clifford Sifton maintained that the government could do nothing without the consent of the tribes.[19] By that time, tribal consent had become largely a formality in the United States, but some Canadian officials seemed genuinely torn between taking unilateral action and adhering to principles of fairness in dealing with the Indians. An examination of the history of the Peigan and Blackfoot surrenders and of efforts to obtain a similar concession from the Bloods reveals the tensions between the two principles that arose after the mid-1900s.

With the appointment of Frank Oliver as head of the Ministry of the Interior, official reticence about obtaining land surrenders from the bands came to an end. In 1908, Oliver announced a modification of existing policy toward the sale of Indian lands. He stated:

> It is now recognized that where Indians are holding tracts of farming or timber lands beyond their possible requirements and by so doing seriously impeding the growth of settlement, and there is such demand as to ensure profitable sale, the product of which can be invested for the benefit of the Indians and to relieve *pro tanto* the country of the burden of their maintenance, it is in the best interest of all concerned to encourage such sales.

Even then, however, DIA officials felt compelled to assure the government that these sales would take place only with the consent of the Indians.[20]

Situated in an area that the government believed was especially attractive to settlers, the Blood, Peigan, and Blackfoot reserves became the prime targets for reduction. The Bloods occupied the largest reserve in Canada, consisting of some 350,400 acres, while the Blackfoot and Peigan reserves contained 300,800 and 116,000 acres, respectively.[21] Efforts to reduce these reserves gave rise to charges of fraud, undue influence, and the kind of high-handedness most often associated with the American style of Indian–white relations. The Peigans were the first band of the confederacy to be asked to surrender a part of their reserve. They formed the smallest group, less than five hundred people, and compared to their tribal relatives, they lived in relative prosperity. In 1904, the DIA instructed J. A. Markle—who served as the Blackfoot agent as well as the inspector of Indian agencies in the North West Territories—to approach the Peigans with the idea of surrender.[22] The situation remained dormant during several years marked by a mounting interest in the reserve lands. The Peigans grew uneasy, and in the spring of 1908, they complained to Markle about rumors that a part of their reserve would be taken away.

Inspector and agent Markle, one of those supremely self-confident, energetic, and dedicated British civil servants, was determined to anticipate as well as fulfill the wishes of his superiors in Ottawa. Prior to his appointment to the Blackfoot agency in 1901 and his elevation to inspector, Markle had served as Indian agent in Manitoba. Engineering the surrender of Indian lands became Markle's obsession. He thought that if Indians relinquished a part of their reserves, the profits from the sale of these lands would relieve the government of the economic burden of providing implements, cattle, and supplies to the land-wealthy Indians and make the lands available to tax-paying citizens. Given his attitude, it is hardly surprising that Markle did not try to quiet the Peigans' fears; instead, he dangled before them the potential benefits of selling their land. He informed the department that he had rejected the Peigans' request for a thresher and farming implements, explaining to them that if they wanted these articles they must surrender the land.[23]

Over the next several months, the band severely divided over this issue, while Markle worked on the vacillators. In the spring of 1909, the Peigans attended two meetings to discuss the cession, but they adamantly opposed any sale. Markle persisted, tantalizing the Peigans with visions of new wagons, cattle, implements, seeds, houses, and rations. On 16 July, a vote of forty-six to thirty-nine turned down any sale, but intratribal animosities ran high. Markle reported that Chief Iron Shield and his followers rode to Fort Macleod to consult a lawyer about blocking any surrender. Some of the young men favoring a sale were married to the daughters of the opposition, and expressed fear that their wives would leave them if they voted for the sale. Markle was exasperated by the opposition of the old warriors, but noting that several of them were in poor health, he believed that once they passed away their place would be taken by more "progressive men," meaning those who favored surrender.[24]

In the summer of 1909, Markle finally swayed enough Peigans to agree to the surrender by a vote of sixty to forty-two. The Peigans relinguished twenty-three thousand acres. Some Peigans, however, never became reconciled to the sale. Indeed, Markle acknowledged that complaints continued about the manner in which the surrender had been accomplished. While never directly denying irregularities, Markle defended the entire transaction on the basis that it had been done for the Indians' benefit.[25]

Obtaining the Peigan surrender, however, did not end the unrest. A part of the band—the majority, as they viewed themselves—decided to block the sale of the ceded land. Notices appeared on the reserve declaring the intention to contest the sale, planned for November 1909, on the grounds that the Peigans had never executed a surrender. When the sale proceeded anyway, another notice appeared in the spring of 1910, inform- ing the purchasers that they would be forcibly ejected if they tried to claim their lands. These announcements were the creation of one Colin Mac- leod, a lawyer consulted by the Peigans before the surrender. Markle immediately dismissed Macleod as an opportunist who preyed on and incited ignorant Indians to oppose the government and to act against their best interests.[26] Despite Peigan protests, the department allowed the sale to stand, and Markle turned his attention to the Blackfoot reserve, whose surrender now became an important objective for government officials.

The Blackfoot occupied the middle of 2.9 million acres granted to the Canadian Pacific Railroad by the Dominion government. After the turn of the century, the railroad decided to open as much land as possible for settlement, and the reserve became an obstacle to the area's systematic development[27]. The decision to develop the region coinincided with the DIA's desire to make reserved lands pay for the Indians' maintenance. J. A. Markle always subscribed to this principle, especially when he dis- covered that after years of reservation life the Blackfoot had not made any progress toward self-sufficiency. His intention to make the Blackfoot self-supporting and the Indians' desire for security enabled Markle to engi- neer the surrender of nearly half the reserve in 1910. The history of the Blackfoot surrender is especially interesting because it illustrates the insis- tence of some DIA officials that the Indians' wishes must be respected.

In one account of the surrender, Blackfoot missionary H. W. Gibbon Stocken painted Markle as a savior of the tribe. Stocken wrote that he approached Markle one day in 1910 with the worrisome problem of his poverty-stricken flock. Stocken recalled that "this led to a sleepless night for the good man and resulted in the careful planning to meet the real needs of the Indian and at the same time prevent the financial burden of it falling upon the overtaxed funds in Ottawa." Since the population of the tribe had declined and left a part of the reserve unoccupied, the Blackfoot indicated a willingness to surrender that portion of their lands. First, however, they asked for guarantees that the surrender would not be a "thin end of a wedge" leading to further reductions.[28] But an exam- ination of the records revealed that Markle's actions were not based on a spur-of-the-moment decision.

Indeed, local interest in obtaining a portion of the reserve existed as early as 1907. The department received petitions from business interests and from the town of Gleichen for a sale of a part of the reserve. Both petitioners argued that the surrender would benefit western development as well as the Blackfoot band. Expecting changes in the Canadian Pacific

Railroad line, which bordered the northern edge of the reserve, the department did not raise the question of surrender until 1908. Meanwhile, Markle tempted the Blackfoot with the usual blandishments—promises of houses, sheds, furnishings, machinery, cattle, and rations. In spite of these promises, Markle reported that there was some opposition to the sale. One of the chiefs even had the audacity to tell the inspector that he would consent to the sale at a hundred dollars per acre.[29]

In the spring of 1910, emboldened by his success with the Peigans, Markle predicted that within four months he could secure the surrender of several townships on the Blackfoot reserve. He was certain that the Peigan surrender had shown the Blackfoot and the Bloods what they too could obtain if they gave up a part of their lands. When the issue came to a vote in the summer of 1910, the prosale faction carried the day. With the surrender of 115,000 acres, the Blackfoot gave up half of their reserve and were transformed from one of the poorest to one of the richest Indian groups in Canada.[30]

This surrender created unexpected problems for the department. Markle secured the Indians' consent by promising the band the 1.8 million dollars to be realized from the sale. A total of 400,000 dollars was to be spent immediately for houses, farm equipment, and rations; the remainder of the proceeds would go to the Blackfoot trust account for the band's future needs. Even before the vote took place, the deputy superintendent cautioned Markle that the surrender terms should be qualified with the phrase "provided sufficient sum [is] received from sale to cover the conditions."[31] Apparently taken with his impending coup, Markle exercised no such caution.

The amount of the sum to be paid was premised on Markle's assumption that the land would sell at a specific price and within a reasonable period of time. Unfortunately, the department soon faced delayed payments from the buyers, and as a result, Ottawa could not meet its promises to the tribe. Indeed, officials soon realized that the Blackfoot sale had fallen short of expectations. At the first sale in 1911 only half of the lands were sold, and the department had to withdraw the remainder from a sale in 1912 because of low bids. By 1912 the sale realized 941,872.25 dollars, considerably short of the expected 1.8 million dollars. Purchasers who decided to keep up payments of the interest while not making payments on the principle compounded the cash-flow problem. Officials grew frantic as the account that paid for Blackfoot rations became seriously depleted. Departmental accountant D. C. Scott summed up the situation: "All expenditure from the account which is at all avoidable, has been stopped, and the whole scheme for the improvement of these Indians is paralyzed." He urged the sale of more land, warning that the government would need to pass legislation granting additional funds for rations.[32]

In the spring of 1914, the band began to complain about delays in the fulfillment of promises. The Indians' disillusionment and bitterness were directed against Markle, their new agent, and tribal members who had voted for the sale. But the Blackfoot were not the only unhappy party to the agreement. Scott, hard pressed to keep up payments from the dwindling funds, was appalled when he learned that officials had made guarantees to the Blackfoot that food rations would be continued as one of the conditions of the surrender. With his office essentially painted into a corner, Scott tried to salvage the situation by reducing Blackfoot beef rations from seven pounds to five pounds per week. He also instructed the agent to explain to the Indians that this reduction was consistent with the terms of the surrender.[33]

When the Blackfoot learned about the reduction, they were outraged. The Indians protested to the government, stating that they had consented to the surrender believing that it would guarantee rations for them and future generations "as long as the river flowed and the sun shone in heaven." The Blackfoot were not responsible for the arrears; they had kept up their part of the bargain. If the money could not be collected, the government should borrow it, they argued. Not only the rations, but the promised farm implements, horses, and wagons also appeared to be in jeopardy. In 1916, the Blackfoot asked when the government would finally begin to provide the promised houses and horses. It was not until 1917, seven years after the agreement, that the remainder of the lands went up for sale, realizing 1.2 million dollars. In the nick of time, this sale saved Blackfoot tribal funds from collapse.[34] Having successfully accomplished two major surrenders in Treaty 7, J. A. Markle turned next to the attempt to reduce the largest reserve in Canada. In the Bloods, however, Markle found formidable opponents.

This band was traditionally wary about allowing outsiders to use their lands. In 1904, efforts to secure grazing leases on the reserve caused an uproar among the Bloods. Although the department had managed to negotiate a grazing lease,[35] the Indians remained suspicious about the department's intentions. When the issue of selling a portion of the reserve arose, some Bloods defended their lands with grim determination.

The first move to reduce the Blood reserve came on 7 March 1907. Inspector Markle told agent R. N. Wilson that the DIA was anxious for the Bloods to surrender two sections of the reserve. Markle asked the agent to evaluate the chances for the success of such a proposal, so that a vote on the issue could be authorized.[36]

Barely two months later, Markle called a council of the Bloods to offer them two choices: to sell a forty-thousand-acre strip at the south end of the reserve, or a four-hundred-acre parcel adjacent to the Mormon town of Cardston. Both proposals met with stiff opposition from a large segment of the Bloods led by Chief Crop Eared Wolf. This man was the adopted son of Red Crow, head chief of the Bloods and a reluctant signatory of Treaty 7.[37] For the next several years, the surrender question became the center of a battle of wills between Crop Eared Wolf and inspector Markle. The inspector was determined to carry out the policy of the Indian department, as he interpreted it, and the chief was equally determined to preserve the land for future generations despite Markle's efforts and opposition from some of his own people.

The issue of surrender came to a vote in May 1907. When a minor chief expressed a willingness to consider the proposition, Crop Eared Wolf broke up the meeting by leading an exodus of his followers. Over the next couple of weeks, the breach widened. At a new meeting, some Bloods were willing to consider a sale of the smaller strip for 100,000 dollars and Markle hastily arranged for a vote to be held at another meeting.[38]

Fearing that some of his wavering tribesmen might consent to the sale, Crop Eared Wolf took the matter into his own hands. He wrote to David Laird, the Indian commissioner, appealing to him as an old friend of the Bloods. The chief told Laird of the assurances, made five years earlier, that the land would never be taken away from the band. Laird gave the chief a chilly reception, informing him that at that time the superintendent had had no intention of asking the Bloods for a surrender; however, the new superintendent obviously had reasons for asking the Bloods for a part of their reserve. Still, as Laird assured Crop Eared Wolf, this surrender would occur only with the consent of the majority of the Bloods.[39]

With no assurances that the department would bar the sale, Crop Eared Wolf searched for a means of preventing a segment of his band from concluding an agreement. He and his adherents arrived at the Fort Macleod police barracks, where they made "protests and complaints" to the police. Not content with these actions, the Bloods met with "one of the lesser legal lights," as their agent put it, to defeat the sale. The agent reported that Crop Eared Wolf and his party were tireless, with the chief using his influence to the utmost in coaxing, pleading, and threatening. The lawyer also filled the Bloods with nonsensical ideas, such as the claim that if any part of the Blood reserve were surrendered, the Indians would be removed beyond Edmonton. On the day of the vote, several antisale chiefs vigorously canvassed each arrival, and the lawyer, a "half drunk pettifogger," as the agent put it, harangued the Indians. The result of the vote was 139 against and 39 for the sale.[40]

Markle lost the battle, but he was determined not to lose the war. He informed the commissioner of his failed mission, pointing out in the same breath that the sale would have carried if the department had removed Crop Eared Wolf and one of his lieutenants under the "incompetency provision" of the Indian Act. When Ottawa informed him that a lack of progressiveness was not incompetence from a legal perspective, and that chiefs could not be removed solely on those grounds,[41] Markle was chagrined.

In the meantime, reorganization of the commissioner's office in Regina further confused the situation. The commissioner's officials informed Ottawa that they were unaware of any instructions issued to Markle to open negotiations with the Bloods. The assistant commissioner also expressed dismay that the inspector would try to remove the chiefs. He wrote to the secretary of the Indian department that "the suggestion to depose the Chiefs appears to be an incident of the unsuccessful negotiations for a surrender of a portion of the reserve." [42] Fortunately for Crop Eared Wolf, the department rejected Markle's solution, and the old chief retained his position while remaining as vigilant as ever of his people's welfare.

Three years later, in 1910, a new furor engulfed the reserve when the department suggested that the Bloods lease the land for petroleum explorations. Crop Eared Wolf was once again in the forefront of the opposition. He accused the government of breaking every promise that it had made to the Bloods since Treaty 7, maintaining that consequently the Indians could not trust any agreement made with the department.

At one of the meetings, Crop Eared Wolf's vehement opposition brought on a "paralytic stroke."[43] At this meeting, Crop Eared Wolf urged the Bloods to boycott the upcoming vote. Unfortunately, the chief did not understand the workings of the white man's democracy. When the time came, only eighty voters arrived, and sixty-eight of them voted to allow the leases. The agent recommended that the DIA approve the vote as a wholesome lesson to the Bloods, even though only a small portion of the eligible voters had participated. Later, when the agent asked some Bloods why they opposed the leases, they told him that they failed to see the difference between leasing the land and selling it.[44] In view of the action of the government during the Greater Production campaign, the Bloods' viewpoint proved to be perceptive.

At first glance, irregularities involving the Peigan and Blackfoot surrenders would seem to indicate that Canadians had an attitude toward Indian rights that was as cavalier as the attitude of their American counterparts. In Canada, however, the lack of agreement about the principles governing Indian surrenders led the department to establish uniform guidelines in 1914. The new guidelines provided that Indians would be properly notified of a proposed surrender, a voters' list would be compiled, a meeting would be advertised, and the vote would be scrutinized and certified.[45] Naturally, such instructions did not guarantee fairness, but they reflected a persistent concern on the part of some DIA officials to preserve the department's reputation for honesty in dealing with the Indians.

This concern led D. C. Scott to veto a surrender of ninety thousand acres of the Blood reserve in 1917. Although the Bloods agreed to the surrender, according to the agent, the document was riddled with so many irregularities that the DIA refused to approve it. Scott took the occasion to lecture to the agent: "I must say that it has always been my policy not to attempt to unduly influence the Blood Indians in this matter, and I do not want them to think that they are being forced to surrender this property. You were so well aware of this fact that I thought you would conduct the negotiations on this basis."[46]

Despite these sentiments, the outbreak of World War I caused a change of heart in the Indian department regarding the legal niceties of surrenders and leases. In 1918, the government modified the Indian Act to allow the superintendent to lease reserve lands for the benefit of the Indian band without obtaining the Indians' consent.[47] On the Blood reserve, some charged that this change of policy caused the ruination of the Blood cattle industry as well as the tribe's economic paralysis.

The disastrous consequences of leasing the reserve became something of a government scandal when ex-agent R. N. Wilson published the muckraking "Our Indian Wards" memorandum in 1921. The Bloods were one of several bands whose lands were leased under the Greater Production campaign, and they found in Wilson their champion. He accused the Indian department of "Prussianism" in trying to force the Bloods to cede their lands and, failing that, of deliberately ruining their cattle business so that poverty would force their acquiescence.[48]

The whole messy affair fell into the lap of D. C. Scott, who was by then the secretary of the Indian department. Scott informed the minister of the interior Arthur Meighen, who was also the head of the Indian department, that the disaster on the Blood reserve resulted from the actions of a succession of several incompetent agents and was not attributable to the Greater Production campaign. This explanation amounted to a roundabout confession of the department's failings. Scott had no desire to submit the affair to public scrutiny and informed Meighen, soon to become prime minister, that "while no doubt the holding of judicial investigation would clear the air, I am not sure that the Department would come out of it very well. While I have no objections personally to this ordeal, I think it would be better policy to avoid it."[49]

During the spring session of 1921, the House launched an inquiry into Blood leases, while Scott adopted a wait-and-see attitude. A year later, Scott sent the bloods a "dear chiefs" letter, telling them that the disaster which had befallen them was the result of bad weather and poor agents, and was not the fault of the department. Scott told the Bloods that the Greater Production campaign was "the most inspiring chapter in the annals of your race." The Bloods, Scott wrote, should not regret the sacrifice they had made to Canada and the civilized world. The Indian department never carried out an official investigation, and the Bloods remained economically devastated. The ultimate irony in this episode proved to be the proposal of W. M. Graham that the tribe sell 160,000 acre to finance their recovery.[50]

Despite the Peigan and Blackfoot land surrenders and persistent efforts to obtain the surrender of a portion of the Blood reserve, Canadians tried to adhere to the principles of obtaining tribal consent. When changes in the Indian Act appeared to lead the Dominion to infringe on Indian treaty rights, prominent members of Parliament rose to defend the treaties.[51] In the United States, on the other hand, Congress took steps to abolish Indian reservations unilaterally with the passage of the Dawes Severalty Act.

The intent of the Dawes Allotment Act, passed in 1887, was to solve the "Indian problem" by terminating federal trust responsibility for Indian affairs. Although the allotment program generated much enthusiasm among Americans, some observers were uneasy,[52] and they looked to Canada for answers to their quandary.

Much to their surprise, the reformers found that Canada eschewed the allotment system, although not as completely as the Americans assumed. Two years after the passage of the Dawes Act, commissioner Hayter Reed instructed the Indian agents in the North West Territories to make surveys of reserves in preparation for allotment. He emphasized that efforts should be made to induce Indians to locate themselves on individual parcels of land in preparation for the eventual issuance of location tickets. That year, the DIA reported that the assignment of land would inculcate in the Indians, through the possession of private property, the spirit of individual responsibility and ambition.[53]

Allotment arrived at the Blood reserve in 1892. A survey team mapped out eighty-acre plots; but the reports are unclear as to how many Bloods availed themselves of this offer. Allotment also took place on the Peigan reserve, with the agent reporting the issuance of thirty-one tickets between 1909 and 1910. On the Blackfoot reserve, a total of 148 individuals became "locatees" in 1918. In 1916, the total number of location tickets issued in Canada stood at 1,948. Obviously, Canadians were not as anxious as the Americans to "individualize" the Indians.[54]

During the same period, Americans proceeded feverishly with allotments of Indian reservations. In time, this system threatened not only the Blackfeet, but many other tribes as well, with the loss of their land base. Indeed, the Dawes Act had inaugurated what has been called, in retrospect, a "carnival of exploitation."[55] Most reservations where allotment took place were situated on the northern plains, and the allotment of the Blackfeet offers a fairly representative picture of the entire process.

The 1907 authorization for Blackfeet allotment came from an act directing the secretary of the interior to order a survey of the Blackfeet reservation, assign to tribal members allotments of 40 irrigable acres and 280 grazing acres, or 320 acres of grazing land, and open the reservation to settlement. Unfortunately for the Montanans, President Theodore Roosevelt subsequently vetoed the opening of the reservation because he believed the move would endanger Blackfeet water rights.[56] Roosevelt's action postponed the actual opening of the reservation for nine years.

The Blackfeet, especially the full-bloods, were considerably bewildered by the entire issue. In 1890, the agent thought that the Dawes Act would have a great civilizing influence on the Blackfeet, although he admitted that the Indians "have no idea in the world in regard to the quantity that each one would be entitled to under allotment." He discovered that some Indians wanted allotment, while others opposed it because the surplus lands would be sold. In 1904, the agent recommended that allotments be made only to mixed-bloods, and he convened a council to discuss the future of the reservation after the 1895 agreement expired.[57]

In the spring of 1908, work began in surveying the reservation and assigning allotments to individual Indians. Given the early arrival of inclement weather, the allotting agents predicted that three or four years would be needed to finish the work. The survey revealed that the reservation contained 1,534,549.24 acres, to be divided among some 2,500 individuals. This left some 800,000 acres as surplus lands.[58]

In 1912, the surveyors and allotting agents completed their work. The bureau immediately inquired about whether a competency commission should be established on the reservation to evaluate the Indians' readiness to accept patents in fee. Agent McFatridge vehemently rejected the idea as premature. He told the bureau that in his judgment the Blackfeet tribe was not ready for citizenship. The agent also told officials that the standards used by the commission for judging the Indians' competence were far too lax, and he added that the issuance of fee patents brought nothing but problems to the Indians.[59]

Fortunately for the Blackfeet, the bureau confined itself to the issuance of trust patents. Only three were issued in 1913, covering some 960 acres. Part of the reason for the delay stemmed from the realization on the part of officials that haste in approving allotments on other reservations often led to loss of land. In 1912, Frederick Abbot, who served as the acting commissioner, pointed to the situation on the Blackfeet reservation as a good example of the unforseen consequences of hasty allotment: the individual owners had no capital to improve their land, and consequently, they could not earn a living.[60]

In the meantime, factions for and against the sale of the surplus lands arose among the Blackfeet. During the winter of 1913, agent McFatridge forwarded to the bureau a petition from several tribal members protesting the opening of the reservation. The Indians reminded the government that two years earlier the agent had recommended the retention of several townships of grazing land. The petitioners stated that allotment and sale of the lands would force the Blackfeet to give up ranching and become farmers, while the soil, climate, and Indian inclination militated against the plan.[61]

In early 1914, the Blackfeet convened a general tribal council to deal with the issue. The three hundred members present voted almost unanimously to petition for an amendment of the allotment bill to enable the Blackfeet to retain the surplus lands. Subsequently, two factions emerged from this debate. One faction, led by one Robert Hamilton, traveled to Washington to persuade Congress to stop entirely the sale of Blackfeet lands. Soon, a second delegation, led by Malcolm Clark, arrived in the capitol to lobby for the sale of the lands.[62]

Thus, almost four years after the completion of allotments, hearings on the future of the Blackfeet reservation opened before the House and Senate Indian affairs subcommittees. Senator Harry Lane of Oregon subjected BIA officials to the most incisive questioning about the proposed sale. Lane asked officials why they did not consider the long-term needs of the Blackfeet rather than reacting to immediate pressures. The two Blackfeet factions also made themselves heard before the committees. The ambitious mixed-bloods headed by Clark supported the sale, arguing that economic salvation of the Blackfeet depended on the sale. Conversely, Three Bears, a member of the opposing party, chastized these views as short sighted: "You fellows don't know what land is. The [white] people I saw are just like this water [the ocean]. They flood the country and I am afraid that some of these days that the people will flood our lands and there will be nothing left for us."[63]

From the same group, Robert Hamilton pointed out to the committee additional reasons why the lands should be retained. The Blackfeet

Indians, he argued, had not yet learned the meaning of individual land-ownership. They knew nothing about mortgages, titles, loans, and fore-closures. Moreover, this allotment act violated the agreement of 1895 because the Blackfeet gave no consent to the measure. When asked about the petition favoring the sale presented by the Clark delegation, Hamilton explained that the signatories had no idea about what they were signing: they were told to sign and promised ten head of cattle in return.[64]

The hearings continued for five days. Senator Thomas J. Walsh of Montana grew irritated with the conflicting arguments. It was useless to try to ascertain the exact views of the Indians, he stated. Obviously, some Indians favored the sale, others did not. In the end their views really did not matter since, after all, the Blackfeet were wards and the government their guardian, and the Indians were "assumed to be incompetent to handle their own affairs." The act of 1907 superceded the promises made in 1895, and that ended the discussion as far as the government was concerned.[65]

Probably, the realization that they were in a no-win situation caused the Hamilton faction to give in. Quite unexpectedly, Hamilton notified the committee that the Blackfeet general council instructed him to accept an offer of 750,000 dollars for economic relief and for the issuance of cattle to the tribe. The agreement also provided for additional allotments to be made to children born after 1912.[66]

Following changes in the new bill regarding the reimbursements for irrigation, the government approved the sale of surplus Blackfeet lands. The bureau immediately stepped up the issuance of trust patents to the Blackfeet; the number grew from 3 trust patents in 1913 to 1,746 issued in 1919. In 1918, the government commenced to issue fee patents, and by the following year, 490 Blackfeet held unrestricted title to their lands. Some refused to accept the fee patents—a rather futile gesture as far as the BIA was concerned. After being informed of the Indians' recalcitrance, the bureau resorted to force-fee patenting. The bureau's chief clerk told the Blackfeet superintendent: "You should inform the Indians that the Secretary has the right to issue these patents, and if they refuse to accept them, you are directed to have the patents recorded and after recording the same, to send them to the patentees by registered mail."[67]

While this solution seemed simple, the consequences for the Blackfeet land base proved to be disastrous. A survey of the reservation in 1921 by a new superintendent revealed that few Indians benefited from their allotments. Joe Tatsey, a fairly well-educated half-blood who had recently received a fee patent, told the superintendent that he had "blown the whole thing." Louie Four Horns, a twenty-one-year-old full-blood, made a poor showing, as had quarter-blood John Morgan, a man fifty-seven years old who had sold not only his own but, in addition, two inherited allotments. Charlie Guardipee, "11/16," and his wife either sold or mortgaged their allotments, and they were not doing well. A leading authority on the Blackfeet summed up the results of the allotment policy: "These patents were issued to debt-ridden, illiterate Indians, who became easy prey for white land-seekers, who acquired some of the best land on the reservation at a fraction of its value." By the end of the next decade, 210,000 acres passed out of Indian ownership.[68] By the beginning of the third decade of the twentieth century, erosion of the Blackfeet land base contributed to the Indians' depressed economic conditions on the reservation, and similar situations arose on virtually all other allotted reservations.

The Dawes allotment program, held up as the solution to the "Indian problem" turned, instead, into the single most vivid example of the poorly planned and executed United States Indian policy. In most instances, the economic damage to Indian tribes was irreparable. The pressure for allotment and fee patenting in the United States caused an economic disaster that has continued to reverberate until the present day.[69]

In Canada, by contrast, no such massive losses of reservation land occurred because the Dominion did not issue fee patents to her Indians. In general, the only way the Canadian government could obtain reserve lands was by cessions, requiring the consent of the Indians. This did not mean that officials had not used unethical means to obtain such consent, or that they had not tried tactics such as leasing the reserves without consent from the Indians. However, in comparison to American officials, Canadians had tried to adhere to the principle of obtaining the Indians' consent. In the United States, legislation even made the pretense of such consent unnecessary. In looking at the confusing "checkerboard" ownership pattern on many of the American reservations and considering the erosion of Indian real estate,[70] many Americans, including John Collier, concluded that the Canadian system of allotted yet "closed" reserves provided a far superior way to manage Indian land policy.

6

Indian Evangelization
and Education

The success of Indian economic development depended not only on weather, proper instructions, and availability of arable lands, but on transforming the attitudes of native people toward the world around them. Concerned Americans and Canadians believed that such a transformation would take place under the tutelage of missionaries and teachers; consequently, after about 1870, federal Indian policy in both countries was directed toward civilization and the ultimate assimilation of native people into the dominant society. "Destroy the Indian to save the man" became the rallying cry of humanitarians.

Most missionaries, philanthropists, and government officials had no doubt that native people would eventually abandon their culture—to adopt the values, attitudes, and beliefs of white society—if only the right policy were implemented. Unfortunately, a lack of awareness about the intricacies of cultural change turned the efforts of Indian civilization and assimilation into a frustrating and bewildering excercise. Even as the nineteenth century drew to a close, all but the most optimistic observers had to admit that the rate of Indian civilization was exceedingly slow. In retrospect, the cause was twofold: first, the objective of assimilating the Indians within a generation or two was simply unattainable; and second, religious institutions proved unequal to the task of native evangelization and civilization. Just as ill-designed government policies as well as administrative and financial shortcomings failed to make the Indians self-supporting, religious denominations failed to shoulder their portion of the white man's burden.

During the "Peace" or "Quaker" policy, the involvement of religious denominations in Indian administration peaked in the United States; but the uneasy alliance officially ended in 1900, with the disengagement of church and state cooperation in native education. A far different situation developed in Canada. Although Canadians never handed over reserve administration to churchmen, even though Father Albert Lacombe recommended such an arrangement in the mid-1870s, the Canadian government expected the denominations to assume the primary responsibility for civilizing Indians. As a result, Canadian churches enjoyed virtual carte blanche in Indian evangelization, education, and health care.[1]

At first glance, churches seemed the most logical institutions to carry out the task of civilizing North American natives, since a powerful nineteenth-century evangelical movement already supported foreign missions in the four corners of the world. In such an atmosphere, one would have expected missionary work among the Indians of North America to flourish. In reality, the opposite proved true.

In his study, Frederick Abbott noted that Canada had frankly acknowledged her dependence on churches for Indian educational and missionary work, whereas the Americans, by insisting on the separation of church and state, had undermined missionary work among the Indians.[2] While it contained a kernel of truth, Abbott's observation oversimplified the situation in Canada. John Maclean, a prominent Canadian Methodist missionary among the Indians, candidly admitted that Canadian Indian missions were in trouble. "It is sad," he wrote, "to be compelled to state that it is much easier to raise funds for missionary work in India, China, and Japan than for missions carried on among the aborigines of our Dominion. 'The child of sorrow' of missions is the work of Christianizing the red man."[3]

Three reasons for this neglect can be cited. First, the largely eastern-based parent churches in the United States as well as in the Dominion had little knowledge or interest in western missions to the Indians. "Out of sight and out of mind" seems to have characterized their attitude. Second, domestic missions with postings in places such as the reservations of the Blackfoot nation could not compete for applicants with exotic stations like China, Africa, or India. Often only those applicants rejected by their mission boards for assignments abroad found themselves shipped to Indian reservations. Finally, Indian missions received nowhere near the funding necessary to carry out a successful civilization campaign. Not surprisingly, therefore, the results of evangelization, education, and civilization of Indian tribes in both countries turned out to be less than a resounding success.

As a mission field, the Blackfoot Confederacy provided an especially challenging problem. As agent John Young observed in 1881, "there are no Indian tribes, either north or west who have had as little intercourse with the whites in the past as the consolidated [Blackfeet] tribes. . . . The out of the way location of their reservation . . . and their [dangerous] reputation . . . account for this."[4] These factors contributed to the difficulty of converting the Blackfeet, but equally significant was the undeniable fact that churches had not pursued their responsibility with sufficient vigor.

The first contact of the Blackfeet with Christianity came through Catholic missionaries in 1840, when Father Pierre Jean de Smet established a mission among the Flatheads, the traditional enemies of the Blackfeet. De Smet and Father Nicholas Point managed to establish contact with several Blackfeet bands, and reportedly they baptized some six hundred individuals, mostly young children. During the next few decades, the roving Jesuit fathers reported baptisms of hundreds of Blackfeet. In 1862, the Jesuits finally found a suitable site for a permanent mission on the Missouri River and named it St. Peter's; but three years later, the outbreak of the Blackfeet War forced the missionaries to abandon their efforts.[5]

In the Canadian North-West Territories, the Catholics were represented by the Oblates of Mary Immaculate, an order that included Father Lacombe. Yet despite the efforts of such illustrious personages as Lacombe and Constantine Scollen, the roving priests visited Blackfoot bands too infrequently to affect any permanent change in the habits of their parishioners. Not until the North Peigans, Bloods, and Blackfoot had settled on reserves could sustained missionary work be mounted. Ironically, it was the Protestants—the Methodists—who first established in the territories permanent mission sites from which to launch the evangelization of the Blackfeet; but the major responsibility for combating the influence of the Catholics fell upon the Anglican Church Missionary Society. During the early 1880s, the society had placed British-born and educated Samuel Trivett and John W. Tims among the Bloods and the Blackfoot. Together with George Mackay, working with the Peigans, the Anglicans began the first sustained mission work among the Canadian Blackfoot bands.[6]

American Protestant missionaries—the Presbyterians—made a brief appearance at Fort Benton in 1857,[7] but for the next several years, the Catholics remained unchallenged in the possession of the South Peigan field. That situation changed in 1870. The Peace Policy assigned the Blackfeet reservation to the Methodists, a denomination which had no previous contacts with the Blackfeet. Since the Methodists had the right to nominate Indian agents, this policy introduced to the reservation a chronic denominational rivalry.

One of the first and most bitter conflicts arose during the administration of agent John Young. As an ordained Methodist minister, Young felt keenly his responsibility to bring Christainity and civilization to his charges. Yet after five years without a regular missionary on the reservation, Young observed bitterly in his annual report: "Liberal sums are expended to better instruct the Hindoo mother that she may not sacrifice her babe to Ganges, . . . but nothing is done to teach *our own* heathens."[8]

Even without a Methodist missionary in residence, conflict with the Catholics soon developed. When Father John Imoda, in charge of St. Peter's Mission some sixty miles south of the reservation, took three boys from the reservation and placed them in his school, the agent accused the priest of abduction. The question of who possessed authority over Indian children—their parents or the BIA—resulted in reams of correspondence between the agent, the bureau, and the Departments of Justice and the Interior. But agent Young obstinately opposed Catholic proselytizing among the Blackfeet.[9] He told the commissioner: "I [have not] seen any good resulting from their [the Catholics'] many years occasional visit to these tribes. None of the heathenish practices abated, no civilization of any shape taught, and the Indians were never shown how to build a house, plant a potato, or raise any kind of crop."[10]

By 1887 no churches, Catholic or Protestant, had opened a mission on the South Peigans' reservation, although the National Women's Indian Association obtained permission in 1886 to open a mission, and the Catholics had received similar approval a year earlier.[11] Finally, in 1890, the Catholics opened the Holy Family Mission with a school for Blackfeet children. Two years later, the Reverend E. S. Dutcher inquired about the feasibility of opening a Methodist mission. Agent Steell welcomed the idea, stressing that "these Indians are not converted to Christainity [and] consequently you will have as great a field as you desire for missionary work."[12]

Despite these queries, until 1893 the Catholics had the Blackfeet to themselves. In that year, the Reverend W. H. Matson, a Methodist minister, became the principal of the government-run boarding school on the reservation. Although Matson, just as Young before him, was not an active missionary, Matson introduced a Sunday school and other religious exercises, thereby setting the stage for future conflicts with the Catholics. In the same year, the Reverend E. S. Dutcher and his wife finally arrived at the agency to begin the first Protestant missionary work from their small house and chapel located next to the government boarding school. Dutcher left six years later, but his successor, the Reverend Francis A. Riggin, remained at his post until 1913.[13] During those years, the condition of the Blackfeet reached its nadir; and the two denominations not only did nothing to alleviate the situation, but contributed to the social strain on the reservation.

The situation at the Blackfeet agency was not atypical. The activities of Christain missionaries among aboriginal people have long been recognized as contributing toward the sociocultural disintegration of the people the missionaries tried to "save." Protestant denominations have received particularly pointed criticism from students of Indian–white relations. Scholars often draw a distinction between Protestant and Catholic attitudes toward native cultures and religions, regarding the Catholic as the more tolerant approach. Contemporary observers also perceived a difference among the churches. Protestants frequently dismissed Catholic reports of numerous conversions as merely cases of "baptized heathenism." This charge sprang from a willingness on the part of Catholics to consider as converts Indians who had not materially changed their life style or personal appearance. In contrast, Protestants considered outer appearance— such as wearing short hair or shirt and pants—as outward signs of inner regeneration.[14]

In general, however, a missionary's attitude toward Indian culture often depended more on the individual than on his religious affiliation. During the early years of their mission, some Jesuits proved more tolerant than their successors. Among the Anglicans, individuals like the Reverend Tims proved rigid toward all forms of native belief and custom, while his coreligionists Trivett and H. W. G. Stocken were less doctrinaire. While most missionaries, Protestant and Catholic, strongly disapproved of the Sun Dance of the plains tribes, the Canadian Methodist John McDougall defended their right to hold this ceremony.[15]

But whatever the differences among individual mission workers, few, if any, grasped fully the importance to the Blackfeet of the customs they tried to suppress. Most missionaries viewed ceremonies such as the Sun Dance as devil worship, or at least, as silly superstitions. On the other hand, Indians lacked the intellectual background to grasp the significance of most tenets of nineteenth-century Christainity. Many Blackfeet, for example, interpreted baptism as new "medicine" to ward off evil spirits.[16] As a result, the attempt to correlate the number of converts with the success of missionary work, or with a degree of civilization, can be extremely misleading.

In Canada, denominational squabbles over Indian missions were as pronounced as those in the United States. On the Blackfoot reserve, the Reverend Tims spearheaded the Anglican–Catholic rivalry. He detailed how "the priests" influenced Chief Crowfoot to refuse Tims's request to be allowed to settle at Crowfoot's camp. Undiscouraged, Tims went to the North Camp, where he was given permission by Chief Old Sun to establish a mission. Tims later recalled how he could not even enter an Indian house to preach because, as soon as he commenced, he was asked whether he had Crowfoot's permission.[17] In reality, Crowfoot's opposition probably stemmed from his desire to keep further interlopers out of his reserve, rather than from the influence of the Catholics.

Despite the earnest appeals of Anglican missionaries to their parent organization for more support to combat "Romanism" as well as to convert the Indians, the Anglicans were slow to respond. In 1900, the Reverend Arthur de B. Owen from the Blood reserve made a public appeal for missions, which echoed the sentiment of the American John Young twenty years earlier about the lavishness with which money was spent on foreign missions, while the "moral degradation as well as physical misery of the Bloods [was] appalling."[18]

Most missionaries tried to carry out their well-intended work of civilizing Indians despite lack of funds and lukewarm support from their parent organization, and sooner or later, all missionaries attempted to change some aspects of their parishioners' lives. Customs such as marriage and divorce, clothing and personal adornment, the activities of the medicine men, the authority of the chiefs, the various Indian dances, and leisure pastimes such as gambling and horse racing became targets of the missionaries. The question was how much pressure missionaries should exert to suppress Indian customs.

Some American observers believed that Canadians demonstrated more tolerance toward Indian culture. Frederick Abbott, for example, claimed that Canada's Indian service officials were able to distinguish far better "between what is real art and religion and that which is a degeneration of art and religion" than most American "sentimentalists," who ignorantly interfered with the Indians' personal and religious rights.[19] In practice, however, Canadians had not been as tolerant as Abbott assumed. In 1895, under pressure from missionaries, the government amended the Indian Act to prohibit certain aspects of Indian culture judged detrimental to the Indians' economic or moral well-being. The Potlatch and the Sun Dance[20] were singled out as especially offensive, but the legislation was not especially effective.

In some instances, the modification of Indian behavior could not be legislated, yet their transformation was considered essential to the natives' success in their new life. For example, traditional gender roles had to be altered before the Blackfeet could succeed in new occupations such as farming. Authorities believed that Blackfeet men should perform all manual labor, while the women should confine their responsibilities to the household; but implementing such changes proved to be difficult. Not unitl 1896 did an American agent report that the men were finally performing the heavy tasks and leaving the women to do housework.[21]

Forcing Indians to conform to the standards of "civilized" people also included the regularization of Indian marital relations. Many officials and all missionaries held as their objective the task of eliminating polygamous marriages, especially among the younger generation, and impressing upon

Indians the seriousness of the marital contract. While authorities in both countries recognized tribal marriages as lawful, by the 1890s Americans attempted to make Indians undergo a civil or a religious ceremony. However, agent Steell opposed the measure, explaining to the attorney general of Montana that, although he was anxious to see the Indians adopt the customs of "white marriages," he did not favor state licenses: "I fear my advance in that direction will be greatly retarded if they [the Blackfeet] are compelled to pay for a license when they wish to marry."[22]

This concern among American officials about Indian marriages reflected the official policy of making Indians subject to state laws. Registering marriages among Indians became especially crucial after the introduction of allotments, since an official record of heirs was necessary to determine equitable distribution of property. Still, despite the obvious need for matrimonial regulations, some critics believed that the BIA was not moving quickly enough. Of the sixty Indian agencies in the United States, the Board of Indian Commissioners complained in 1901, only eight or nine kept marriage records. A bill to regulate Indian marriage had been submitted to Congress in 1901, but by the 1920s no legislation had been implemented.[23]

Although a DIA circular of 1893 forbade plural marriages, Canadian officials paid only sporadic attention to Indian marital relations, preferring to leave that area to the churches. Indian agents usually tried to prevent a married man from adding another wife, but not always successfully. In 1897, agent James Wilson reported that six Bloods had added second wives to their households and refused to give them up. As a rule, the offending husbands received only a mild punishment, such as having their rations withheld until they complied with the norm of one husband, one wife. As a rule, agents left undisturbed the plural marriages contracted before and during the early years of reserve life, but missionaries often encouraged the husband to set aside a plural wife before performing baptism.[24]

While some Americans demanded a regularization of Indian marriages, Canadians took an opposite view. In 1907, for example, the DIA declared that the department fully recognized aboriginal marriages, adding that it would be improper to force upon the Indians a religious or civil ceremony that had no meaning to them. The following year, the secretary reiterated that even though officials were cognizant of the sometimes lax marital relations among the natives, the department rejected the idea of replacing tribal with "legal" marriages. The result, officials feared, would be absence of any form of marriage.[25]

Ironically, while the DIA recognized Indian marriages, it did not recognize tribal divorces. The Americans, on the other hand, recognized both. R. N. Wilson, the Blood agent, reported on the difficulty created by this lack of consistency. He wrote about a young married couple who had separated, with the wife refusing to return to her husband. The husband declared that since the department was powerless to help him in his marital difficulties, he was asking for permission to remarry. The young man was only twenty-five years old, Wilson wrote, and to expect him to remain single for the rest of his life was unrealistic. Wilson reported that there were many such couples on the reserve.[26]

The government's answer proved to be singlularly unhelpful. After listing some platitudes about the need to maintain the sacred and permanent nature of marriage, the deputy superintendent ruled against recognizing an Indian divorce. "The best hope of discouraging these separations," he wrote, "will be found in endeavoring to punish bigamists, for probably if these Indians find that after separation they can not without danger of punishment contract fresh alliances, they will hesitate about leaving each other." He concluded that this problem would fade in time, as the Indians acquired the habits of Christian civilization. Meanwhile, as far as marriage was concerned, Indians were in the same position before the law as other citizens of the Dominion.[27]

Faced with such unrealistic advice, the Indians ignored the department and married and divorced as they pleased. Many DIA officials, especially the agents, knew of this situation and turned a blind eye, and eventually the department tacitly agreed that it had no power to enforce its own regulation.

Even though both countries attempted to regulate most aspects of Indian life, efforts gravitated toward suppressing the most visible evidence of "barbarism." The Sun Dance, an important religious ceremony for the plains tribes, came under attack on both sides of the border. The reasons for its suppression were threefold: officials saw the aspect of self-torture in the ceremony as particularly pagan and offensive; since the ceremony took place during the summer, officials believed that the Indians neglected their stock and crops; and finally, officials objected to the Indians giving away their possessions as part of the ceremony.

The Sun Dance on the Blackfeet reservation—or the "Medicine Lodge," as some agents called it—came to the attention of American authorities in 1881, following the accidental shooting of an Indian by an agency employee. Commissioner Hiram Price issued a severe reprimand to the agent for allowing the Sun Dance to take place, and while the commissioner felt that it would be imprudent simply to forbid such ceremonies, he told the agent that Indians should be informed that the bureau wished to end the dance. Despite the wishes of the bureau, however, the Blackfeet continued to hold the Sun Dance for the next several years. Not until

1888 was the agent able to report that the "Medicine Lodge" had been abandoned.[28] However, the passage of years showed that this obituary for the Sun Dance had been premature.

Canadian officials also sought to end the Sun Dance, and they were equally reluctant to abolish it by force among the Blackfoot. Yet as the 1880s drew to a close, some missionaries, including Father Lacombe, thought that the time had come for the DIA to take a stand. In 1889, Lacombe submitted to the department a plan for civilizing the prairie bands, prominently featuring the suppression of the Sun Dance. He called the dance "one of the greatest obstacles against [the Indians'] being christianized and civilized," and he assured the department that "you are strong enough by your moral influence and your Mounted Police to make the Sun Dance die out."[29]

At about the same time, agents and missionaries joined to prevent Indian participation in the dance. Agent Magnus Beggs reported from the Blackfoot reserve that he had managed to prevail upon Chief Crowfoot to have the Indians abandon the part played by mutilation in the ceremony. Yet even though the Blackfoot and Blood chiefs agreed to abandon it at that time, evidence indicated that the last Sun Dance in Canada involving self-torture took place on the Blood reserve in 1894. As a result, the Canadian Bloods were apparently the last of the plains Indians to observe this form of the ceremony. In the meantime, the Canadian Peigans found the aspect of torture in the ceremony distasteful, and they gave up that part in the 1870s; the Blackfoot made a similar decision in 1890.[30] Yet the ceremony persisted in its modified form.

In addition to attempting to quash aboriginal celebrations, officials tried to promote patriotic amusements as substitutes. In the United States, agents tried to induce the Blackfeet to observe the Fourth of July instead of the Sun Dance. This substitution did not fool the Blackfeet, who wanted to practice their ceremonies as well as celebrate Independence Day, despite notices, such as those posted in 1901 by agent James H. Monteath, declaring that "the probabilities are that the 'Sun Dance' on July 4th [would] be prohibited by instructions from the Department."[31]

The Canadians also tried to provide civilized amusements for their Indians. On many reserves, department officials introduced summer fairs, which included horse races and prizes; and at the Blood reserve, the agent customarily butchered a steer for a feast. However, in 1900, when the agent decided to end this practice, he precipitated a revolt among the Bloods that revealed a deep-seated resentment on the part of the Indians toward official interference with their customs. On 7 June, some dozen minor chiefs and head chief Red Crow and Mrs. Red Crow, accompanied by a number of tribesmen, arrived at Fort Macleod. Through an interpreter, the disgruntled delegation presented their complaints to the puzzled policemen. It soon became obvious that complaints about the steer were only the tip of the iceberg.

One of the spokesmen, Day Chief, stated that four years had lapsed since the DIA had tried to put an end to the Sun Dance and had offered various substitutions. Since the officials had obviously reneged on their promise, the Bloods wanted to resume their celebration—after all, *they* had never agreed to give it up. Other speakers presented more compelling arguments, pointing out that various churches dotted the countryside and it was lawful for everybody but the Indians to pray as they wished. Bull Shield wanted the ceremonies of the Horn Society, one of the most sacred religious ceremonies, to go on uninterrupted, and he stated flatly that "the Horn Society is as good as the Bible." The interpreter also translated the statements of Green Grass, who voiced the Indian view most succinctly: "There is praying all over the world. . . . Red Crow believes in his own praying. He wants to be allowed to have his own prayers. [The Bloods] have been asking so long, they want to get it this time."[32] The Bloods did get their wish. The Sun Dance took place, and they continued to practice the ceremony, despite opposition from missionaries.

In 1902, Rev. A. de B. Owen echoed Father Lacombe's pleas of thirteen years earlier in urging the police to put an end to the gathering. He complained, "[The Bloods] ought to be made to comply with what the law commands, and not allowed to do just as they like, laughing at the Police and the agent for their (they say and think) inability to stop them." In his reply, a Mountie inspector took a more philosophical view of the situation. He informed the agent that if the police complied with the reverend's request and dispersed the Indians, it would undoubtedly lead to a confrontation.[33]

Apparently encouraged by the authorities' reluctance to use stringent measures to suppress the ceremony, the North Peigans, who rarely did anything to attract official attention, decided to hold a Sun Dance in 1905. Agent J. H. Gooderham felt helpless to stop the proceedings, explaining to his counterpart on the Blood reserve that once these Indians made up their mind to hold the dance, his persuasive powers were insufficient. Gooderham's only action involved asking the Blood agent to refrain from giving passes to his Indians.[34]

Eventually, reports of the continuation of Sun Dance reached the upper echelons of the Indian department. In 1908, the officials noted the "recrudescence" of the ceremony, but dismissed it as only a partial revival, lamely declaring that the department's policy was to prohibit its most objectionable parts.[35] Six years later, when the Bloods once again held the Sun Dance, the department admitted its defeat in trying to stamp out the ceremony. Agent Dilworth informed the commissioner that he had no objections to the Sun Dance because the Indians had promised to finish their farm work before joining the camp. The commissioner replied that his primary concern was the attendance of white men—presumably for immoral purposes. As long as the dance did not interfere with the Indians' work, he had no objection to it.[36]

The Blackfoot bands were not the only tribes who managed to evade the ban on the Sun Dance. The Crees also managed to continue their Sun Dance, despite government opposition. Thus, by the first decade of the twentieth century, Canadian officials had tacitly acknowledged defeat over the Sun Dance issue. In part, the defeat resulted from a flurry of legal petitions filed by Indian bands against the prohibition. While some officials, like the Indian inspector W. M. Graham, railed against the government's laxness in enforcing regulations, others considered the ceremony innocuous. Commissioner Laird overlooked the issue, especially since the Indians simply ignored the regulations.[37]

Among the South Peigans, the suppression of the Sun Dance depended largely upon the inclination of the agents. Some, like L. W. Cooke, proved unsympathetic to all facets of Blackfeet culture, including face painting, horse racing, gambling, bead work, and, of course, native dances. Others, like Dare and Monteath, used permits to regulate social dances. As a rule, after an unsympathetic agent left the Peigans returned to forbidden practices. Sometimes, the Indians even found allies like agent C. Churchill, who saw nothing wrong with the Sun Dance and defended the ceremony before the commissioner. In 1912, when Father P. C. Bourgis complained that the Indians were "praying to the Sun," agent McFatridge dismissed the complaint as unfounded.[38]

At the end of the teens, the South Peigan's Sun Dance took up a full month during the summer. This situation would not have been tolerated by Canadian officials, but on the Blackfeet reservation a procession of new agents prevented a successful campaign against the practice. Finally, in 1921, the new agent Frank C. Campbell persuaded the Peigans to confine their festivities to one week, and in that way, the Indians' ceremony was preserved while they also found ample time to tend their crops and stock.[39]

Missionaries experienced as many difficulties in converting the Blackfoot Confederacy as in suppressing the Sun Dance. In 1899, Merrill Gates, the president of the Indian Rights Association, visited the reservation, and produced a rather embarrassing reflection on the status of the South Peigans' Christianization. He telegraphed the agent to say that he would like to give a Sunday talk to the Indians and to agency employees. The agent responded by sending to Gates the Indians' reply: they would welcome a council with their white brother, but "they could not come that day, because on Sunday they prayed to the Beaver god, from sunrise to sunset," and they invited Gates to pray with them. Gates declined this ecumenical offer, expressing hope that when they did worship together, "we could get nearer to the center than the Beaver god."[40]

On Canadian reserves missionaries fared no better. In 1898, the agent for the North Peigans observed:

> With a single dubious exception, these Indians are pagan and bid fair to remain so for at least another generation. They are or until recently were intensely religious in their own way, and seem to have failed to perceive any attraction in Christianity, in spite of the fact that it has been expounded to them incessantly for about twenty years.

The Bloods also showed little interest in the white man's religion. Even the department noted, with dismay, that a "considerable number of Indians still [refuse] even a nominal adherence to Christianity."[41]

Although missionaries generally chose not to advertise their failures, John Maclean revealed the status of Indian work in the Canadian West in 1892: "Indian mission work in Manitoba and the North West has been successful, but it is not the kind of success desired by those who know nothing of life and labor among the Indians. The average Christian's idea of success is impossibility." In 1909, Samuel Blake, a critic of Anglican missions, stated the case even more bluntly: the Peigans, Bloods, and Blackfoot were still almost entirely heathen after twenty-five or thirty years of missionary effort.[42]

Not only had the churches failed to harvest Indian converts, but the teachings of Christianity had failed to alter materially the Indians' behavior and cultural attitudes. The Blood agent noted that his wards maintained a "proud and imperious spirit which after twenty-eight years of reservation life is still the dominant characteristic of the Bloods." Furthermore, a team of anthropologists studying the Bloods in 1939 concluded that the Bloods had managed to preserve "perhaps most completely, those mechanisms of aggression that characterized them in the first three quarters of the nineteenth century."[43]

Despite the wishful thinking of earnest missionaries, most of their converts did not understand, much less internalize, the teachings of Christianity, largely because of the cultural and linguistic differences that existed between the two groups. Canon Stocken, a respected minister on the Blackfoot reserve, recounted that one of his Indian parishioners— an intelligent and well-educated Christian man—failed to deliver a message one night because he was afraid of ghosts. Stocken was dismayed by the man's reaction, and as an object lesson against Indian superstition, he decided to deliver the message himself. However, the Blackfoot people remained unimpressed, offering a perfectly logical explanation. "I was told," Stocken wrote, "that ghosts were afraid of white men."[44]

Even missionary efforts with the best intentions often proved to be more damaging than helpful to the Indians. Conversions among individuals divided families and created tensions and factionalism within the band. Some converts tried to suppress the "heathen" practices of their neighbors by giving away or destroying sacred paraphenalia, which only exacerbated tensions. Missionaries like Stocken, while joyously reporting the activities of their converts, remained completely oblivious to the problems they had caused.[45]

Fights among rival religions on a single reservation also hampered efforts toward Christianization. Some Indians found a simple solution to this confusing religious pluralism. When Three Suns, a prominent Canadian Blackfoot, was asked to convert to Christianity, he replied "that he had found it was two religions; the one on the west side (Anglican) and the other on the east (Catholic); the representatives were nice fellows and seeing he could not join both he preferred to be a good neighbour by sticking to his own."[46]

On the South Peigan reservation, a form of religious segregation had developed by the turn of the century. The Methodists, who had operated their mission since 1893, relocated to the agency town of Browning in 1909. In the same year, the Presbyterians opened a church in town and soon built up a non-Indian congregation. In fact, neither of these churches made any special effort to reach the reservation Indians, so the mission field remained in Catholic hands. As a result, Catholic–Protestant tensions, which had plagued the reservation during the 1870s, continued into the twentieth century,[47] especially in the area of education.

Missionaries experienced similar failures on the Canadian reserves. In part, failure here stemmed from the Anglican society's inability to fulfill its goal of training a native clergy as well as from the unwillingness of the mother body to allow missionaries to adapt general policies to local conditions. The high-handed approach practiced by some missionaries also alienated many Indians. For example, Rev. J. W. Tims, a stickler for doctrinal purity, found himself hastily transferred to another reserve when a child at his hospital died, nearly precipitating a violent response from the Blackfoot. Already angry at Tims's arrogant attitude and disregard for Blackfoot social niceties, the Indians demanded and got his removal.[48]

Due to recent changes in attitude among many Americans and Canadians toward native people, few would praise unreservedly the work of Christian missionaries among the Indians. Even scholars who present a sympathetic picture of missionary activities cannot help but conclude that the legacy of the missions was often hostility and resentment on the part of the native people.[49] Yet while missionaries generally received bad press, one cannot ignore the fact that some, such as Canon Stocken, devoted their lives to the Indians. In 1921, inspector W. M. Graham called Stocken a dangerous man to have on an Indian reserve, concluding: "He has been there altogether too long, and he feels that he is called upon to protect the Indians from those on the reserve whose business it is to advise them." Stocken remained on the reserve for two more years before retiring after thirty-one years among the Blackfoot. An indication of the respect that Stocken earned among his parishioners came when he died in 1955. He was buried in the Blackfoot cemetery overlooking North Camp.[50]

Efforts to educate native people yielded results as unspectacular as the efforts to Christianize them. Yet officials regarded Indian education as essential for their assimilation. "Education and civilization are practically synonymous, . . . the last is impossible without the first . . . ," observed the commissioner of Indian affairs in 1902, a sentiment that his Canadian counterpart echoed. Ironically, the failure of evangelization and education resulted, in large part, from their interdependence.[51]

An American writer remarked in 1911: "In the matter of education of her Indian population, Canada is following the system we abandoned years ago. Nearly all the schools are denominational, maintained jointly by the government and the church and missionary societies." This system intrigued American students of the Canadian Indian administration, leading some to conclude that the education of Canadian Indians by religious societies was superior than the predominantly secular education in the United States.[52] In fact, however, neither system proved successful.

In the United States, denominational education received the first government support in 1819, with the establishment of a ten-thousand-dollar civilization fund. The BIA had not opened its first strictly government-supported Indian day schools until 1873; but because the Indian bureau could not provide enough schools, it contracted with the churches for the education of Indian children.[53] These contract schools were either situated on a specific reservation or located hundreds of miles from the reservation from which they drew their pupils.

In Canada, Indian schools were called "mission schools" because they were staffed and administered by denominations. These denominations had assumed a prominent role in Indian education during the pre-Confederation period, and they did not begin to relinquish it until the early 1960s.[54] Canadian churches managed to maintain their position in Indian education because of the absence of legal barriers to church–state cooperation. In the United States, however, the constitutional principle of the separation of church and state, along with animosities between Protestants and Catholics, forced the two institutions to sever their ties.[55]

Unlike the American government, Canadian federal authorities had not paid attention to Indian education until 1875–76, when Parliament provided a fund of two thousand dollars for Indian schooling. Prior to this arrangement, the legislatures of the various provinces gave no financial aid for native education, leaving the denominations to conduct Indian education in conjunction with their missions. Acquisition of the North West Territories and the conclusion of the Indian treaties, which often included schools for the Indians, forced the government to face for the first time the question of native education.[56]

In the meantime, a lively debate arose in the United States over the types of schools best suited for the aboriginal population. The Americans considered three kinds of schools: the nonreservation boarding or "industrial" schools; the reservation boarding schools; and day schools. The first two were similar, for in addition to the "three Rs" they taught manual skills and tried to instill in pupils "the habits of industry."[57] Reservation day schools provided the least satisfactory method of education because of the difficulty in securing pupils' regular attendance.

By the late 1880s, the industrial school system championed by Richard Henry Pratt, the founder of Carlisle Indian School, came under attack.[58] Opponents of industrial schools charged that students often were secured by "cajolery, threats, bribery, fraud, persuasion, force, and transported thousands of miles from their homes." Indian parents bitterly resented being separated from their children, often for years; moreover, many school children contracted tuberculosis and other diseases from which they frequently died. Those who graduated returned to reservations where their education proved to be useless, and many reverted "back to the blanket." In observing the less-than-spectacular success rate of these schools, the bureau decided that civilization should be carried to the Indians rather than transporting the Indians to civilization; thus, a system of reservation boarding schools was born.[59]

Reservation boarding schools provided manual training without removing the children completely from their families, while simultaneously ensuring regular school attendance. However, many humanitarians began to attack the boarding schools as an anomaly, since these schools segregated Indians from the white population. To these critics, the ultimate step in the integration of Indians into the American society was the enrollment of children in public day schools.[60]

Canadian officials experienced similar confusion about what types of schools were best suited for educating prairie Indians. At first, many thought that native education in the West would be simply a matter of introducing the eastern system of day schools, and officials only belatedly recognized the enormity of the problem. In the midst of the 1879 crisis in Indian affairs, Nicholas Flood Davin admitted, "Guaranteeing schools as one condition for surrendering the title to land, was, in my opinion, trifling with a great duty."[61]

Davin was the man charged by Prime Minister Macdonald to find a school system for the prairie tribes. Davin took the simplest solution: he went to the United States to inspect their schools. Davin's visit was significant for the future of Canadian Indian education because he arrived at a time when Pratt's system of industrial boarding schools was enjoying its heyday. In his subsequent report, Davin recommended the adoption of the American system of industrial boarding schools in the North West Territories. His second recommendation involved the placement of mission schools under government contract[62] but while the government began to implement the first suggestion in the early 1880s, it did not act on the second recommendation until 1910. Between those years, chaos reigned in Canadian Indian education.

Drawing on Davin's report, Macdonald proposed the establishment of nineteen schools in the West, to be managed by religious denominations and supported by an annual appropriation from Parliament of three hundred dollars for each school. The churches would provide teachers with a salary each quarter of three dollars per student.[63] The government anticipated that the bulk of Indian school funding would come from churches, supplemented by federal funds. This arrangement was predicated on the assumption that churches would pay their share and that the government's portion would be sufficient to cover expenditures. Unfortunately, these assumptions, which proved to be erroneous, became the major cause of conflict between the government and the churches.

In 1883, the first Indian industrial school in the territories opened at Battleford. During the next two years, two more schools opened at High River near Calgary, and at Qu'Appelle. Meanwhile, denominations opened both day and boarding schools on the reserves. After these schools had been operating for a time, churches began to make persistent appeals for financial aid from the government. The department usually relented, and began to contribute to their maintenance on an ad hoc basis.[64] This arrangement, however, satisfied neither side.

In 1887, a confidential report submitted by Deputy Superintendent General Lawrence Vankoughnet to the prime minister presented an uninspiring record by Indian schools: low attendance, low salaries for teachers, an insufficient number of schools, and inadequate government funding. Like many of his contemporaries on both sides of the border, Vankoughnet remained puzzled about the causes of this situation. "There is difficulty," he remarked, "in coming to a conclusion as to the exact changes which should be made in order to improve on the [Indian education]." Even if drastic changes were needed, Vankoughnet concluded that the department had no money to make them. Yet the situation must have been serious because the normally parsimonious Vankoughnet recommended the appropriation of more than 500,000 dollars for Indian education, with 158,000 dollars earmarked for the North West Territories. The government responded with a dramatic, but still inadequate, increase in funds for Indian education. In 1879, the total funding for Indian education in Canada amounted to 16,000 dollars, and ten years later the total was increased to 172,980 dollars, which was only slightly more than Vankoughnet's request for the territories alone.[65]

Despite the periodic increase in school funding, which had never kept up with the actual expenditures, the department continued to be besieged by requests from churches for more funds. When they were unable to obtain increases, the churches simply went into debt.[66] This practice greatly upset Ottawa because government officials felt that denominational appeals to bail out the schools amounted to blackmail.

Prompted by Vankoughnet's pessimistic school report, Canadians once again looked to the United States for help. In 1889 two Canadian officials, including the Indian commissioner Hayter Reed, visited the United States to inspect Indian schools. They returned impressed with Carlisle's system of industrial education—especially the removal of students from their "savage" environment, the "outing system" and the suppression of native languages.[67] By then, however, the United States had begun to move toward substituting day schools for boarding schools.

Unfortunately, the arrangement between the churches and the government made changes in the Canadian educational system impossible. Each denomination clamored for the establishment of more industrial schools, clung tenaciously to every existing school and every pupil, and lived in fear that a competing denomination would enter "their" field if these schools closed. Canadian denominations also transported Indian children long distances to fill the rosters of their institutions and to receive government grants.[68] With every child representing an investment, there were virtually no critics of this system among the denominations.

The Anglicans were particularly strapped for funds, and even though their educational system was in deep trouble, they became vocal defenders of their school. In 1894, the Anglican Church Missionary Society, which funded the Anglican missions in western Canada, began a fifteen-year phaseout of funding for Indian schools. During this period of declining resources, however, no Canadian Anglican body filled the gap. Not until

1903 did the Toronto-based Missionary Society of the Church of England in Canada begin to fund Indian education; but this organization refused to support Indian boarding and industrial schools, believing that they were the responsibility of the government.[69]

Finally, in 1905, the government was forced to face this crisis in Indian education during a rare debate in the House of Commons. Minister of the Interior Clifford Sifton took the floor to call the industrial schools a failure and to urge the expansion of reserve boarding schools.[70] But five more years passed before the churches and the government finally came to an agreement. A government official delicately explained the situation: "The missionary societies were dissatisfied with the financial grants the Department was making, we, on the other hand, were dissatisfied with the nature of the appeals which reached us, and the difficulties of administration in the absence of any definite understanding." Representatives of Catholic and Protestant denominations agreed to place all denominational schools under a government contract that stipulated clearly the responsibility of each party. Government grants to schools would be increased, with the main purpose being the improvement of school plants, many of which proved "inadequate, . . . unsanitary and . . . undoubtedly chargeable in a very high death rate among the pupils."[71] Unfortunately, the outbreak of World War I scuttled these promising beginnings of reform.

The agreement of 1910 merely formalized church–state relations, but it had little effect on the quality of instruction in Indian schools. Low salaries, which attracted mediocre teachers, contributed to the high turnover in school staff, and dedicated individuals frequently left their positions because of uncongenial working conditions. In many schools, teachers frequently resorted, in their frustration, to the physical abuse of children. Some children made repeated efforts to escape, and the problem of runaways became chronic in both countries.[72]

Around the turn of the century, Indian educational philosophy in the United States underwent a change, principally as a result of the scientific racism of the 1890s. In 1899, the commissioner of Indian affairs declared that Indian education must be based on the "well-known inferiority of Indians in religion, intelligence, morals, and home life." No longer would the Indians be educated to be "elevated" to a place beside their white brethren. Influenced by the conviction of many "experts" that Indians had limited intellectual abilities, many Indian industrial schools introduced vocational training to prepare their pupils to fill certain limited occupations.[73]

At about the same time, DIA officials in Canada also began to question the ultimate purpose and value of Indian industrial schools. The deputy superintendent general declared in 1897 that "education must be considered with relation to the future of the [Indian] pupils. . . . To educate children above the possibilities of their station, and create a distaste for what is certain to be their environment in life would be not only a waste of money, but doing them an injury." A year later, the superintendent proposed that education in industrial schools be offered only to a limited number of pupils because the future of the graduates from these institutions remained uncertain. Vested denominational interests, however, made curriculum changes difficult to implement. Ironically, the refusal of some denominations to adjust their curricula to DIA demands may have helped to maintain a higher academic level and to instill leadership in the Indian graduates.[74]

The history of educational efforts among the Blackfoot Confederacy provides a vivid illustration of many of the problems encountered by Canadian and American Indian schools. The concept of classroom education was first introduced to the Blackfeet in the Treaty of 1855. Seventeen years later, the first day school opened at the Teton River agency, but shortly thereafter it closed because of irregular attendance. During the early 1870s, agent John Young's two daughters taught in a day school at the Badger Creek agency, with disappointing results. Of the eight hundred eligible children, Young reported that only eighty-seven attended school, and their parents frequently withdrew them. If the Blackfeet were to be educated, Young stated, a boarding school had to be established.[75]

Commissioner E. A. Hayt announced in 1879 that he was also "desirous of having a large, flourishing manual labor boarding school established among the Blackfeet,"[76] but another two years would lapse before a school at Willow Creek was near completion. Even before the doors of the school opened, Blackfeet education became embroiled in a denominational squabble between Protestants and Catholics over Father Imoda's "abduction" of three Blackfeet boys. Needless to say, such a situation did not encourage the Blackfeet to seek an education.

The development of education for the three Blackfoot nations in Canada was beset with problems much like those across the border. In addition, the frequent adversarial relations between the churches and the department complicated the situation. The government became involved in Blackfoot education through the promises of Treaty 7. Signed in 1877, this treaty stipulated that "Her Majesty agrees to pay the salary of such teachers to instruct the children of said Indians . . . when said Indians are settled on their reserves and shall desire teachers."[77] Since the decision about establishing schools was left up to the Indians, the Dominion took no steps to establish schools until 1883.

In the meantime, in 1879, Anglicans opened a day school at the Peigan reserve; a year later, the Reverend Samuel Trivett started a school among the Bloods; and the Reverend Tims opened a day school among the Blackfoot in 1884.[78] The Catholics did not formally begin to educate the Blackfoot bands until the government opened the High River (or St. Joseph's) industrial school and placed it under Catholic control.

Keen competition soon developed between Protestants and Catholics over government funding for Indian education. The venerable Father Albert Lacombe demanded that the DIA turn over to the Catholics one of the schools built for the Methodists and Anglicans on the Blood reserve. The commissioner explained that a school promised to another denomination "cannot be handed over to you," but his explanation did not stop Father Lacombe's complaints. The Protestants kept an equally vigilant eye on their own interests. Anglican Bishop William Cyprian Pinkham of the diocese of Calgary, which encompassed Treaty 7, complained bitterly to the department that the Catholic church had been granted seven hundred dollars toward the building of a school on the Peigan reserve, despite the fact that the Peigans had requested a "Church of England man."[79]

In their haste to claim more schools than their rivals, churches often paid little attention to the conditions of these institutions, which were dismal as a rule. An Anglican day school at the Blood agency in 1888 resembled an Indian log shanty, measuring eighteen by sixteen by nine feet, with five desks, five benches, a stove and a blackboard, and accommodating twenty-seven boys and thirteen girls. An inspector found five or six pupils who knew the alphabet; the rest, he said, had no more idea than their teacher about what they were doing. At the Peigan reserve, the Reverend H. T. Bourne's school was described as completely unsuitable for its purpose. No wonder the department balked when requests poured in from the churches for funds to patch up structures that were "far from the class expected on reserves."[80]

Schools among the South Peigans were in no better condition. A few years after its construction, the agency boarding school at Willow Creek became seriously overcrowded, a condition that plagued it into the new century. Already in 1889, the school superintendent reported that he had to turn away twenty-three children and that thirty-four children used a dining room measuring fourteen by sixteen feet. He faced the choice of lodging twenty boys in a dormitory measuring thirteen by thirteen feet, or discharging some of them. Such conditions, of course, contributed to the poor health of the pupils and to the school's high death rate. The school was eventually relocated to Cut Bank Creek, and a second school opened on the reservation in 1890. Catholic sisters ran the new Holy Family School, which provided accommodations for some one hundred pupils.[81]

The government school at Cut Bank continued to be plagued by problems. Several inspectors condemned the plant for lacking a sewage system and running water and for using wood stoves and coal oil lamps. Finally, in October 1905, a new school opened with proper sewage disposal, gas lighting, steam heating, and hot and cold water. In the meantime, the old Willow Creek School was retained as a day school, but attendance dropped dramatically and the place closed in April 1908.[82]

Although students filled both agency and Catholic boarding schools, with four day schools in operation and nearly a hundred students attending nonreservation schools in such places as Fort Shaw, Carlisle, and Genoa, these facilities could not accommodate all school-age children. Some alleviation of the crowding problem occurred in 1913, when the Blackfeet agency school opened two new buildings, doubling its capacity. The agent was pleased, but he commented that while the Indians had a school, the school lacked teachers. Even these enlargements did not fill the needs of the Blackfeet. In 1916, the school superintendent noted that there were more than three hundred children without schools, some of whom could not even speak English.[83] Similar problems of inadequate educational facilities were also evident on the three reserves in Canada. Here, however, denominational rivalry aggravated the situation.

In 1899, Catholics opened the Crowfoot Boarding School at the Blackfoot reserve, and Emile Legal, the bishop of St. Albert, mounted a compaign to secure as many pupils and as much money as possible. He also asked for an increase in appropriations for the Sacred Heart School at the Peigan reserve, arguing that the school could accommodate forty or fifty pupils even though government appropriations allowed for only twenty. The DIA rejected his request after discovering that if the increase were granted, the Catholics would have in their school three more children than the total school roll of Peigan children—some of whom the Anglicans claimed.[84]

In 1909, Bishop Legal reapplied to the department for permission to increase the number of pupils in Catholic schools. The department again rejected the request because, as chief accountant D. C. Scott pointed out, twenty-two of the thirty-nine Catholic pupils at Sacred Heart School had contracted tuberculosis and seven had died in school, one after leaving it—which did not bode well for the remaining students. Instead of remedying the situation, Catholic authorities called the medical findings a "specious pretense" to prevent the admission of more children to Catholic schools.[85]

Conditions at the Anglican schools were no better. In 1912, the DIA judged the Peigan boarding school (Victoria Home) to be well below departmental standards. The plant was run down and dirty, the children were neglected, and only seven of the nineteen children enjoyed good health. Displeased, Ottawa threatened to withdraw its grants,[86] but the threat did not materialize, and the Anglicans made no improvements.

Poor conditions at the Peigan and Blood boarding schools paled in comparison to the White Eagle and, especially, the Old Sun's schools on the Blackfoot reserve. Both schools fell under the management of the Anglicans, and like many other denominational schools, they experienced financial difficulties. While DIA and church accountants squabbled, the structures as well as the health of the pupils deteriorated so badly that the Old Sun's school became somewhat notorious among officials and missionaries.[87]

After a prolonged dispute that lasted until 1912, the department built a new school for the Blackfoot, but unfortunately the Anglicans continued to mismanage it. An inspection conducted four years later found the plant to be dirty and overrun with mice; the principal and his wife were nice people, "but without the faintest idea of managing an institution of this sort." By then, the department was accustomed to such reports. In 1920, Scott observed, with resignation: "Anglican schools in the diocese of Calgary [have] been unfortunately always badly managed."[88] Not only were the living conditions in many of these schools deplorable, but untrained and factious staff also provided substandard instruction.

An investigation of the South Peigan boarding school by the agency physician soon revealed that the school superintendent Charles A. Robinson and his formidable wife Caroline had mismanaged the school. In March 1892, Dr. Z. T. Daniels visited the school and labeled it as essentially a hovel. The doctor reported that the boys' clothing was "dirty, ragged, unpatched and they reminded me of street gamins more than school pupils." Bath water was changed only once every twenty-four hours, and a single towel was used for the entire week. "It is stiff and emits a rank odor," his report concluded.[89]

Robinson and his wife finally resigned, but a change in personnel did not bring improvement or harmony to the school. Seven years later, agent Logan issued orders to school employees to cease the "discord, strife, backbiting, [and] immorality." At the turn of the century, a new teacher had beaten and choked an Indian pupil, and in 1913 another ill-tempered employee mauled the son of the agent, an Indian woman, and two Indian boys. The rapid turnover of personnel contributed to the chaos. In 1900 there were seventeen staff changes, and numerous agents pleaded in vain for an increase in teacher salaries.[90]

In addition to low salaries, inadequate appropriations plagued the schools. In 1912, the principal of Blackfeet school submitted a budget estimate of $11,301.11 for 76 pupils, but he was informed that the allowance would be $8,323.08 for 144 pupils. To make up the difference, the bureau advised him to supplement the childrens' diet with produce from the school garden. Shortages in staff and inadequate funding often forced the children to assume a disproportionate load of the housework, and at times children became the school's main labor force. The principal of the Blackfeet boarding school complained that only eight out of twenty-four girls were old enough to do housework, requiring the boys to work in the laundry and the kitchen.[91] Obviously, the necessities involved in running the school kept many children out of the classrooms. But this did not mean that they missed much by way of education.

The curriculum at the Blackfeet school reflected a general lack of imagination on the part of the teachers. When the agent submitted several examples of pupils' work to a show in the east, the commissioner of Indian affairs returned some of the samples with these caustic comments:

I also return the cluster of graduated pyramids. They are very neatly and carefully made and show considerable pains on the part of the pupils; but the trouble is that they do not stand for anything special in the way of education or cultivation. They are not artistic, they are not useful, they are not made by kindergarten pupils but by pupils of comparatively advanced years who could be taught in some more practical way form and care and neatness and thereby their time be put to much better use. . . . I trust that the ingenuity and good sense of your employee force will devise something by which boys and girls from twelve to sixteen can spend their time in learning what can be of some use to them in their future lives.[92]

Given the conditions at the school and the enforced separation of parents and children, the school obviously did not prove to be popular with the Blackfeet. To secure children for the school and then keep them there provided the agent with a continuous problem. In fact, two-thirds of the children who attended school in 1893 were brought in by Indian police, and the runaway problem was chronic. Girls in their early teens often slipped away at night, traveling as far as twenty miles to reach their families. Some runaways paid dearly. In 1895, two boys ran away in the middle of January; one was found frozen to death, and while the other was alive, his feet were badly frostbitten. Nonreservation boarding schools were no more attractive to Blackfeet children than reservation schools. When one pupil refused to return to the Fort Shaw school, the agent shipped him back in shackles, with an ex-policeman in charge of him. The agent hoped "that by the time [the pupil] arrives at his school his idea of education will be more in consonance with those of the Department."[93]

In Canada, schools under religious auspices also suffered from badly trained teachers as well as from the problem of runaways. At the Peigan Victoria Home, one Anglican teacher called, inappropriately, P. W. Gentleman whipped a boy and was transferred to the Old Sun's school on the Blackfoot reserve in 1919. The commissioner recommended that Gentleman be dismissed, but the church authorities replied that corporal punishment was justified. Two more years elapsed before the man was relieved of his post.[94]

To handle runaways, school principals called on the North West Mounted Police. In November 1920, the Mounties chased nine runaways, one of whom had already been returned to school eight times. This youngster led the police on a chase of 322 miles. No sooner had he been returned than he fled again, followed later by seven other boys. The distraught principal reported that the exodus had left the school without any male students.[95]

The Catholic institutions were not immune to such problems. During the Gentleman episode, a complaint reached Ottawa from a nurse inspecting the Crowfoot school. The children told her that they were chained to benches as punishment, and some were whipped by the sisters. In reply to an inquiry from the DIA, the principal stated that the department merely invited trouble by encouraging the Indians to voice "pretended grievances."[96]

In addition to these numerous problems with school administration, officials in both countries faced the ultimate and vexing question of what to do with the graduates, especially those from nonreservation institutions. Both Canadian and American officials worried that ex-pupils would revert to their old habits after they returned to the reservations. To solve this problem, the Canadian government instituted for graduates a support system that was meant to "bridge over the dangerous period of renewed contact with the reserve." Male students received a loan of cattle or horses, implements, tools, and building material. The department gave female students between thirty-five and fifty dollars at the time of their marriage, money toward the purchase of "useful articles" such as a sewing machine and household furniture. To prevent recidivism, officials even became matchmakers, encouraging and arranging marriages between ex-pupils and providing brides with dowries. To ensure further that the graduates did not regress, the department established a farming colony for Cree students, which was set up at File Hills, Saskatchewan; and the department tried to expand this project to other reserves.[97]

But such a system did not work for all Indians. The Reverend W. R. Haynes, principal of the Victoria Home on the Peigan reserve, reported that few among the eight graduates had found gainful employment, and the rest "spen[t] most of their time in idleness and dancing." Graduates who did not want to live in idleness encountered difficulties in finding employment. In 1911, the "Blood Pupils Association" complained to Ottawa that after having been taught the value of education and work they could find no employment on the reserves; and they protested the department's employment of white men in various capacities on the reserve when educated Indians were available. "The consequence for us," the pupils complained, "is a lack of opportunity for work, so that many gradually get discouraged and thus do not derive any profit from the education so generously dispensed to them by the care of the Government."[98]

Yet observers like Frederick Abbott found the Canadian Indian educational system to be highly commendable, especially since the BIA had no comparable plans to aid Indian ex-pupils. Officials who sometimes inquired about the fate of returned students did not find the reports from the Blackfeet agency encouraging. In 1896, the agent reported that he had offered the position of a laborer at twenty dollars per month to a graduate from Carlisle, but "this was not suited to his idea of what he would have," and the young man turned down the job. Most returned Blackfeet graduates had few options. By the midteens some took up their allotments, worked on the construction of irrigation ditches, or helped their parents. Jobs off the reservation were largely seasonal, and in general, returned students had few choices and faced a bleak future.[99]

Children who stayed on the reservation and attended the Blackfeet boarding school encountered conditions that had not improved much in forty years. Poor plant conditions, underpaid staff, and inadequate facilities proved impossible to remedy. In 1920, an inspection by a member of the Board of Indian Commissioners found the place ill kept, with an outdated and dangerous heating system and bad plumbing. The report concluded that teachers' salaries were so low that "competent people will not accept the position." Among nearly 1,000 school-age children, 139 attended the agency school and about 400 went to reservation and non-reservation schools, leaving over 300 children without schools. In short, the lack of schools made the BIA's rule of compulsory education virtually meaningless.[100]

Indian schools on Canadian reserves fared no better. Government officials knew of the poor conditions of Anglican schools, but they did nothing to remedy the situation. Securing the regular attendance of children continued to pose a problem, and educational results proved to be equally discouraging. In 1918, a Peigan agent reported that the five pupils who had graduated after ten or eleven years in school still could not speak proper English. The agent had no praise for the Catholics either, for similarly disappointing reports came from the Catholic schools on the Blood reserve. Still, some officials remained optimistic about educational progress and the future of the pupils.[101]

When Americans reviewed their Indian administration in the mid-1920s, they also labeled the educational system a failure. The Meriam Report, for instance, called the boarding schools "grossly inadequate," offering a poor diet and overcrowded, dirty surroundings that undermined the children's health. Moreover, poorly trained and underpaid teachers taught trades that were useless to the graduates. For Indians over twenty-one years of age, illiteracy stood at an estimated 48 percent, and a National Literacy Crusade was launched to remedy the situation. This crusade was but one part of a new Indian reform movement in the United States.[102]

In Canada no reexamination of Indian education policy took place because the church–state arrangement made changes difficult. The DIA was content to let the churches deal with Indians, and it interfered only when things got out of hand. The churches viewed any criticism by the department or by others as an attack on their faith. In 1915, an inspection of the Catholic boarding schools on the Blood reserve found the children barely able to speak English, with their reading, writing, spelling and arithmetic well below average, and most of their class work consisting of memorizing and reciting lessons. The school principal responded to the criticism by telling the department that it should ignore such reports.[103] And the department usually did ignore them.

By 1920 impartial observers were forced to admit that members of the Blackfoot Confederacy on both sides of the border were not about to be assimilated into Canadian or American society. The Blackfoot demonstrated only a nominal adherence to Catholicism and the various Protestant confessions, and they continued to carry on the aboriginal ceremonies, albeit in modified form despite periodic efforts to stamp them out. Thus, these differently administered systems of evangelization and education produced a general failure in Indian Christianization and education. Yet in the United States these problems eventually sparked an interest in reform, while the Canadian system became so fossilized with vested interests that reform became impossible.

7

Reservations, Law, and Order

The evangelization and education of the Indians—the standard planks in the platform to civilize the native people—have received considerable attention from students of Indian–white relations. By contrast, far less attention has been paid to the role of the white man's law and justice in bringing about Indian assimilation. In general, in both Canada and the United States those who argued for the extension of the white man's law to Indian reservations had three complementary aims: to establish a new law enforcement agency, to introduce a new legal system on the reservations, and to use the law to protect natives from exploitation by avaricious white men. The two countries chose different paths toward the same goals.

Considering the repeated declarations by Americans of the need to civilize and assimilate the Indians, the Indian bureau moved surprisingly slowly in imposing American ideas of justice upon Indian reservations. Part of the reason stemmed from the legal position of Indian tribes as domestic dependent nations exercising sovereignty over internal matters. In 1883, the commissioner of Indian affairs deplored the situation:

> Indians in the Indian country are not punishable for crimes or offenses committed against the persons or property of each other. Such offenses are generally left to the penalties of tribal usage, involving personal vengeance or pecuniary satisfaction, or the offenders are subjected to a few weeks or months of arbitrary confinement in an agency guard house or military fort. It is high time that crimes among Indians should be defined by United States laws.[1]

Because the American government experienced difficulty in providing law and order for the areas settled by white people, it is hardly surprising that legislators showed little interest in providing law for Indian reservations.

Canadians, on the other hand, did not subscribe to the concept of tribal sovereignty, and therefore, they faced no legal barriers to the imposition of Canadian law upon Indians living on reserves. Unlike the United
States, the Dominion established a law enforcement agency—the North
West Mounted Police—to oversee all of the prairie West, including the
reserves, beginning well before the arrival of settlers. Hence, law enforcement involving Indians became simply a matter of cooperation between
the DIA and the police.

By contrast, until the inauguration of the Peace Policy in 1870, the army
was the only body in the United States that could impose law and order
on the reservation, but its deployment depended largely on the decision
of the officer in charge. After 1870, the army withdrew from most reservations, confining itself to chasing "renegades" who had left their reservation without permission. Although the agent could call on the army to
quiet disturbances, civilian agents and their staff had, as a rule, the principal responsibility for maintaining law and order on the reservations and
for punishing miscreants. Since the United States government did not
create a law enforcement agency for the reservations, American agents
were forced to improvise a reservation law enforcement and justice system. In the late 1860s and early 1870s, agents on a couple of reservations
in the Southwest organized a police force composed of tribal members.
The most famous of these organizations became the Indian police, established by John P. Clum on the San Carlos Apache reservation.[2] These ad
hoc arrangements became formalized in 1878, with the passage of federal legislation authorizing the establishment of Indian police forces.

The duties of Indian policemen included the maintenance of order on
the reservation, the prevention of the sale of liquor, and general assistance to the agent. The Indian bureau hoped to make the Indian police
an instrument of civilization by enforcing school attendance, punishing
polygamists, and suppressing Indian dances. Indians usually made up
the force, but a non-Indian could serve as its chief officer. Recruits received
monthly salaries, ranging from five dollars for privates to eight dollars
for officers, a paltry sum considering the duties required in the job.[3]

Five years after the establishment of an Indian police force, the secretary of the interior authorized the creation of a "court of Indian offenses"
on the reservations. This tribunal possessed the authority to enforce rules
prohibiting "sun-dance, scalp-dance and war-dance, polygamy, theft, &c."
In addition, the court had jurisdiction over misdemeanors committed by
reservation Indians as well as other matters brought before it with the
agent's approval. In civil cases, the court wielded powers similar to those
of the justice of the peace. The Indian court usually consisted of three
Indian judges nominated by the agent and approved by the bureau. The

judges could pass sentences consisting of a fine, imprisonment, hard labor, or loss of rations. In the absence of federal laws regulating Indian conduct, these tribunals provided the means of imposing non-Indian concepts of proper behavior.[4]

In 1883, the case of *Ex parte Crow Dog* publicized the fact that the United States could not legally punish an Indian who had murdered another Indian on a reservation. The case resulted in the passage, in 1885, of the so-called Major Crimes Act, which made Indians subject to federal law in the commission of seven crimes: murder, manslaughter, rape, assault with intent to kill, arson, burglary, and larceny. In 1909, incest, assault, and robbery were added to the list.[5]

In spite of these changes, the legal status of American Indians remained unclear. A final solution to their anomalous status appeared to come with the passage of the Dawes Act, which would eventually make the Indians subject to the state's jurisdiction in civil and criminal matters. However, this process turned out to be long and complicated, and periodically, impatient Americans demanded that all Indians be made subject to the civil and criminal laws of the country.[6] In the meantime, the system of tribal courts and federal involvement in certain cases continued to exist side by side.

In attempting to formulate a system of reservation law enforcement, Americans once again turned to Canada for a solution. In 1877, the commissioner of Indian affairs reported that Canadians had controlled their Indians with a police force, indicating that a similar method might be used in the American West.[7] These statements suggest that Americans based their idea of a reservation police on the North-West Mounted Police. More likely, however, Americans misunderstood the Canadian system, for the commissioner urged the recruitment of such a force from Indians, to be commanded by white men. Consequently, Americans established an Indian police force that bore little resemblance to the Canadian Mounties.

Meanwhile, the exploits of the Mounties in the West became a Canadian legend, even though academics have now disposed of the image of clean-living defenders of the queen's law. Historians have also reexamined the commonly held assumption that the force was dispatched to the West to protect Indians from rapacious whiskey traders, as well as the belief that the police facilitated a relatively trouble-free settlement of the West.[8] Whatever the motivations, however, the very presence of the police eliminated many of the problems that faced American Indians and government officials.

The creation of the North West Mounted Police led to a system of law enforcement on Canadian reserves that differed from the system established in the United States. For one, the Mounties were not an "Indian" police: the force was neither composed of Indians nor stationed on individual reserves. Second, the jurisdiction of the police extended over non-Indians and Indians alike, regardless of whether the latter were living on reserves. Except for Indian or mixed-blood scouts, recruits came largely from eastern Canada and included English- and French-speaking men. During the early years, officers came from Britain, and were often veterans of the British law enforcement establishment.[9] This composition may have contributed to the force's generally amiable relations with the plains tribes, since neither the officers nor the recruits felt the contempt and animosity toward Indians so prevalent among American frontiersmen.

In comparison to American lawmen, the Canadian police could dispense justice swiftly and surely. Senior officers served as magistrates; and lawbreakers were not only apprehended, but also tried and sentenced by the police, and many were even jailed in police barracks. This system prevailed until 1886, when the Dominion created a Supreme Court for the territories, making the judges independent of the police. Prevention and persuasion appeared to be the two methods that enabled the Mounties to curb lawlessness on the prairies. Regular patrols visited ranches and settlements where settlers signed "patrol slips" and informed officers of any problems or suspicious characters in the vicinity. Under this policing system, most rural crime was nearly eliminated by 1892.[10]

Unlike Americans, Canadians created neither a special Indian police force nor a tribal court system. Law enforcement on the reserves became part of the general Indian administration. The Indian Act spelled out penalties for lesser crimes, such as selling liquor to Indians, trespassing on reserves, cutting timber illegally, and procuring Indian women for prostitution. On reserves with an elected tribal council, the act specified that councillors could frame additional regulations pertaining to reserve management.[11] In cases of major crimes, such as murder, assault, or theft, the Mounties tried to impose penalties according to the Canadian justice system.

Moreover, Canadian Indian agents played a vital role in maintaining law and order among Indians and between Indians and settlers. In the North West Territories, Indian agents possessed the powers of magistrates and the authority to try cases arising from violations of the Indian Act, particularly cases involving liquor offenses. Frederick Abbott, visiting the West in 1915, found the combination of the Mounted Police and the agent–magistrate to be a powerful tool for fighting liquor.[12]

Yet Canadians believed that their law enforcement could be improved, and on several occasions the Indian department came close to establishing a Canadian Indian police. In 1889, the department approved, under the Dominion Police Act, the hiring of "reliable and intelligent" Indians to help in the suppression of illicit liquor sales to Indians. Although Ottawa made no reference to the American Indian police, the department's justification of the employment of Indians reflected sentiments similar to those in the United States: "The presence on an Indian reserve of an officer of the law cannot but have a good moral effect on an Indian band generally . . ." The department concluded that "the expense is very much lessened by employing Indian police."[13]

Some agents already employed Indian police on their reserves. During the unsettled early 1880s, agent Denny organized an Indian police force on the Blood reserve to control horse stealing. Denny's force was patterned after South Peigan tribal police, but it remained a local and informal arrangement. In the meantime, the Mounted Police hired Indians as guides and scouts. Seven members of the Blackfoot Confederacy served as special constables in the Mounties; two were stationed with the detachment at Lethbridge, three at Fort Macleod, and two at Blackfoot Crossing. They were doing a splendid job, even though one of them, a man named Young Pine, soon went astray.[14]

In 1891, commissioner Hayter Reed toyed with the idea of creating a separate Indian troop of the Mounties. Reed thought that such an organization would provide young Blackfoot men with employment, and he submitted evidence from the United States of the efficacy of such police. However, the comptroller of the Mounted Police rejected this proposal, explaining the difference between the American reservation police and the semimilitary nature of the Mounties. The comptroller recommended, instead, the creation of a strictly Indian police on the western reserves, separate from the Mounties.[15] Once again, nothing came of this idea, although Indians and mixed-bloods continued to serve as special constables in the Mounted Police.

Obviously, neither Canadians nor Americans understood the other's system of reservation law enforcement. But even if they had, given the political realities, it is doubtful that Americans would have accepted an authoritarian organization such as the North West Mounted Police. On the other hand, even though prime Minister Macdonald had originally contemplated a police force composed of the Metis as well as whites, the Riel uprising put an end to that idea. With the Mounties at their disposal, Canadians saw no reason to create a separate reserve police.[16] In view of these different approaches to law enforcement, the Blackfoot reservations offer a good comparison of the efficacy of the two systems.

The first major law enforcement problem faced by Canadian and American authorities revolved around the restrictions in the free passage of Blackfeet across the "medicine line." The original intention was to suppress horse stealing and intertribal warfare. These two pursuits formed a part of plains Indian culture, and they continued even after the tribes had settled on reservations. Raids and thievery became an international problem when raiders took advantage of the "medicine line" to dispose of property stolen on the other side. Indeed, in the early 1880s, complaints that "Canadian" Indians indulged in horse stealing and cattle killing on the American side were common, as were complaints about Cree harassment of the South Peigans.[17]

Raids and intertribal warfare involving the Blackfoot Confederacy and its ancient enemies on both sides of the border continued until the late 1880s. Although such incidents were supposedly eliminated by an 1887 "international agreement" between the Bloods and three American tribes,[18] two years later a Blood raiding party stole horses from the Crows. But the reception given to the raiders upon their return illustrated how times had changed.

In returning from the United States, the Bloods encountered a group of Gros Ventre, and a fight ensued in which two Gros Ventre died. When the raiders, led by the Indian policeman Young Pine, returned to the Blood reserve with five horses and two scalps, agent W. B. Pocklington took them to task. Young Pine explained that they had fought the Gros Ventre to avenge the death of six Bloods at the hands of other members of that tribe. Young Pine was upset at what he perceived to be the agent's groundless complaints, for the raiders had not stolen any horses from white people. Pocklington had a different view: he lectured Young Pine on the evil of his ways, warning him to stop the raids across the border or his men would be handed over to American authorities and hanged.[19]

Pocklington's threat was not an idle one. At times, agents of the Blackfoot Confederacy found it necessary to cooperate with each other and with the Mounties in order to subdue their adventuresome charges. Moreover, American agents called on the police for assistance in returning stolen property and sometimes in apprehending American criminals. In 1885, the Mounties expressed a desire to make cooperation closer and more official between American agents and Canadian authorities.[20] Agent George Steell relied the most on the help of the redcoats. He and Major Samuel B. Steele, who commanded the Fort Macleod detachment, exchanged information on Indian and white lawbreakers, and tried to keep each other abreast of possible trouble.[21]

In addition, officials tried to restrict Blackfeet movement in order to prevent the issuance of rations to Indians who officially "belonged" to the other side. In the early 1880s, officials recognized that a problem existed, and the bureau sent frequent inquiries to the Blackfeet agent about steps taken to exclude northern Indians. Canadian officials also worried about unregulated comings and goings. In 1889, the Dominion, acting upon a request from the DIA, asked imperial authorities to contact the Americans to work out a system of Indian passes.[22] Although an international pass system never materialized, agents on both sides of the border did institute their own pass system, but the scheme was never very effective.

As early as 1891, Sam Steele recognized that the Blackfoot, Bloods, and Peigans went south whenever the spirit moved them, pass or no pass. He reported that a few of the policemen spoke Blackfoot and tried to explain to the Indians the pass system, but he admitted that "the Indians when it suits their purpose can be very obtuse." In 1894, American agent L. W. Cooke reported that he had adjusted the Blackfeet tribal roll with those of the Canadian reserves. From then on, he promised, Canadian Indian visitors to his reservation would need to show passes. If they arrived without one, they would be arrested, sentenced to hard labor, and then forced to walk back to Canada.[23]

Such cooperation between agents served in 1895 to put an end to the escapades of a Blood named Black Looking. Black Looking "took treaty" in Canada, but then went to the American agency where he married a South Peigan woman. Subsequently, he returned north only to abscond with the wife of a man named Hairy Face. Black Looking's first wife complained to George Steell about the new arrangement, and when the agent found out that the second wife was a Canadian Indian, he wrote to James Wilson at the Blood agency:

> Black Looking and his second wife—"Three Cuts," were tried by our Indian Court and sentenced to two months confinement at hard labor. At the expiration of the two months it was agreed that the woman, —"Three Cuts" was to return to your Reservation. Under the circumstances I would suggest that the woman be allowed to serve out her time in our Agency jail, and at the end of two months she will be returned to you.

Steell hoped that this punishment would serve as a warning to the rest of the Indians.[24]

Efforts to restrict the movement of the Blackfeet were not entirely successful, since they depended on the initiative of the individual official. In 1897, George Steell complained to the Canadian Indian commissioner that the Blood agent not only granted far too many passes to his Indians, but many of them went to Montana without permission. Steell believed that these visits led to discontent, and he advocated the further limitation of contacts between these groups. The Blood agent made similar complaints about American Blackfeet coming to the Blood reserve in large numbers, especially at issue time.[25]

By the turn of the century the two governments had recognized the extent of the problem posed by this cross-border tribe. In 1899, David Laird wrote to the Blood agent that the existing ad hoc pass system could not be enforced by law. This realization followed complaints by customs agents that Blackfeet on both sides of the border were evading customs regulations. In 1902, with the problem of the free movement of Indians across the border still unsolved, the DIA wrote to the BIA, advocating a formal agreement to limit the number of passes and to turn back those without passes. The bureau agreed to this proposal and instructed agents to comply. However, as with most other legislation emanating from Ottawa and Washington, these directives proved easier to issue than to enforce. Several years later, the Blood agent asked Ottawa to remind the Americans of the arrangement in order to enforce the agreement,[26] but it would have been easier to plug a sieve. The pass arrangement turned out to be a dead letter.

Those who violated the pass rule faced only mild punishment. In cases of more serious offenses, however, Canadian Indians in the United States faced the full brunt of the American justice system. For example, three Bloods caught with stolen horses on the South Peigan reservation in 1891 were sentenced to imprisonment for eight years.[27]

The habit of crossing the boundary to escape punishment backfired even more tragically for one Canadian Indian. In the fall of 1879, the body of a murdered white man was found at Cut Bank Creek, and a Blood Indian named Spopee was arrested at the Blackfeet agency. He was tried and given a death sentence. Because of extenuating circumstances, the judge commuted his sentence to life imprisonment in the Detroit House of Correction. His jailers did not seem to realize that they had in their custody a plains Indian who neither spoke nor understood English. Since Spopee did not communicate with them, the jailers concluded that he must be insane and transferred him to St. Elizabeth's Hospital in Washington, D.C. In 1914, a Blackfeet delegation to Washington heard about a strange Indian in an insane asylum, and they went to visit him. One of the women in the group managed to communicate with Spopee and learn his story. After appeals to the president, Spopee was released from the asylum and returned to the Blackfeet reservation, where he died a year later.[28]

For American agents, the Indian police provided some means of law enforcement on the reservations. Organized in October 1878, this force consisted of a captain, a lieutenant, three sergeants, and ten privates, with the agency physician serving as police chief. In 1884, agent Allen reported that prior to his arrival, the police had mustered out "wrapped in their blankets and wearing pants, or with leggins instead of pants, or dressed in any peculiar style they saw fit to adopt." Allen not only put the men in uniform, but he also ordered them to cut their braids, which caused a momentary revolt. Eventually, most of the policemen submitted or found themselves replaced.[29]

For years, the police force worked with various degrees of success. Agent Logan had only praise for his policemen in 1899. He called them "a most efficient body of men, perfectly trustworthy, and to be depended upon in any emergency." At times, however, the force posed problems. Some policemen occasionally refused to obey orders and it was not uncommon for the entire police force to get drunk.[30]

A more serious situation arose during the closing years of the 1910s, when the Blackfeet police force became a law unto itself. The man responsible for this development was the head of the police—an Indian—who allegedly not only connived to introduce whiskey on the reservation, but also extorted money and property from the Blackfeet and wreaked his private vengeance on the people. When an inspector uncovered the situation, the superintendent informed him that another Indian could not be found to fill the position. The inspector recommended that a white man be hired, and he stated that "the Blackfeet reservation is another proof positive of the imperative need of immediate legislation . . . for establishing and enforcing well-defined law on Indian reservations."[31]

In the meantime, the bureau did try to provide law for the reservations. In 1891, for instance, the National Bar Association passed a resolution urging the establishment of "courts and a system of law in and for the Indian reservations." The association believed that although the system of police and Indian courts had been successful, many Indians should have been "brought under the influence of some simple system of courts and laws by which they might be instructed in the methods of civil and orderly government." The association recommended that certain tribes, which were not sufficiently civilized to comprehend the new legal system, should be excluded from the plan. The Blackfeet fell into this category.[32] While nothing came of this suggestion, the reservation courts of Indian offenses continued to play an important role in the enforcement of order and the suppression of "barbarous practices."

Most of the time, these courts experienced considerable difficulty in carrying out their mandate. They operated without funding or legislative authority until 1888, when the government appropriated five thousand dollars to pay judges' salaries ranging from three to eight dollars per month. The commissioner deplored the paltry remunerations, and he urged that the appropriations be tripled.[33] In spite of these obstacles, reservation courts carried out their duties.

The exact date of the establishment of the Indian court on the Blackfeet reservation is uncertain, but some sort of tribunal probably operated between 1884 and 1889, for in 1889 the commissioner questioned the agent about stories of "sometimes ridiculous decisions of the present Judges of the Court of Indian Offences." The agent replied that the reports were based on hearsay, but if the complaints proved to be true the judges would be replaced. Ten years later, the agent reported that the three judges, all full-bloods, "while not having the wisdom of a Solomon, . . . dispensed justice impartially and intelligently, according to the Indian's idea of justice."[34]

The court handled all reservation disputes, including liquor infractions and domestic disputes. While visiting the reservation in 1899, the secretary of the Board of Indian Commissioners observed the proceedings in settling a marital spat between a young couple, and he returned charmed and amused by the deportment of the judge named "Shorty White-Grass."[35]

Illicit liquor traffic posed the most difficult and time-consuming challenge to the justice systems in both countries. Historically, alcohol remained a bane to the Indians. Governments in both countries prohibited its sale to Indians in an effort to help in forestalling the exploitation and social disentegration of the tribes; nevertheless, the illicit sale of whiskey to Indians remained a perennial problem in both Canada and the United States. Canadians tried to control the use of liquor by imposing a prohibition in the North West Territories from 1873 to 1892. Lawbreakers faced a relatively swift punishment at the hands of the Indian agents or the Mounties. One Mountie recalled that traders were never fined less than two hundred dollars and served no less than six months in jail.[36]

In the late 1870s, American federal law imposed a slap-on-the-wrist penalty for introducing liquor to Indian country, calling for imprisonment for not less than a year and a fine of not less than one hundred dollars. In the early 1880s, the penalty was raised to not more than two years imprisonment and a fine of not more than three hundred dollars. At the same time, American officials realized that the law was unenforceable because local juries refused to convict one of their neighbors for engaging in one of the most lucrative examples of private enterprise.[37]

The Blackfeet suffered from the whiskey plague as much as other tribes. During the 1870s, American whiskey traders infested the plains of southern Alberta, with their activities leading to murder and mayhem within the Blackfoot Confederacy. News of the impending arrival of the North West Mounted Police sent the traders scurrying back across the border, where they wreaked havoc among the South Peigans. When agent John Wood arrived in the mid-1870s, one of his first acts was to put an end to drunken brawls and to establish a code of law, modeled after the American system, to end the disintegration of the demoralized Peigans.[38]

Enforcing the reservation liquor law posed a problem that neither country solved satisfactorily. In 1914, American reformers still considered whiskey to be the greatest menace to the Indians, and questions of the best way to put an end to the traffic occupied reformers as well as BIA officials. During Prohibition, the federal government increased funds aimed at suppressing the liquor trade to Indians to 150,000 dollars, but by 1921 the amount had been cut in half, with predictably disastrous results for law enforcement.[39]

Although the violation of Canadian liquor laws was a clearly defined offense, the Mounted Police nevertheless had its hands full. The legal system allowed magistrates to convict the accused on evidence presented by the informer alone, and since the Canadians in the West had dispensed with jury trial, a conviction was far more certain than in the United States. Despite these advantages, in 1907, the DIA declared the idea of enforcing total abstinence on the reserves amounted to nothing but a utopian dream.[40]

In the meantime, Americans had an even more difficult time in enforcing liquor regulations. Until the arrival of George Steell in 1890, agents gave the liquor problem on the South Peigan reservation only cursory attention. A report by George B. Grinnell to the Indian Rights Association, regarding the difficulty of securing conviction for this offense in Montana, illustrated why agents were reluctant to prosecute the peddlers. Steell, however, thrived on difficulties. His declaration of war against whiskey sellers came as the result of a mishap at the town of Robare, just outside the boundaries of the reservation. After a political meeting in Robare, a group of Peigans got drunk, and during the ensuing fracas a saloon proprietor shot one of the Indians. Shortly thereafter, an Indian froze to death following a drinking spree in the town.[41]

Robare was not the only place where the Peigans could easily obtain liquor. The town of Cut Bank, located a mile from the eastern boundary of the reservation, also provided liquid refreshments. With a population of about three hundred, it boasted two mercantile stores and eight or ten saloons. In addition, about a hundred people and three saloons made up the town of Dupuyer, which, like its counterparts, supported itself largely by the sale of liquor to Indians.[42]

Not surprisingly, liquor caused its share of problems on the reservation. Of the 116 cases that came before the Indian court in 1906, 25 were for drunkenness and 25 for being drunk and disorderly. The cases remaining involved assaults, disputes, and thefts.[43]

Even with prohibition in the North West Territories, Canadian authorities fought an uphill battle to suppress the lively Indian liquor trade. Blood agent Wilson tried to end clandestine imbibing by imposing a jail sentence, rather than a fine, on Bloods who broke the law. David Laird, the Indian commissioner, fully supported Wilson's efforts, commenting that "this will prevent them from squandering their money and give them time to think over the evils of intemperance."[44]

Despite the advantages of their legal system, Canadian officials found that it was difficult to secure evidence against traders selling whiskey to the Indians. Among the Bloods, the tribe closest to the border, the whiskey traffic flourished. The department attempted to hire two detectives to learn the identities of the traders, but no one suitable could be found for the job. The intrepid agent Wilson launched his own campaign, giving money to Indians to purchase liquor and then using them as witnesses against the sellers. However, the DIA warned him that his action amounted to de facto participation in the trade. Inspector J. A. Markle warned him: "You will find in time that the liquor dealers and friends will try to create the impression that you, the Indians, and others are prosecuting them for the money there is in it, i.e. fines."[45]

Yet the situation among the Bloods must have been serious enough for the usually parsimonious department to authorize in 1905 a fifty-dollar reward for each conviction, particularly since the fines collected usually produced less than this amount. Because the department benefited from each conviction, Ottawa made provisions for someone other than the agent to try the liquor cases. Two police constables were also detailed to suppress the Blood liquor traffic. Nevertheless, five years later, the department continued to receive reports of drunkenness among the Bloods, and again it considered the possibility of hiring detectives, this time to keep an eye on the citizens of the town of Macleod.[46]

Such efforts to quash the liquor traffic met with disapproval from white residents. In April 1906, an editorial in the *Macleod Gazette* attacked agent Wilson for sentencing "a woman with a two month's old child at her breast to pay a fine of $450 or go to jail for nine months for selling a bottle or more of whiskey to an Indian." The editorial charged that the penalty imposed was "out of all proportion to the offence and out of the bounds of reason and against the dictates of christianity and civilization and illustrates the danger of permitting unqualified and irresponsible persons exercising and abusing the judicial power." Wilson had already given a nine-month sentence to another woman "with a sucking child at her breast," and the child had died in a Calgary jail. The newspaper wanted to rouse the people of Canada against such conduct by an "official understrapper."[47] In the United States, similar attacks by the public on an Indian agent would have led to a lengthy investigation by the bureau, and ultimately to his dismissal. To its credit, the DIA ignored these complaints, knowing well that the agent's action was justified.

South of the border, the Blackfeet agent experienced a much more difficult time in getting officers of the law to act in liquor cases, let alone in securing convictions. In 1897, George Steell wrote to a state senator to appeal for his support in passing a stringent piece of antiliquor legislation. Steell wanted all law officers to arrest any drunken Indian and mixed-blood found off the reservation, and to impose severe penalties against whiskey pedlars. "There are laws against all this, but you know that the State law stands as a dead letter," Steell complained. "You know that there are no arrests made by State, County, or City governments, of anyone selling whiskey to these people."[48]

The American justice system repeatedly proved to be too ponderous to deal effectively with liquor traffic. Whiskey traders and witnesses often disappeared before the trial; and the Department of Justice refused to allow the Indian bureau to employ officers of the U.S. Marshal's office to "ferret out" whiskey sellers, explaining that these officers were neither policemen nor detectives and their only duty was to serve papers. The Justice Department maintained that only special agents could investigate the liquor problem.[49]

In Canada, at least, the North West Mounted Police was given latitude to deal with liquor infractions, and did not become an obstacle to justice. In the early years of its existence, the Mounties largely succeeded in retaining the goodwill and respect of Canada's native people; but when a tight-fisted government policy led to starvation among the Indians, and insensitive department officials took over many of the functions of the police, the situation changed. In 1879 came the first fatality among the police, possibly at the hands of an Indian. A Blood, Star Child, was accused of killing Marmaduke Graburn, a constable, but Star Child was subsequently acquitted for lack of evidence. The murder, however, damaged the image of the police as untouchable defenders of justice. After the Graburn episode, Indian resistance and attacks on members of the Mounties still occurred, but they remained comparatively isolated.[50]

Nevertheless, in the late 1880s a rash of altercations between settlers and Indians alarmed DIA officials. Most of the incidents occurred when towns like Lethbridge and Macleod increased in population, following the completion of the railroad. In 1887, there were three clashes between whites and Indians, with one involving a Peigan shot by a settler for allegedly robbing his cabin. The three bands saw the shooting as unjustifiable, and they voiced stong complaints to the authorities.[51]

Commissioner Edgar L. Dewdney worried about these developments, noting that some of the newcomers did not think the Indians were worthy of the same consideration as white people. Dewdney wrote to Ottawa, "I fear some of the complications which have arisen between our neighbours and the Indians across the line, brought about by such causes, will obtain here."[52] Fortunately, Dewdney's fears proved to be unfounded, and the violence against Indians did not spread, but his reaction indicated the Canadian officials' sensitivity to any departure from law and order.

During the mid-1890s, another series of serious incidents occurred, revealing the strained relations between whites and Indians. In 1891, a couple of Peigans attempted to murder a rations issuer when he testified against several Indians who had broken into a storehouse. In 1895, a Cree named Almighty Voice managed to murder several white men, including a police officer, before being killed himself two years later. Also in 1895, the refusal to give a meat ration to a Blackfoot with a sick child resulted in another tragedy on this reserve. When the child died, the grief-stricken father blamed the issuer for his son's death. Three weeks later, the Indian shot and killed the issuer, an ex-policeman. In turn, the police were called out and proceeded to shoot and kill the distraught man.[53]

Another tragedy stemming from clashes between Anglo-American and aboriginal concepts of justice took place on the Blackfoot reserve in October 1896. A forty-year-old Blackfoot named Charcoal shot and killed the lover of one of his wives. Until then, Charcoal had been a model reservation Indian, who appeared to have abandoned the old ways. But his wife's lover was also a close relative, making the liaison a matter of incest, and both Charcoal and his errant wife were members of important religious societies. After the first killing, Charcoal was convinced that he too would be killed, and so he decided to go out in a blaze of glory. After failing to kill Red Crow, the Blood head chief, Charcoal wounded the farm instructor and then fled with his family. The Mounties, guided by Indian scouts, began the manhunt. Finally, Charcoal's brothers, pressured by the police, turned him over to the authorities. He was sentenced to death for the two killings, and hanged in March 1897.[54]

The imposition of alien concepts of crime and punishment on the plains tribes also caused a tragedy on the South Peigan reservation. In 1887, the sheriff of Choteau County arrived at the agency with an arrest warrant for a Peigan called Two Foxes, who allegedly had killed a white man. The Indian police found their man, but Two Foxes escaped. The police gave chase, and Two Foxes killed himself before he could be apprehended. "He told [the police]," the agent wrote, "he would not be arrested, that his body was his own."

Most of the Peigans believed that Two Foxes committed suicide rather than face arrest for murder, but agent Baldwin maintained that Two Foxes had not been involved in the murder, and actually feared being arrested for stealing a horse a year earlier. Most likely, his fear of white man's justice had driven Two Foxes to take his own life.[55] However, such tragic incidents were more unusual than typical of problems in law enforcement on Indian reservations.

The majority of law enforcement problems were quite mundane, yet some solution to them was imperative for the welfare and prosperity of the natives. One of the most vexing problems faced by American agents concerned the removal of pernicious individuals from reservations. These persons were often white men who had married Indian women, and according to American law, they possessed the right to reside on the reservation. While some men worked hard to support their families, others became sources of trouble when they interfered with agency administration, or more seriously, when they indulged in cattle stealing and selling whiskey.[56] Since Americans had no uniform law to define tribal membership, U.S. Indian agents were virtually powerless to remove these individuals from reservations. Once evicted, most simply returned to the reservations to resume their activities. By contrast, because the Indian Act required an Indian woman who married a non-Indian to leave the reserve, this problem of pesky "squaw men" never materialized in Canada.

Preventing trespass on Indian reservations also presented constant law-enforcement challenges to American Indian agents. The American justice system consistently failed to provide a remedy against enterprising cattlemen, lumbermen, and miners who intruded on Indian reservations. Like the "squaw men," many trespassers either ignored eviction orders or returned to the reservation once the authorities had relaxed their vigilance. On the other hand, those who trespassed on Canadian reserves faced certain punishment, and the Indian Act even singled out the prevention of trespass as one of the agents' duties. Penalites imposed on violators consisted of a mandatory thirty-day sentence for the first offense, and an additional thirty days for each subsequent offense.[57]

On the Blackfeet reservation in Montana, the agent and the police force spent considerable energy in trying to prevent trespassing on the reservation by neighboring cattlemen. These trespassers were extremely injurious to the Indians' welfare because illegal cattle grazing robbed the tribe of thousands of dollars in grazing fees. John Young, for example, complained in 1883 that some twelve thousand head of outside cattle grazed on the reservation. Agent L. W. Cooke reported that there were ten to fifteen thousand head on the reservation when he arrived in 1893. Cooke had frequent altercations with the cattle ranchers, who audaciously complained to the BIA when the agent removed their cattle from the reservation. "They should realize this reservation is for the Indians and not for them," Cooke snapped back at the commissioner when asked to explain his actions.[58]

Fencing the reservation would have solved the problem, but for many years the BIA rejected the suggestion as impractical because of the high cost per mile of fence, between one and two hundred dollars. When agent J. A. Monteath revived the proposal in 1900, the bureau again turned down his request. At the same time, the commissioner instructed the agent: "This does not mean, however, that you are to cease your efforts to prevent trespass on the reservation or to prevent the Indian stock from wandering off." Unfortunately, Monteath and his police force were not able to prevent trespass. During the especially severe winter of 1900, outside cattle herds, ranging from fifteen to twenty thousand head, foraged on the reservation. Monteath sarcastically told the commissioner: "I am not prepared to state thay they were herded onto the reserve, but it is a fact that they are now overrunning us."[59]

Indian reserves in southern Alberta also suffered from intrusions by non-Indian cattle. Fortunately for the Canadian Indians, agents were able to prosecute this type of trespass more successfully than their American neighbors. In fact, Canadian Indians themselves considered these incidents to be serious, protesting loudly to the department and the police. For example, the Peigans made a protest in 1911 with the full backing of their agent, E. H. Yeomans, who wrote to his superiors: "These ranchers possibly thought that the treatment given to Indians south of the International line to be good enough for the Indians within the Canadian territory."[60] He made clear that such attitudes would not be countenanced in Canada.

Stealing and killing livestock presented yet another law enforcement problem to officials on both sides of the border. The offenders in these instances could be both whites and Indians. Ranchers in Canada complained that Indians killed their cattle, and in the late 1890s, the Mounties managed to arrest a number of Bloods for this offense. By contrast, on the South Peigan reservation, the cattle industry suffered heavily from depredations committed by white cattle rustlers.

One agent, in complaining that most white men regarded the "Injun critter" as fair game, reported that Indian cattle regularly vanished. Many of the rustlers crossed the borders to Canada to escape prosecution, and the agent complained that he had no travel funds to follow them and bring them to justice. In 1909 alone, the agent reported, the Blackfeet lost fifteen thousand dollars worth of stock and recovered only a third. Therefore, agent McFatridge was especially pleased when he managed to secure the conviction of three sons of a "squaw man" who had been stealing cattle from Indians.[61]

By the 1910s, depredations against Blackfeet livestock became so serious that some agents feared the Indians would be driven out of the cattle business. To combat the problem the Indians organized the Blackfeet Stock Protection Association, modeled after the ranchers' stock associations. Forty-three members of the group were deputized as special officers and deployed to prevent cattle theft and to apprehend rustlers.[62] This organization supplemented the tribal police in limiting the number of cattle thefts.

In retrospect, neither country found a perfect system of law enforcement for Indian reservations. The Mounties proved to be an effective organization, but nevertheless Canadian concepts of law clashed with aboriginal ideas of justice, sometimes tragically. However, because of the broad powers granted to them, the Mounties were more capable of suppressing disorders than American law enforcement agencies such as county sheriffs, federal agents, Indian police, and Indian agents.

The Canadian Indian Act also provided a less complicated way of dealing with some offenses by giving the Indian agent the powers of a magistrate. At least, Indian agents in Canada did not experience the frustrations of trying to stop whiskey traffic or punish trespassers with an obstructive and cumbersome legal system. Cooperation between Indian agents and the Mounties ensured relatively speedy punishment for transgressors, producing a situation vastly different from relations between Blackfeet agents and sheriffs or district attorneys in Montana.

On the other hand, one could argue that, even with all its faults, the American system of Indian police, tribal courts, and judges allowed the Blackfeet a measure of independence and self-respect. The absence of these institutions in the context of Canadian Indian administration was undoubtedly the result of the conservative attitudes of department officials. The rejection of the idea of an Indian police illustrated the Canadian fear of innovation and experimentation. As a result, Americans had a system of law enforcement that partially integrated native people into the legal system, but proved largely ineffective against trespassers and whiskey traders. The Canadians, on the other hand, rejected the participation of the natives, but managed to combat lawbreakers with more vigor and, in some instances, with more success.

8

Welfare and War

After decades of attempts by humanitarians and government officials to educate, evangelize, and civilize the Indians, as well as to make them economically self-sufficient, a group of new academics emerged in the United States. The social scientists pointed out that native population would not be absorbed into American society as swiftly and as thoroughly as previously anticipated. Although they did not abandon the idea of eventual assimilation, this group, along with many like-minded officials, argued, instead, that the federal government as well as American society should reconsider to what degree Indians could be integrated. Thus, lower expectations about what Indians could accomplish became one clear trend in molding native people into permanent second-class citizens.[1] Similar developments took place in Canada. While officials and academics mulled over the future of the natives, others who were more intimately involved with the residents of reservations most likely thought that such discussions would shortly become literally academic for the simple reason that overwhelming evidence indicated that unless something was done quickly, few Indians would survive to be assimilated.

Although many observers had pointed for decades to the decline in native population, by the end of the nineteenth century the depiction of Indians as a "vanishing race" became a reality. While intermarriage played an important role in changing the genetic makeup of North American natives, diseases served as the primary agency in the overall decline in Indian population. Diseases such as smallpox had decimated tribes since their first contact with the Europeans; typhus, diphtheria, pneumonia, tuberculosis, and trachoma subsequently became the scourge of many reservation Indians. Still, although the two governments were aware of the health crisis on most Indian reservations, they showed little interest in providing systematic health care for native populations until after the turn of the century.[2] As in other areas of Indian affairs, native health care suffered from the usual problems of staffing, funding, and administration.

In hiring reservation physicians, the American government recognized its responsibility for providing health care, as set forth in some Indian treaties, but staffing medical posts with competent personnel proved to be difficult because of poor pay, overwork, a lack of facilities and drugs, and uncongenial working conditions. Doctors who stayed in the Indian service often remained because they were incompetent and could not find employment elsewhere.

In the meantime, conscientious physicians wrote reports to the commissioner describing appalling health conditions on their reservations, but since the BIA maintained no health statistics, authorities found it easy to ignore such reports. By the turn of the century, Indian health conditions had deteriorated so much that only government-supported intervention could begin to deal with the situation. Not until 1909, however, did the United States fund the first government-sponsored campaign against trachoma, an eye disease that blinded and disfigured many Indians. Two years later, the bureau finally used general appropriations for the prevention and treatment of diseases among Indians; a year later, the government appropriated ten thousand dollars for the Public Health Service to survey reservations for contagious diseases. There, researchers found that Indian mortality topped 30 percent per one thousand people, a rate about double that of the general population. Despite such alarming statistics, the situation did not result in drastic action. In fact, in 1928, the Meriam Report concluded that Indian health care had fallen "below a reasonable standard of efficiency."[3]

While the American government dragged its feet in the area of Indian health, the subject became a frequent topic of discussion among concerned Americans. Some reformers believed that the issue required a larger perspective, and at the meeting of the Eastern Association on Indian Affairs in 1925, a statistician speaking about American Indian health urged a comparative study of American and Canadian Indian longevity. In citing the annual reports of the Canadian Indian department, the speaker stated that "there are some reasons for believing that the Department of Indian Affairs in Canada is more successful in conserving the health of Canadian Indian population than our own Indian office." At the same time, the speaker noted that high mortality among Canadian Indians indicated that steps should be taken before some bands completely died out.[4] However, while the speaker was correct about his second observation, his first statement could not have been more wrong.

In fact, Ottawa paid even less attention to Indian health matters than Washington because the Canadian government believed that systematic native health care did not fall within its area of responsibility. This attitude was not an unusual one, considering that only private, philanthropic, and religious Canadian institutions had provided health care until after World War I. Consequently, although on some large reserves the DIA employed physicians on a full-time basis, in most instances the department reimbursed physicians for services occasionally rendered. To some extent, missionary societies filled the void by hiring physicians and nurses and building hospitals on the reserves. The Canadian government did not act on the problem of Indian health until 1904, when the deputy superintendent created the office of medical inspector in the Department of the Interior and the Department of Indian Affairs. Dr. Peter H. Bryce occupied this position until 1914, when his irritating and depressing reports of health conditions among the Indians led the government to relieve him of his post. One student of the history of Canadian Indian health care has observed that "one can only conclude that the Superintendent General was less interested in the health of the natives than remaining free of the agitation of a conscientious Medical Officer."[5] Ignoring the problems, however, did not cause them to go away.

In 1907, Dr. Bryce conducted an inspection of Indian schools in the prairie West and presented a damning report of physical conditions among the pupils. He noted that children had been admitted into schools who were suffering from various infectious diseases—usually some form of tuberculosis—and principals, teachers, and physicians "were at times," as Bryce put it, "inclined to question or minimize the dangers of infection from scrofulous or consumptive pupils." Since the department did not supply Dr. Bryce with reliable statistics, he compiled his own. The numbers spoke eloquently: information on 1,537 pupils from fifteen different schools, which had been operating for an average period of fourteen years, revealed that one-quarter of their pupils had died. The cause of most of the deaths was tuberculosis. One school's mortality rate among former pupils was 69 percent. In the same year that Bryce was relieved of his post, he wrote to the deputy superintendent to declare that from the reports of Indian agents one might conclude that Canadian Indians lived in a state of "arcadian simplicity." They were not, Bryce stated flatly; they were dying of tuberculosis. Seven years later, after being passed over for a government appointment, Bryce gave full vent to his frustrations. In a privately published pamphlet, entitled *The Story of a National Crime*, Bryce detailed the disinterested attitudes of government officials who pigeonholed his reports and postponed decisions during a time of dire need in Indian health care.[6]

The physical condition of Indian school children was fully as bad in the United States as in Canada. Although officials noticed that tubercu-

losis claimed a large portion of the children's lives, some authorities pointed out that if accurate statistics existed they would show that three out
of four children in boarding schools died within five years. The bureau
did try to control some infectious diseases, such as smallpox, by issuing
instructions that all children attending schools should be innoculated;
but tuberculosis and trachoma proved to be beyond control, not only
because of the state of contemporary medical knowledge but because of
living conditions among the native population.

In 1913, a survey of Indian reservations for tuberculosis, trachoma,
and smallpox, conducted by the Public Health Service and the Marine
Hospital Service, revealed that the bureau's efforts in the area of Indian
health care had been largely wasted. The report blamed a lack of proper
sanitation in Indian schools, substandard reservation housing, and an
inadequate supply of nutritious food for the alarming conditions. The
death rate from tuberculosis among Indians reached 35.4 percent per one
thousand, compared to 12.1 percent per one thousand for the white population. Trachoma afflicted nearly one-fifth of the native population.[7]
Investigators summed up all of these problems in the following statement: "The important problem is not so much the medical treatment of
Indians for disease as the improvement of sanitary conditions caused by
such disease." Ironically, the recommendations that inspectors placed
above all others revealed how difficult it would be to improve Indian health
conditions. The report urged an elevation in the economic status of the
Indians so that they would be able to secure a regular and sufficient food
supply. The investigators did not seem to realize that if the government
could accomplish that goal the "Indian problem" would be solved.[8]

The plains tribes may have been more susceptible to the white man's
diseases because they had no experience in sedentary living. Once the
plains tribes were confined to reservations, officials tried to persuade them
to abandon their teepees for permanent houses. Most of these houses,
however, became death traps for their residents. Families generally crowd-
ed into one structure, especially during the winter, and as a result, contagious diseases spread among the occupants. American investigators
found that the typical Indian house in the North and Northwest consisted of either a small, one-story frame or a log structure, where the family
cooked, slept, and received visitors in a common living room with a dirt
floor. Investigators also discovered that the diet of many reservation Indians, which consisted of coffee, baking-powder biscuits, or fried bread,
but rarely beef, led to chronic malnutrition.[9] These findings were fairly
descriptive of living conditions within the Blackfoot Confederacy.

The confederacy had not flourished under the care of either government, although living conditions on the Blackfeet reservation were no

better or worse than at other agencies. In 1891, an agent reported that the South Peigans lived in "the very poorest of little cabins," and a medical examination revealed that the various forms of tuberculosis were the primary cause of death. In their annual reports, Indian agents usually noted that schoolchildren, in particular, suffered severely from this disease. In 1898, agent Thomas P. Fuller wrote that nearly all schoolchildren suffered from some form of tuberculosis. This situation had not improved with the passage of years. Agent McFatridge noted, in 1914, that during the past ten years there had been an unusually high death rate due to tuberculosis among children who had been released from school because of the disease.[10]

Although the bureau had provided a doctor for the Blackfeet at least as early as 1877, the presence of physicians generally did little to alleviate the tribe's medical problems. The bureau opened a hospital at Willow Creek in 1895, and until 1899 the institution operated as a combined hospital and school since many of its patients were school-age children. But the hospital, situated three miles from the school, had experienced problems from the time of its construction. One agent stated that during the winter the place might as well have been in Alaska, for it was haphazardly built, badly equipped, and poorly located. In 1899, the BIA closed the hospital because of the small number of patients and because of the "delapidated conditions of the building."[11]

If Blackfeet health-care facilities proved to be inadequate, its medical personnel were equally deficient. In 1909–10, the bureau provided two doctors to care for the tribe, but both turned out to be worse than useless. The agent described one doctor as incompetent and the other as a drunkard who was brutal to his patients. Their replacements turned out to be just as bad. One doctor was a drunkard, as was his partner, who was also addicted to morphine and had not passed a state licensing examination. One of these men was forced to resign two years later when he got drunk and set fire to his office.[12]

Authorities were not unaware of the deplorable conditions on the Blackfeet reservation. In 1916, during an appropriations hearing, Senator Franklin Lane painted a distressing picture of living conditions among the Blackfeet.

> The housing of those people on certain portions of that reservation is in shacks; poor, miserable, wretched shacks, and without bedding except such scraps and rags as they can pick up. The majority of them are tuberculous and living in those shacks, crowded and huddled together, with tracoma[sic] and tuberculosis among; . . . The conditions seem hopeless; there ought to be something different done

there. We ought to make larger appropriations and house them properly, and put them under proper conditions.

Lane recommended that all houses be burned and new ones built.[13]

In 1913, reports of the poor physical conditions among American Indians moved the new commissioner of Indian affairs, Cato Sells, to direct the BIA to devote more attention to the Indians' medical needs. Part of his approach included health inspections of reservations and efforts to remedy the conditions. In 1916, an inspection team visited the Blackfeet reservation; the inspectors had originally expected to clean every house, but they soon found that this was impractical because 80 percent of the structures, most often their roofs, were in need of repairs. With a fund of 1,400 dollars, they tried to provide the lumber for repairs, in some instances razing the structures completely and relying on Indian labor to cut and haul logs. A physician examined 950 Blackfeet, in a population of some 2,700, and found that 64.3 percent suffered from trachoma. His estimates of tuberculosis among the total population ran at 30 percent.[14]

While the United States government made at least periodic attempts to deal with native health problems, Canadian officials refused to recognize that the Dominion's Indians suffered from alarming incidents of disease. Some authorities even maintained that no problem existed. As late as 1940, Diamond Jenness, a leading Canadian anthropologist, declared that the Blackfoot suffered less from ravages of diseases than other prairie bands.[15] In reality, nothing could have been further from the truth. The Blackfoot Confederacy in Canada suffered grievously from disease because of a lack of adequate health care. Scattered statistics about a population decline in the confederacy indicate how perilously close the Blackfoot came to extinction.

The smallest group, the North Peigans, living on their reserve on Old Man River, came the closest to extinction. A census taken in 1888 placed the Peigan population at 932; eleven years later, the numbers had dropped to 536. Around the turn of the century, smallpox and the "grippe" claimed a number of young children, and in 1909 the population hovered at 471. That year, agent E. H. Yeomans wrote that the Peigans' health was satisfactory—except that they suffered from tuberculosis.[16]

The second group, the Blackfoot, experienced an erratic demographic pattern in which the population growth of a decade could be wiped out by a sudden epidemic or by the slow advance of the dreaded tuberculosis. In 1889, the Blackfoot population stood at 815; in 1896, it reached 1,226; but since the death rate was nearly double the birth rate, the future did not look auspicious. Indeed, in 1901, the population dropped to 975; two years later, it had declined by another one hundred; and by 1910 the number dropped to 768. Although the Blackfoot were vaccinated against smallpox in 1910, no one had the means to cure tuberculosis. For the family of Chief Crowfoot, this disease proved to be especially tragic. In 1886, agent Magnus Beggs observed casually that "the health of the Indians during the year [had] been generally good, Crowfoot being the principal sufferer in his own family, having lost all of his younger children, and being constantly in mourning." In the year following his release from the penitentiary, tuberculosis was probably what claimed Poundmaker, Crowfoot's beloved adopted son.[17]

The Bloods, with the largest population of some 3,200 in 1883, experienced the highest mortality rate when compared to the Blackfoot and the Sarcee. The department knew about the problem by the turn of the century. Dr. F. X. Girard, physician on the Blood reserve, reported the "enormous death rate" among the Bloods and ranked the causes, as follows: (1) overcrowding in small, dirty, ill-ventilated, and badly lighted houses; (2) overcrowding in these houses during dances; (3) the lack of personal cleanliness and sufficient clothing; and (4) the improper preparation of food. The secretary of the Indian commissioner made pointed comments on the Blood situation:

> The Department is well aware that the conditions just described are incidental to the early stages in the process of reclaiming Indians from their natural conditions, and the introduction among them of civilized methods of living, but it was not prepared to learn that at this distance of time they still prevail among the Indians in question to the extent to which it must be inferred from the Doctor's report they do. Now, if it be true that the result of expenditure of money and labour upon these Indians for the last twenty years is that they continue in such a condition as to threaten their extermination at no distant date, the gravity of the position can hardly be exaggerated, and urgently calls for the most serious consideration with a view to remedial measures.[18]

Such pleas, however, fell on deaf ears.

In 1900, the Blood population stood at 1,247, with a mortality rate of 83 percent per one thousand people; ten years later, the numbers had declined to 1,149. In its official report, the department usually ascribed the high death rate to the Indians' living conditions, pointing especially to overcrowding and the lack of ventilation in Indian houses as the cause of the spread of disease. In 1904, the assistant Indian commissioner concurred with agent R. N. Wilson in declaring that the Bloods needed better housing than their "rude and unsanitary shacks." But he believed that the Indians should provide the building funds from their own earnings, and only after they had fed themselves first, again with their money. Ironically, even when officials recognized that forcing Indians to live in permanent structures contributed to their health problems, most officials believed that the benefits of Indians living in houses outweighed the dangers. In 1909, the department stated that the transition from the teepee to the cabin, or hut, formed the "initial stage in the fixity of adobe which is the first essential step towards civilization."[19]

As a rule, the department eschewed preventive health care, but it acted only in response to an emergency. Thus, in 1884, when an apparent typhoid epidemic claimed many Indian lives in the North West Territories, the department appointed one physician for the entire Treaty area.[20] In the absence of a resident physician, missionaries with various degrees of medical training or doctors from nearby communities rendered aid as occasions for it arose. Thus, in 1886, Dr. J. D. Lafferty of Calgary occasionally treated the Blackfoot. Canon Stocken recalled that "tuberculosis and scrofula were rampant and medical attention was at rare intervals. A medical man visited the reserve once a month and remained for only an hour or so, according to the train service." Between these visits, Canon Stocken and the Reverend Tims doctored their flock with a "good supply of ordinary drugs and stock remedies" that the government kept at the agency. But stock remedies proved to be useless against tuberculosis, and Canon Stocken's reminiscences are replete with stories about losing promising students and converts to the disease.

In the mid-1890s, the Toronto Women's Auxiliary opened a small hospital on the reserve, and shortly thereafter a seventy-year-old retired physician from Toronto, with the help of four nurses, provided the first systematic health care. But tuberculosis, fueled by an inadequate diet, continued to claim lives. To forestall a further decline in population, Stocken, with the support of inspector Markle, came up with the idea of surrendering a portion of the reserve to buy, literally, some form of future for the Indians. Three years later, the department noted an improvement in Blackfoot health while observing disingenuously that it might be due to new houses and regular rations of flour, beef, and tea obtained from the tribal fund.[21]

Although American visitor Frederick Abbott found, in 1914, that the Bloods, Peigans, and Blackfoot were in better physical condition than their cousins across the line,[22] his observation was not so much a reflection of the success of the Canadian Indian administration as a commentary on the poor conditions among the American Blackfeet. Yet another difference existed between the American and Canadian Indians, which

Abbott did not mention: there was a sizable presence of mixed-bloods on the South Peigan reservation.

Anthropologists noted that the mixed-blood population in the United States had been steadily increasing because of their higher birth rate and their resistance to diseases that caused havoc among the full-bloods.[23] Intermarriage with whites had been changing not only the appearance of the population on many Indian reservations, but it also had an effect—for better or for worse—on the rate of Indian assimilation. Since Americans allowed a white man who married an Indian woman to reside on his wife's reservation, the situation led to a rapid increase in the number of reservation mixed-bloods. The allotment policy also accelerated the intermarriage process by giving opportunistic white men a chance to seek out an Indian wife in order to secure title to reservation lands as well as encouraging enterprising individuals to claim a tribal affiliation. Agent Steell wrote about one white man who came to the reservation with the object of "marrying a squaw so as to enable him to take land." This was not an unusual event, and similar incidents attracted the attention of officials.[24]

Northern plains Indians experienced a change in their racial composition, which began with the first marriages between fur trappers and Indian women, a process that accelerated toward the end of the century. Although accurate statistics regarding the exact percentage of mixed-blood population are difficult to obtain, existing figures are revealing. In 1912, for example, the entire Blackfeet population consisted of 2,613 individuals: 1,234 were full-bloods, 1,095 were half-blood or more, and 284 individuals had less than half Indian blood. In 1905, agent J. Z. Dare summarized the impact of intermarriage on the Blackfeet. He noted that general sanitary conditions among the Indians were slowly improving, and he attributed this development to the increase in the mixed-blood population. He feared that the full-bloods might be exterminated by tuberculosis, but he also observed that "the mixture of white blood seems to make [the Blackfeet] physically stronger, which, coupled with the fact that the part bloods observe better the laws of good sanitation, have better homes, better and more food, renders the part blood much less subject to this disease."[25]

Agents also found the mixed-bloods to be more "progressive" than their full-blood relatives, even though their so-called progressivism was directed, at times, against their tribal members. The full-bloods, on the other hand, often bore the label of "conservatives," which in official parlance, denoted backwardness and resistance to change. Some agents considered the full-bloods, especially the older generation, to be beyond redemption, and consequently, this diminishing segment of the Indian population demonstrated the most serious economic and physiological handicaps. Not surprisingly, then, when F. C. Campbell assumed his position as the new Blackfeet agent in 1921, he directed most of his energy toward rescuing the full-bloods from years of neglect.[26]

Unfortunately, years of neglect of the Indian population by governments on either side of the border could not be easily remedied by the efforts of a few dedicated men. For a time, it appeared that the outbreak of World War I would inaugurate a new chapter in Indian administration, but this hope did not materialize either. Although the American and the Canadian governments encouraged Indians to utilize their lands fully, and in some cases expropriated reservations for the purpose of increasing food production, hopes were soon dashed that this trend would lead to further economic advances and raise the tribes out of their depressed status. Increased food production did not improve the economic conditions of the Blackfoot Confederacy because, even though some Indians sold their cattle to take advantage of high prices and enjoyed a brief period of prosperity, a series of natural disasters dealt a severe blow to the entire Indian economy. A member of the Board of Indian Commissioners wrote about the South Peigans in 1920: "These Indians are now in a discouraged and destitute condition, as are many white people in that section . . . [and] the Indian can not leave, but he must live."[27]

However, officials remained optimistic about the war's overall benefits to the Indians. These benefits would come through the opportunities afforded to Indians who served in the armed forces. Although native people in both countries were not citizens and therefore were excluded from the draft, about ten thousand American Indians and some four thousand Canadian Indians eventually served in the army during World War I. In several instances, American Indians from reservations in the northern parts of the country enrolled in the Canadian forces because the United States did not enter the war until 1917.[28]

Native responses to the crisis won praise from officials in both countries, who drew attention to the willingness of Indians to fight for their homelands. American observers found the participation of Canadian Indians especially interesting, and Canadians were no less pleased with this development. In 1917, the deputy superintendent general observed rather smugly that the Indians' willingness to sacrifice their lives for the preservation of the ideals of Western civilization was a tribute to the beneficent character of British rule over the aboriginal people. In reality, most Canadian Indians responded to the call to arms out of personal loyalty to the Crown rather than gratitude to the Dominion government. American officials were equally pleased with the performance of their Indian population. Commissioner Sells observed, in 1918, that "it is something to challenge attention when 8 to 10,000 of a race which within the memory of living men knew little beyond the restraints of barbarism [has crossed] the ocean as crusaders of democracy and civilization."[29]

Ironically, Indian soldiers most often claimed attention and received praise for behavior that Indian service officials tried to obliterate. For example, Indians most often won applause for their marksmanship, but one newspaper, among others, also praised the Indian soldier for being clever "in procuring information." This particular writer did not elaborate on the means by which Indians secured such "information." An article reprinted in an American newspaper reverted to the stereotypical image of American Indians brandishing tomahawks to "scalp the Huns," in describing their valiant conduct on the battlefields of France. Other newspapers noted that many Indian soldiers underwent tribal ceremonies formerly conducted before warriors engaged in battle. This time, the ceremonies did not elicit disapprobation for being heathen customs, but were received with curiosity and praise.[30]

Many officials believed that the war experience would have a beneficial effect on Indian soldiers. Commissioner Sells referred to war as a "civilizer," and he felt sure that "from the equal opportunity they had with white comrades for gaining knowledge, for maturing judgement, for developing courage . . . the same sort of splendid initiative and self-reliance should find expression in action wherever the Indian soldier returns to his people.[31]

A few members of the Blackfoot Confederacy enrolled and served in the armed forces, some with distinction. During the early years of the conflict, the department discouraged those who desired to enlist, and local officials had their own reasons for refusing the Indians' requests. In 1915, agent Dillworth reported that thirty Bloods wanted to enlist, but he opposed the idea because of his belief that they would develop tuberculosis if they left Alberta's climate. Three Bloods eventually managed to enlist anyway, but the agent had them released. In 1917, eleven Bloods enlisted, but five aspiring soldiers were turned down for medical reasons. Albert Mountain Horse of the Blood tribe became one of the first Canadian Indians to join the army, and he saw action in France, where he was gassed three times. He died on his return to Canada, and his funeral at St. Paul's mission was attended by his tribe and the citizenry of Fort Macleod. Those who stayed behind contributed generously to the Canadian Patriotic Fund and purchased American Liberty Bonds.[32]

The valiant performance of Indians on the battlefield inevitably raised questions about their legal status. Many Indians, American and Canadian officials, and the public alike advocated the enfranchisement of the native population in recognition of their role in saving democracy. While

such a gesture appeared to many as a boon to the Indians, enfranchisement unfortunately also carried the distinct possibility, especially in the
United States, that the government would terminate its responsibility
toward them once they had been granted the privileges of citizens. In
1924, the United States granted citizenship to its Indian population without abandoning its role as trustee; Canada did not take such a step until
1960. When a Canadian Indian agent inquired about the legal status of
Indian veterans in 1922, the assistant secretary of the department replied,
"These returned Indian soldiers are subject to the provisions of the Indian Act and are in the same position as they were before enlisting."[33] This
statement summed up well the legal as well as the social and economic
status of North American Indians.

Technological innovations introduced during the period of World War
I brought about changes that left the native people further behind in economic development than before the war. Most Indians had neither the
capital nor the knowledge to take advantage of these wartime innovations. The Blackfeet of Montana were once again dependent upon rations,
and a government official, albeit a well-meaning one, once again directed their future. A similar situation arose at the Blood reserve in Alberta,
where a disastrous winter and an ill-advised wartime government policy
led to the collapse of the Blood economy.

Yet, in comparison to their American relatives, the Blackfoot of Alberta made a remarkable economic recovery, which was due largely to the
sizable tribal trust fund from the land cession of 1910. Without the cession, the tribe would have been in a situation as precarious as what the
other groups experienced. But prosperity had its own problems. Under
the direction of G. H. Gooderham, who succeeded his father as agent to
the Blackfoot, the Indians had their needs taken care of by a government
employee. For the next several decades, officials continued the paternalistic approach of a government-managed tribal economy. This approach
bred dependence and a lack of initiative not only on the part of the
Blackfoot,[34] but among other reservation tribes as well—a fact that officials
only belatedly acknowledged.

Conclusion

Canada and the United States followed an Indian policy, which, while sharing the objective of assimilation, differed in the methods that each country employed to reach that goal. Concerned people in both countries believed that eventual absorption of the native people into the dominant society was the only humane way to deal with them. Officials disagreed largely on the specific steps that should be taken.

For decades, Americans believed that Canadians had found a better solution to the "Indian problem"; Canadians, as a rule, concurred. While Americans implemented a succession of legislative and administrative reforms to bring about Indian assimilation, Canadians relied on routine and tradition. While concerned citizens in the United States clamored for reform in the Indian bureau, the Indian service, and founded various humanitarian organizations on behalf of the Indians, Canadians saw no reason to delve into the workings of their Indian department.

Examination of Indian policies and their administration in the two countries reveals that Canadians possessed several advantages over the Americans. Some of these advantages had nothing to do with official design, but were products of the historical development of the two countries. In the United States, for example, Indian issues often became a platform for various individuals who sought to make their political mark by agitating for the passage of legislation that appealed to a land-hungry electorate. This need to cater to public pressure was comparatively absent in Canada because only the government—that is, the party in power—had the right to legislate in Indian matters. Consequently, for better or for worse, the Dominion government retained a firmer hand on such issues as reserve surrenders. Canadian officials also accepted—if they did not always adhere to—the principle that in matters concerning reserve lands the government needed to obtain the consent of the Indians. With the passage of the Dawes Act in 1887, this idea became officially obsolete in the United States.

Without doubt, in comparison to the United States, Canada's brightest idea was her conservative reserve-lands policy. Although allotted yet "closed" reserves did not, as the DIA had hoped, produce a desirable degree of ambition and acquisitiveness among the "locatees," this policy avoided the staggering loss of Indian real estate that occurred under the American version of Indian allotment. No wonder Americans displayed such great interest in this aspect of Canadian Indian administration.

Canada's Indian Act gave it another advantage over United States Indian administration. Concise and detailed, the document was obviously superior to the overwhelming body of Indian legislation that had accumulated in the United States. Americans found the act the most admirable and imitation-worthy part of Canadian Indian administration. The act's provision depriving Indian women who married non-Indians of their Indian status has been the source of much controversy in Canada, until amended in 1985 by the passage of Bill C–31. Even though the act's provision undeniably represented a case of sexual discrimination, in retrospect, the measure prevented the situation that arose in the United States, where white men married to Indian women gained access to tribal property.

In managing Indian reserves, Canada also implemented a system which proved to be better than the American method. Reservation administration in the United States suffered from frequent changes among politically appointed agents who were often corrupt and incompetent. Officials dedicated to the welfare of the Indians could find themselves hounded out of office on trumped-up charges of corruption. Canadians avoided these problems by providing the security of civil-service appointments for their Indian agents and Indian department employees. Unfortunately, the Indian service in Canada as well as in the United States fell prey to centralization and regimentation, to the point where field workers were deprived of their discretionary powers and the flexibility to react to local situations.

Decentralization, on the other hand, did not necessarily produce efficiency and flexibility. Law enforcement on Indian reservations is a case in point. By establishing tribal police, courts, and judges on many reservations, the Americans allowed the native people a measure of self-rule, although all three were intended as means to assimilate the Indians. The Canadians, however, excluded Indians from law enforcement roles on their reserves, relying instead on the North-West Mounted Police. This force proved to be superior to the American system in quashing liquor traffic and, at least in the early period, in maintaining an amicable relationship with the Indians. American law enforcement, by contrast, remained at the mercy of locally elected sheriffs and judges who had little inclination to protect the Indians or their property from avaricious white men.

Despite the several advantages that Canadians possessed over the Americans in some areas of Indian administration, after forty years of reservation life the Blackfoot Confederacy found itself in similar straits in both countries. The problem was that even the best-laid plans did not turn out as expected when theory encountered the reality of reservation life. One of the most frustrating failures lay in the area of economic development.

In both countries, after the disappearance of the buffalo in the early 1880s, the Blackfeet ceased to be self-sufficient and became dependent upon the government. A recent study of the collapse of aboriginal economies has found the "roots of dependency" in an interplay of cultural, political, economic, and environmental factors.[1] The crucial issue, however, is why the Blackfeet, like many other Indian tribes in the United States and Canada, remained in a dependent status after decades of efforts to provide them with a viable economy.

Explanations can be found in a historical chain of causes and effects. First, the decision to make all Indians self-sufficient through farming, while understandable in the context of the times, proved to be more difficult than anticipated. Many reservations were not suited for agriculture, nor did their occupants have any inclination or experience to take up this pursuit. In addition, funds appropriated invariably fell far below the needs of establishing and sustaining a productive agricultural operation. Conversely, much time, money, and energy were wasted on projects that were of dubious value to the Indians.

After experiencing repeated failures due to weather, inadequate instructions, and bureaucratic bungling, many Blackfeet simply gave up on farming. Cattle raising eventually enjoyed more success, but the unequal distribution pattern of livestock established in the late nineteenth century perpetuated a class of the permanently poor. When well-intending reservation officials decided to step in and take over the management of farming and ranching, their actions did little to encourage the Indians. Finally, reservation allotments and surrenders further impeded the development of a reservation economy.

The inability to make many Blackfeet flourish under a competitive, individualistic economic system stemmed from failures in the crucial area of education and Christianization. Not only did teachers and missionaries lack an understanding of the slow process of culture change, but their efforts suffered from the usual handicaps. For example, funding for education was ultimately inadequate, with an insufficient number of schools staffed by disinterested or incompetent teachers. Many boarding schools were so poorly operated that they caused a high death rate from disease among their pupils. In Canada, the school situation became particularly reprehensible because of the involvement of churches in the educational process.

The failure to transmit the cultural values of Western civilization to the Indians was another reason for the disappointing economic situation. On the whole, the civilization efforts by the several denominations working among the Blackfoot Confederacy could not be called notable attempts. Indian missions never gained the popularity of overseas service, and as a result, inadequate funding left missionaries to struggle with what little financial support they had received. While missionaries had gained Indian converts, many of whom undoubtedly believed sincerely in their new faith, it is still a matter of controversy as to what extent the parishioners internalized Western values.

In fact, forty years of activities by missionaries, teachers, and various officials working among the confederacy raise the question of the degree of assimilation that the Indians had achieved by 1920. By that time, however, the Blackfeet were not a homogeneous group. Many Blackfeet, especially the mixed-bloods, had little in common with their full-blood relatives of 1880. The mixed-bloods more readily accepted evangelization efforts, and their aggressive pursuit of economic gain also set them apart from their ancestors and full-blood relatives. By the same token, many of the full-bloods retained their aboriginal spiritual beliefs and their aversions toward labor and the white man's education and religion. Yet this scenario does not preclude the existence of successful, "progressive" full-bloods and traditionally oriented individuals of mixed ancestry. In general, however, Blackfeet on both sides of the border were not about to disappear into the "melting pot."[2]

As this century draws to a close, it has become obvious that native people in the United States and Canada are not about to vanish. If anything, they have become more vocal about their rights, especially in Canada. This situation occurred partly as a result of explorations for new sources of energy in Canada's northern "frontier." Problems in how to deal with aboriginal land rights and the status of native people within the structure of Canadian federalism are current issues in Canada. To find answers, Canadians have even made rare, though tentative sallies into a comparative study of aboriginal policies in other nations, including the United States.[3]

In their efforts to solve these problems, Canadians have adopted a typically American approach of looking for "new solutions." This is an ironic development since American students of Canadian Indian administration have believed that Canada already possessed all the right tools

to implement a satisfactory Indian policy. Whatever his misunderstand-
ings of the Canadian Indian system, Allan Harper made an astute comment regarding Indian administration in Canada, when he observed in
1944:

> If there is any one criticism which I would make of the Indian sys-
> tem in Canada, it would be that the Indian Service has missed almost
> all comprehension of the potentialities which are inherent in the Indi-
> an Act. Indian affairs, it has seemed to me, have been approached
> with appalling lack of imagination and with a strong assumption of
> Indian inferiority. Hence, there is definite stagnation and unoriented
> administration in Indian affairs in Ottawa. In these circumstances, it
> is not surprising that outside suggestion is unwelcome and that field
> employees are discouraged in the use of their initiative.[4]

Students of Canadian Indian administration watched these trends developing in the nineteenth century, but the Department of Indian Affairs,
wedded to an administrative tradition, ignored all of the warning signals.

Unfortunately, Canada is now unwittingly headed for a disappoint-
ment in her "new" native policy because she still lacks an objective, historical perspective in analyzing her Indian administration. Largely because
of the immediacy of native issues, lawyers, anthropologists, political scientists, sociologists, and journalists, will no doubt be asked to elucidate
the past strengths and weaknesses in the Indian administration, and to
advise the "technocrats" in the Indian and Northern Affairs department
on the future direction of native policies. And even though many of these
professional observers have produced some pathbreaking studies drawing
upon historical evidence, their works, as a rule, unfortunately, tend to
shortchange firmly grounded historical research into their subject matter.
Some scholars even believe that such research is redundant in understanding the current situation.[5] This attitude is especially unfortunate
because evidence from comparative historical studies indicates that expectations that the "Indian question" would be permanently settled
once new policies were implemented have been incorrect.

Undoubtedly, American administration of Indian affairs will continue
to stumble thorough cycles of reform and reaction that have typified American Indian policy throughout the past century, and probably with as little success in solving the "Indian problem" in the twenty-first century as
the United States experienced in the past. If there is one clear trend in
American Indian administration, it is the continuing litigiousness of Indian tribes looking to courts of law to protect, among other things, their
water rights and mineral resources. And if Canada continues to fail to

satisfy native demands, increasing litigation, rather than negotiation, of outstanding issues is more than likely to occur there as well.

In any case, it is a safe bet that Americans, or for that matter, Canadians, will not be completely successful in dealing with native poverty, unemployment, alcoholism, and suicide, no matter what policies they adopt. Both countries are burdened not only with ill-advised programs or policies, but also by the persistence of basic irreconcilable differences between aboriginal and Western cultural values. As a rule, the formulators of Indian policy do not recognize that most non-Western cultures do not share the basic ethos of Western society: individualism, acquisitiveness, and competitiveness. This is not to argue that Western civilization is therefore superior and non-Western cultures are inferior, or vice versa, but that they are different. The belief that non-Western people could, within a relatively short period of time, abandon their cultures and adopt the values that Western society had acquired over centuries has proved to be wrong not only on Indian reservations, but also in the so-called Third World countries. And unless the Indian policymakers realize the basic incompatibility of certain aboriginal and Western values, and learn to approach reforms in Indian administration as an ongoing process, a hundred years hence Americans and Canadians will still be trying to formulate the perfect Indian policy as the only solution to the "Indian problem."

Abbreviations

BIAC	Blood Indian Agency Correspondence (Canada)
BIC	Annual Reports of the Board of Indian Commissioners (United States)
CIA	Annual Reports of the Commissioner of Indian Affairs to the Secretary of the Interior (United States)
Denver FARC	Denver Federal Archives and Records Center
DIA	Annual Reports of the Department of Indian Affairs (Canada)
DP	Edgar L. Dewdney papers
DSG	Deputy Superintendent General (Canada)
GAI	Glenbow–Alberta Institute, Calgary
IRA papers	Indian Rights Association papers
MPI–A	Museum of Plains Indians Archives (United States)
NA	National Archives, Washington, D.C.
NWMP	North West Mounted Police
PAC	Public Archives of Canada
Seattle FARC	Seattle Federal Archives and Records Center

Notes

Introduction

1. Christopher C. Joyner, "The Hegira of Sitting Bull to Canada: Diplomatic Realpolitic, 1876–1881," *Journal of the West* 13 (April 1974). See, also, Frank C. Turner, *Across the Medicine Line, The Epic Confrontation between Sitting Bull and the North-West Mounted Police* (Toronto: McClelland and Stewart, 1973).

2. George F. G. Stanley, "Displaced Red Men: the Sioux in Canada," in *One Century Later: Western Canadian Reserve Indians since Treaty 7*, ed. Ian A. L. Getty and Donald B. Smith (Vancouver: University of British Columbia Press, 1978), pp. 55–81.

3. Garrick Mallory, "The Indian Systems of Canada and the United States," *The Nation* 636 (6 September 1877):148.

4. Ibid., p. 147.

5. Frederick H. Abbott, *The Administration of Indian Affairs in Canada, Report of an Investigation made in 1914 under the Direction of the Board of Indian Commissioners* (Washington: Government Printing Office, 1915). Allan G. Harper, "Canada's Indian Administration: Basic Concepts and Objectives," *America Indigena* 5 (April 1945); idem, "Canada's Indian Administration: The Indian Act," *America Indigena* 6 (October 1946); idem, "Canada's Indian Administration: The Treaty System," *American Indigena* 7 (April 1947). The various published proceedings of the Lake Mohonk Conference held at the turn of the century included discussions of Canadian Indian affairs, as did publications such as *The Red Man*, published by the Carlisle Indian School. Recent comparative studies of "racial frontiers" include Frances Svensson, "Comparative Ethnic Policy on the American and Russian Frontiers," *Journal of International Affairs* 36 (Spring–Summer 1982). Ronald G. Knapp and Laurence M. Hauptman, " 'Civilization over Savagery': The Japanese, the Formosan Frontier, and United States Indian Policy, 1895–1915," *Pacific Historical Review* 49 (November 1980). William E. Unrau, "An International Perspective on American Indian Policy: The South Australian Protector and Aborigines Protection Society," *Pacific Historical Review* 45 (November 1976). Donald G. Baker, "Color, Culture, and Power: Indian–White Relations in Canada and America," *The Canadian Review of American Studies* 3 (Spring 1972).

6. The quotation is from W. Turrentine Jackson, "A Brief Message to the Young and/or Ambitious: Comparative Frontier as a Field for Investigation," *Western Historical Quarterly* 9 (January 1978):13. Comparative works include A. L. Burt, "If Turner Had Looked at Canada, Australia, and New Zealand when He Wrote about the West," in *The Frontier in Perspective*, ed. Walker D. Wyman and Clifton B. Kroeber (Madison: University of Wisconsin Press, 1957), pp. 59–77; Paul F. Sharp, "Three Frontiers: Some Comparative Studies of Cana-

dian, American, and Australian Settlement," *Pacific Historical Review* 24 (November 1955). Sharp, *Whoop Up Country, the Canadian–American West, 1865–1885* (Norman: University of Oklahoma Press, 1978; first published by the University of Minnesota Press, 1955). David H. Miller and Jerome O. Steffen, eds., *The Frontier: Comparative Studies* (Norman: University of Oklahoma Press, 1977). Leonard Thompson and Howard Lamar, eds., *The Frontier in History, North America and Southern Africa Compared* (New Haven: Yale University Press, 1981).

7. George M. Fredrickson, "Comparative History," in *The Past Before Us: Comparative Historical Writing in the United States,* ed. Michael Kammen (Ithaca: Cornell University Press, 1980), pp. 457–73. For an overview of comparative studies and their problems, see, also, Peter Kolchin, "Comparing American History," *Reviews in American History* 10 (December 1982):64–81. See, also, Morris Zaslow, "The Frontier Hypothesis in Recent Historiography," *The Canadian Historical Review* 24 (June 1948); Michael S. Cross, ed., *The Frontier Thesis and the Canadas; The Debate over the Impact of the Canadian Environment* (Toronto: Capp Clark Publishing Co., 1970). Francis Paul Prucha, *Indian Policy in the United States, Historical Essays* (Lincoln: University of Nebraska Press, 1981), pp. 13–19.

8. A notable exception to this trend is Paul Stuart, *The Indian Office, Growth and Development of an American Institution, 1865–1900* (Ann Arbor, Mich.: University Microfilms International Research Press, 1978), yet this study does not go beyond the turn of the century. The classic treatment of the BIA remains Lawrence F. Schmeckebier, *The Office of Indian Affairs, Its History, Activities, and Organization* (Baltimore: Johns Hopkins Press, 1927). The most recent work by Frederick E. Hoxie, *A Final Promise, the Campaign to Assimilate the Indians, 1880–1920* (Lincoln: University of Nebraska Press, 1984), studies changing attitudes toward Indians during this period rather than Indian policy. A recent study by Francis Paul Prucha, *The Great Father: The United States Government and the American Indians* (Lincoln: University of Nebraska Press,1984), covers the entire history of Indian policy. Prucha, *Indian Policy,* p. 5; Randolph C. Downes, "A Crusade for Indian Reform, 1927–1934," *Mississippi Valley Historical Review* 32 (December 1945).

9. Robert J. Surtees, *Canadian Indian Policy, A Critical Bibliography* (Bloomington: Indiana University Press, 1982), p. 1. See, also, Surtees, "The Changing Image of the Canadian Indians: A Historical Approach," in *Approaches to Native History in Canada: Papers of a Conference Held at the National Museum of Man, October 1975,* ed. D. A. Muise (Ottawa: National Museum of Man, 1977), pp. 111–23. W. Peter Ward, "Western Canada: Recent Historiography," *Queen's Quarterly* 85 (Summer 1978):272–74. James W. St. G. Walker, "The Indian in Canadian Historical Writing," *Canadian Historical Association History Papers* (1971).

10. These new Canadian studies include J. E. Chamberlain, *The Harrowing of Eden, White Attitudes toward Native Americans* (New York: Seabury Press, 1975), which is a study of American and Canadian attitudes toward native people. For a general overview of Canadian and native relations, see E. Palmer Patterson, *The Canadian Indians: A History since 1500* (Don Mills, Ontario: Collier–Macmillan, 1972). James Douglas Leighton, "The Development of Federal Indian Policy in Canada, 1840–1890," 2 vols. (Ph.D. diss., University of Western Ontario, 1975); John L. Taylor, "The Development of an Indian Policy for the Canadian West, 1869–1879" (Ph.D. diss., Queen's University, 1975); Anthony J. Looy, "The Indian Agent and His Role in the Administration of the North West Superintendency, 1876–1893" (Ph.D. diss., Queen's University, 1977); John Jennings, "The North West Mounted Police and Indian Policy, 1874–1896" (Ph.D. diss., University of Toronto, 1979); W. K. Regular, "The Plains Indians and the Application of the Federal Government's Indian Policy during the Laurier Era" (Master's thesis, University of Calgary, 1980); N. E. Dyck, "The Administration of Federal Indian Aid in the North West Territories, 1979–1885" (Master's thesis, University of Saskatchewan, 1970). Growing interest in Canadian Indian policy is expressed

in reprints of scholarly articles: see Leroy Little Bear, Menno Boldt, and J. Anthony Long, *Pathways to Self-Determination: Canadian Indians and the Canadian State* (Toronto: University of Toronto Press, 1984). J. Rick Ponting and Roger Gibbins, *Out of Irrelevance: A Sociopolitical Introduction to Indian Affairs in Canada* (Toronto: Butterworth, 1980); Sally M. Weaver, *Making of Canadian Indian Policy, The Hidden Agenda, 1968–1979* (Toronto: University of Toronto Press, 1981); Adrian Tanner, ed., *The Politics of Indianness, Case Studies of Native Ethnopolitics in Canada* (St. John's, Newfoundland: Memorial University of Newfoundland, 1983).

11. For a view of Canadian Indian policy by an Indian, see Harold Cardinal, *The Unjust Society* (Edmonton: Hurting, 1969). For the concept of Indian irrelevance to Canadian history, see Ponting and Gibbins, *Out of Irrelevance*, pp. xvii, xi.

12. Some of these studies of frontier development include Stanley, "Western Canada and the Frontier Thesis," *The Canadian Historical Association Papers* (1940); Zaslow, "Frontier Hypothesis," p. 111; J. M. S. Careless, "Frontierism, Metropolitanism, and Canadian History," *The Canadian Historical Review* 35 (March 1954):1–21. See Douglas Robb Owram, " 'White Savagery': Some Canadian Reaction to American Indian Policy, 1867–1885" (Master's thesis, Queen's University, 1971)" p. 68.

13. C. T. Loram and T. L. McIlwraith eds., *The North American Indian Today: University of Toronto–Yale University Seminar–Conference, Toronto, September 4–16, 1939* (Toronto: University of Toronto Press, 1943).

14. Prucha, *Indian Policy*, p. 37. American Indian laws are contained in Charles I. Kappler, ed., *Indian Affairs, Laws and Treaties*, 5 vols. (Washington: Government Printing Office, vols. 1–2, 1904; vol. 3, 1919; vol. 4, 1929; vol. 5, 1941). The series continues as *Kappler's Indian Affairs, Laws and Treaties*. See, also, Henry E. Fritz, "The Last Hurrah of Christian Humanitarian Indian reform: the Board of Indian Commissioners, 1909–1918," *The Western Historical Quarterly* 16 (April 1985). William T. Hagan, *The Indian Rights Association, the Herbert Welsh Years, 1882–1904* (Tucson: University of Arizona Press, 1985).

15. Lewis Meriam et al., *The Problem of Indian Administration*, Institute for Government Research, Studies in Administration (Baltimore: Johns Hopkins Press, 1929). The decline of reformers' expectations about how far the Indians could be assimilated forms the theme of Hoxie's *Final Promise*. One American Indian called the years between 1900 and 1930 the "Great Indian Depression"; see Herbert Hoover, "Yankton Sioux Experience in the 'Great Indian Depression,' 1900–1930," in *The American West: Essays in Honor of W. Eugene Hollon*, ed. Ronald Lora (Toledo, Ohio: University of Toledo Press, 1980), pp. 51–71.

16. *Report of the Thirteenth Annual Lake Mohonk Conference of Friends of the Indian and Other Dependent People* (Lake Mohonk: 1912), p. 99 (hereafter cited as *Lake Mohonk*).

17. The quotation is from Desmond Morton, "Cavalry or Police: Keeping Peace on Two Adjacent Frontiers," *Journal of Canadian Studies* 12 (December 1977):27. Also see this observation in D. Aidan McQuillan, "Creation of Indian Reserves on the Canadian Prairies, 1870–1885," *The Geographical Review* (Canada) 70 (October 1980):379, 396.

18. *Report on the Management of Indians in British North America by the British Government*, House Misc. Doc. 35., 41st Cong., 2d sess., 1870, pp. 32–33, serial 1433.

19. "Great Britain's Solution to the Indian Problem," *The World of New York* (New York, 7 August 1874), newspaper clipping in the files of the DIA, Public Archives of Canada (PAC) volume 3611, file 3676, microfilm C10106 (hereafter cited by volume, file, and microfilm numbers). The Canadian writer conveniently forgot the Red River Rebellion five years earlier which indicated that all was not well with Canadian western policy.

20. Joyner, "Hegira of Sitting Bull," pp. 11–12.

21. Mallory, "Indian Systems," p. 448.

22. Nelson A. Miles, "The Indian Problem," *The North American Review* 10 (Winter 1973):42 (First published in the *Review*, 1879). Carl Schurz, "Present Aspects of the Indian Prob-

lem," *The North American Review* 19 (Winter 1973):47 (originally published in the *Review*, 1881). Contrast, for example, the explanations of Leighton, "Federal Indian Policy"; Morton, "Cavalry or Police"; and John Jennings, "The Plains Indians and the Law," in *Men in Scarlet*, ed. Hugh A. Dempsey (Calgary: McClelland-Stewart West, 1974), pp. 50–65.

23. Helen Hunt Jackson, *A Century of Dishonor, A Sketch of the United States Government's Dealings with Some of the Indian Tribes* (Minneapolis: Ross and Haines, 1964), p. vii.

24. House of Commons (Canada), Debates (1886), p. 772.

25. *Regina Leader* (Regina, Saskatchewan), 27 March 1886; *The Globe* (Toronto, Ontario), n.d. Newspaper clippings in files of the DIA, PAC, v. 3743, f. 29448–2, C10106.

26. John Maclean, *Canadian Savage Folk* (Toronto: William Briggs, 1896), p. 291; *The Canadian Indian* 5 (February 1891):133, and ibid., 6 (March 1891):170; William Trant, "The Treatment of the Canadian Indians," *Westminster Review* 144 (July–December 1895):527 for the quotation.

27. Egerton, R. Young, "The Indian Question in Canada," *Lake Mohonk* (1900):131.

28. Frank Pedley, "The Indian Question from a Canadian Standpoint," *Lake Mohonk* (1912).

29. D. C. Scott, "Civil Service in Its Relation to Indian Administration," *Lake Mohonk* (1914):43–44.

30. Scott, "Some Features of Indian Administration in Canada," *Lake Mohonk* (1916): 95, 97.

31. Pliny Earle Goddard, "The Indian Problem in Canada," *The Red Man* 4 (December 1911):133–34.

32. *The Christian Science Monitor* (Boston, Mass.), 14 May 1915, a newspaper clipping in DIA files; George Vaux to Frank Oliver, n.d., PAC, v. 3186, f. 464–314A, C11336; Abbott, *Administration of Indian Affairs*, p. 12.

33. Abbott, *Administration of Indian Affairs*, p. 20.

34. Ibid., pp. 24–31.

35. Ibid., pp. 23, 88–89.

36. F. A. Abbott to D. C. Scott, 24 February 1915, PAC, v. 3186, f. 464–314A, C11336; *Codification, Annotation, and Revision of Indian Laws, Prepared in Compliance with House Resolution 134, 1917* (Congressional Committee Prints, House 2793, 1917). "Canada Shows Best Way of Managing Her Indian People," *Toronto Daily News* (Toronto, Ontario), 24 June 1915, and *The Gazette* (Montreal, Quebec), 22 June 1915, clippings in the DIA files, PAC, v. 3186, f. 464–314A, C11336.

37. Downes, "Crusade for Indian Reform," pp. 334–43. Another proposal for reform of the BIA along the Canadian example is Warren K. Moorehead, *Plan of Reorganization of the Indian Service* (Andover, Mass., 15 December 1925), pp. 27–28.

38. In 1935, Allan G. Harper, the executive secretary of the new American Indian Defense Association conducted a study of Canadian Indian administration with the full support of the new commissioner of Indian affairs, John Collier. Harper thought that the proposed study should consider not only general Indian policy, but also examine its implementation on particular reservations. For example, Harper wrote that the Blackfeet of Montana and those of Alberta were useful subjects for comparing approaches, especially in the area of tribal land history. Harper received a grant from the Carnegie Foundation, and in the summer of 1935 he visited the Blackfeet of Montana and Alberta; he also spent a few days with an Indian department official in Calgary. The following year, Harper entered the American Indian service, and thus a formal report of his visit apparently was not completed. A. G. Harper to Diamond Jenness, 13 May 1935; A. G. Harper to H. W. McGill, 21 May 1935, both letters in PAC, v. 3186, f. 464–314A, C11336. A. G. Harper to John Collier (?), (?) September 1935, Collier Papers II–151, frame 5, reel 15.

39. Loram and McIlwraith, *North American Indian Today*, pp. 4–16.

40. Esther S. Goldfrank, *Changing Configuration in the Social Organization of a Blackfoot Tribe during the Reserve Period, the Bloods of Alberta, Canada*, American Ethnological Society Monograph Series, no. 8 (Seattle: University of Washington Press, 1966). See, also, Goldfrank, "Administrative Programs and Change in Blood Society during the Reserve Period," *Applied Anthropology* 2 (January–March 1943):19–23. Lucien M. Hanks, Jr., and Jane Richardson, *Observations on Northern Blackfoot Kinship*, Monographs of the American Ethnological Society, no. 9 (Seattle: University of Washington Press, 1945); Hanks and Hanks, *Tribe Under Trust, A Study of the Blackfoot Reserve of Alberta* (Toronto: University of Toronto Press, 1950); Oscar Lewis, *The Effects of White Contact upon Blackfoot Culture with Special Reference to the Role of the Fur Trade*, American Ethnological Society Monograph Series, no. 6 (Seattle: University of Washington Press, 1942).

41. Some anthropologists insist upon using the term *complex* rather than Confederacy. See Goldfrank, *Changing Configuration*, p. 4. John C. Ewers, *The Blackfeet, Raiders of the North Western Plains* (Norman: University of Oklahoma Press, 1958), p. 5. Problems with tribal names are discussed in Hugh A. Dempsey, "Blackfoot or Blackfeet?" *Glenbow* 4 (May–June 1971):7–8.

42. Ewers, *Blackfeet*, pp. 5–6, 196, 124–25. Peter W. Dinwiddie, "The Nature of the Relationship between the Blackfeet Indians and the Men of the Fur Trade," *Annals of Wyoming* 46 (Spring 1974).

43. Ewers, *Blackfeet*, pp. 205, 217, 226.

44. Ibid., pp. 239, 245. Kappler, *Indian Affairs*, vol. 1, p. 998.

45. Ewers, *Blackfeet*, pp. 247–51. Wesley C. Wilson, "The U.S. Army and the Peigans, the Baker Massacre of 1870," *North Dakota History* 32 (January 1965); Paul Hutton, "Phil Sheridan's Pyrrhic Victory: The Peigan Massacre, Army Politics, and the Transfer Debate," *Montana* 32 (Spring 1982).

46. Kappler, *Indian Affairs*, vol. 1, p. 855. Ewers, *Blackfeet*, pp. 270–73.

47. Sharp, *Whoop-Up Country*, pp. 133, 156.

48. Ewers, *The Blackfeet Indians, Ethnological Report of the Blackfeet and Gros Ventre Tribe of Indians*, American Indian Ethnohistory Series (New York: Garland Publishing Co., 1974), pp. 188, 147, 136, 149 (hereafter cited as *Blackfeet Indians*).

49. A good discussion of the relationship between the Hudson's Bay Company and the Indians is in Arthur J. Ray, *Indians in the Fur Trade* (Toronto: University of Toronto Press, 1974), pp. 59–60, 140–41. Stanley, *The Birth of Western Canada, A History of the Riel Rebellions* (Toronto: University of Toronto Press, 1961).

50. Ewers, *Blackfeet*, pp. 254–61. C. P. Stacey, "The Military Aspects of Canada's Winning of the West, 1870–1885," *The Canadian Historical Review* 21 (March 1940).

51. Ewers, *Blackfeet*, p. 262. Sharp, "Three Frontiers," p. 373. Stacey, "Military Aspects," pp. 7–15. Morton, "Cavalry or Police," p. 51.

52. Dempsey, *Crowfoot, Chief of the Blackfeet* (Norman: University of Oklahoma Press, 1972), pp. 77–86, 93–107.

53. C. Scollen to A. G. Irvine, 13 April 1879, PAC, v. 3671, f. 10836–2, C10118. See also John L. Taylor, "Two Views of the Meaning of Treaties 6 and 7," in *The Spirit of Alberta Treaties*, ed. Richard Price (Montreal: Institute for Research on Public Policy and Indian Association of Alberta, 1980), pp. 9–45. Dempsey, *Crowfoot*, pp. 105–6.

Chapter 1

1. Francis Paul Prucha, *American Indian Policy in the Formative Years* (Lincoln: University of Nebraska Press, 1962).

2. For example, the settlers of Quebec made no demands for additional lands between

1760 and 1774. See David T. McNab, "Research Report on the Royal Proclamation of 1763 and British Indian Policy, 1750–1795," Treaties and Historical Research Center, Department of Indian and Northern Affairs, Ottawa, 1979 (hereafter cited as DIAND). D. C. Scott, "Indian Affairs, 1763–1841," in *Canada and Its Provinces*, ed. Adam Shortt and Arthur G. Daugherty, vol. 4 (Toronto: Glasgow, Brook and Co., 1914), p. 717.

3. Prucha, *American Indian Policy in the Formative Years*, p. 215.

4. D. C. Scott, "Indian Affairs," p. 724. L. F. S. Upton, "The Origin of Canadian Indian Policy," *Journal of Canadian Studies* 7 (November 1973):56.

5. Unrau, "An International Perspective," p. 525.

6. An exception was, of course, Governor Francis Bond Head's removal of Indians to Manitoulin Island in the 1830s.

7. John L. Tobias, "Protection, Civilization, Assimilation: An Outline of Canada's Indian Policy," *The Western Canadian Journal of Anthropology* 6 (1976):18.

8. See, for example, arguments for Indian sovereignty presented in Russell L. Barsch and James Youngblood Henderson, *The Road, Indian Tribes and Political Liberty* (Berkeley: University of California Press, 1980).

9. Neil H. Mickenberg, "Aboriginal Rights in Canada and the United States," *Osgood Hall Law Review* 9 (1971).

10. "The Indian Difficulty," *The Nation* 7 (31 December 1868): 545.

11. Schmeckebier, *Office of Indian Affairs*, p. 270.

12. DIA 1897, p. xxvii. Loram and McIlwraith, eds. *The North American Indian Today*, p. 56. Ponting and Gibbins, *Out of Irrelevance*, pp. 14–15. In Canada the Department of Indian Affairs was part of the Interior Department until 1936, when it was transferred to the Department of Mines nd Resources. In 1949 the Indian Affairs Branch went to the Department of Citizenship and Immigration. In 1966, it was transferred to the Department of Northern Affairs and Natural Resources, and, in 1966, the present Department of Northern Development and Indian Affairs, (called Indian and Northern Affairs) was established.

13. *The Indian Act, 1876*, S. C. 1876, c. 18 (39 Vict.). The various versions of this statute are compiled in *Indian Acts and Amendments, 1868–1950*, Treaties and Historical Research Center, DIAND, 1981.

14. Tobias, "Protection, Civilization, Assimilation." Loram and McIlwraith, *North American Indian Today*, p. 157.

15. See section 3(3) of the 1876 Indian Act.

16. A law passed in 1888 aimed to prevent white men who were not tribal members from acquiring tribal property through a marriage to an Indian woman. This law was however rarely enforced. CIA 1888, p. 340. The nature of sex discrimination in the Indian Act is described in Kathleen Jamieson, *Indian Women and the Law in Canada: Citizens Minus* (Ottawa: Minister of Supply and Services Canada, 1978). For problems in defining who is an Indian in the United States, see Barsch and Henderson, *The Road*, pp. 241–49.

17. CIA 1914, p. 315. For discussion of the need to define "Indian" in the United States and questions regarding the legal status of Indian women married to non-Indians, see CIA 1892, pp. 31–36.

18. Schmeckebier, *Office of Indian Affairs*, pp. 282–84. CIA 1907, p. 9; SI 1903, p. 17. Francis E. Leupp, "Spoilsmen and Indian Agencies," *The Nation* 65 (28 October 1897):333–34. BIC 1897. William S. Washburn, "The Application of the Civil Service Law Examinations," *Lake Mohonk* (1914); William T. Hagan, "Civil Service Commissioner T. Roosevelt and the Indian Rights Association," *Pacific Historical Review* 44 (May 1975):189, 192. Necah Furman, "Seed Time for Indian Reform: An Evaluation of the Administration of Commissioner Francis Ellington Leupp," *Red River Valley Historical Review* 2 (Winter 1975):498.

19. SI 1912, v. 1, p. 50.

20. Schmeckebier, *Office of Indian Affairs*, p. 87. *CIA* 1912, p. 3. *CIA* 1914, p. 317.

21. *SI* 1903, p. 20. Abbott, *Administration of Indian Affairs*, pp. 25–26.

22. Leighton, "Federal Indian Policy," vol. 2, p. 551. D. J. Hall, "Clifford Sifton and Canadian Indian Administration, 1896–1905," *Prairie Forum* 2 (November 1977):129.

23. Abbott, *Administration of Indian Affairs*, pp. 29–39. Margaret Garretson Szasz, "Indian Reform in a Decade of Prosperity," *Montana* 20 (Winter 1970):20. S. D. Grant, "Indian Affairs under Duncan Campbell Scott, the Plains Cree of Saskatchewan, 1913–1930," *Journal of Canadian Studies* 18 (Fall 1983):24.

24. D. C. Scott, "Civil Service," *Lake Mohonk* (1914), pp. 44–45. Leighton, "Federal Indian Policy," vol. 2, p. 551. "List of Employees and Dismissals in the North West Territories between 1896–1898," PAC, v. 3984, f. 168–921, C10169. Henry A. Carruthers to C. E. Sifton, 2 January 1898, PAC, v. 3877, f. 91839–1, C10155. Memorandum from the Treasury Board, 28 January 1899, PAC, v. 2277, f. 55412–1, C10193. L. G. Vankoughnet, "Departmental Regulations," 27 June 1887, PAC, v. 2380, f. 77736, C11211. "Dismissal of Agents and Employees for Political Partisanship," 15 April 1901, PAC, v. 2905, f. 185–723A, C11295.

25. Leighton, "Federal Indian Policy," vol. 2, pp. 367, 547. D. C. Scott, "Civil Service," p. 43 and "Some Features," *Lake Mohonk* (1916), p. 97.

26. Memorandum of N. McNeil, Chief Clerk, 12 April 1898, PAC, v. 2580, f. 117–593, C11243. Leighton, "Federal Indian Policy," v. 2, p. 547.

27. Leighton, "Federal Indian Policy," v. 2, p. 540. Abbott, *Administration of Indian Affairs*, p. 21, provides statistics for 1913. "List of Questions Asked in the House of Commons Relating to the DIA, 1906, PAC, v. 2905, F. 185–723, C11295. See, for example, the attitude of then minister of the interior Arthur Meighen in Grant, "Indian Affairs under Duncan Campbell Scott," p. 26.

28. Furman, "Seedtime for Indian Reform," p. 497. Sharp, "Three Frontiers," p. 373, describes Canadian Indian policy as being "orderly, well-planned, and honorable." *SI* 1914, p. 5. "Address of the Honorable Robert G. Valentine," *Lake Mohonk* (1912), p. 81. The Canadians also thought that the Americans had no definite Indian policy until after 1900. See F. Pedley, Memorandum to C. Sifton, 24 March 1904, PAC, v. 3635, f. 6567, pp. 37–38, C10111.

29. Statement by Senator Henry Dawes, cited by D. S. Otis, *The Dawes Act and the Allotment of Indian Lands*, ed. F. P. Prucha (Norman: University of Oklahoma Press, 1973), p. 83.

30. *BIC* 1897; D. C. Scott, "Civil Service," p. 43.

31. D. C. Scott, "Indian Affairs, 1867–1912," in Shortt and Daugherty, *Canada and Its Provinces* vol. 8, p. 621. Grant, "Indian Affairs under Duncan Campbell Scott," p. 21.

32. Robert T. Handy, *A Christian America: Protestant Hopes and Historical Realities* (New York: Oxford University Press, 1971). For studies of Indian missions, see Robert F. Berkhofer, *Salvation and the Savage: An Analysis of Protestant Missions and Indian Response 1787–1862* (Louisville: University of Kentucky Press, 1965); Francis Paul Prucha, *American Indian Policy in Crisis: Christian Reformers and the American Indian, 1865–1900* (Norman: University of Oklahoma Press, 1976); R. P. Beaver, *Church, State and the American Indian* (St. Louis: Concordia Publishing House, 1966); Prucha, *The Churches and the Indian Schools, 1888–1912* (Lincoln: University of Nebraska Press, 1979); and Robert H. Keller, *American Protestantism and United States Indian Policy, 1869–1882* (Lincoln: University of Nebraska Press, 1983). The first study of missionary involvement in Canadian Indian administration is by John Webster Grant, *Moon of Wintertime, Missionaries and the Indians of Canada in Encounter since 1534* (Toronto: University of Toronto Press, 1984). Several biographical works have also touched on this topic. See, for example, James Ernest Nix, *Mission among the Buffalo: The Labours of the Reverends George M. and John C. McDougall in the Canadian North West, 1860–1876* (Toronto: Ryerson Press, 1963); H. W. Gibbon Stocken, *Among the Blackfoot and Sarcee* (Calgary: Glenbow Alberta Institute, 1976); and Elizabeth Graham, *Medicineman to Missionary: Missionaries as Agents*

of Change among the Indians of Southern Ontario, 1784–1867 (Toronto: P. Martin Associates, 1975).

33. Fair Play [pseudonym], "The Future of Our Indians," *The Canadian Indian* 1 (March 1891):160.

34. One indiviudal who urged the government to leave the American Indians alone was Warren K. Moorehead, *The American Indian in the United States, period 1850–1914* (Andover, Mass.: The Andover Press, 1914), p. 241. Abbott, *Administration of Indian Affairs*, p. 28. Brian W. Dippie, *The Vanishing American, White Attitudes and U. S. Indian Policy* (Middleton, Conn.: Wesleyan University Press, 1982). In Canada similar sentiments were voiced. See Bleasdale Cameron, "The North West Redman and His Future," *The Canadian Magazine* 14 (January 1900):24. Diamond Jenness, the leading Canadian anthropologist, also believed that Canadian Indians would die out. See Jenness, *The Indians of Canada* (Toronto: University of Toronto Press, 1977), p. 264 (first published in 1932). Frederick Hoxie, "The End of the Savage, Indian Policy and the United States Senate, 1880–1900," *Chronicles of Oklahoma* 55 (Summer 1977). In general, after the turn of the century Indian reformers clashed with many BIA officials who saw the disastrous consequences of federal withdrawal from Indian affairs. See John F. Berens, "Old Campaigns, New Realities: Indian Policy Reform in the Progressive Era, 1900–1912," *Mid-America* 59 (January 1977):64. See, also, Commissioner Leupp's statements in "Outlines of an Indian Policy," *Outlook* 79 (April 1905).

35. Abbott, *Administration of Indian Affairs*, p. 28. Harper, "Canada's Indian Administration: Basic Concepts," p. 313. See *Indian Advancement Act, 1884*, S. C. 1884, c. 28 (47 Vict.). This legislation bears the subtitle "An Act for conferring of certain privileges on the more advanced Bands of Indians of Canada with the view of training them for the exercise of municipal powers." Abbott, *Administration of Indian Affairs*, p. 27. Scott, "Some Features," p. 97.

36. American Indians did not gain the right to vote in all states until 1948. Malcolm Montgomery, "The Six Nations and the Macdonald Franchise," *Ontario History* 57 (March 1965):13–22. T. R. L. MacInnes, "History of Indian Administration in Canada," *Canadian Journal of Economics and Political Science* 12 (1946):391.

37. John Leslie and R. Maguire, eds. *The Historical Development of the Indian Act*, 2d ed., Treaties and Historical Research Center, DIAND, Ottawa, 1978) pp. 26–28, 31. "Blue Book," PAC, v. 10020, p. 45, C11059. Tobias, "Protection, Civilization, Assimilation," p. 98. *An Act to Amend the Indian Act*. S. C. 1919–1920, c. 50 (10–11 Geo. V). *An Act to Amend the Indian Act*. S. C. 1922, c. 26 (12–13 Geo. V). Leslie and Maguire, *The Indian Act*, pp. 115–18.

38. Tobias, "Protection, Civilization, Assimilation," p. 93. Hall, "Clifford Sifton," p. 137. Abbott, *Administration of Indian Affairs*, p. 26. Loram and McIlwaith, *North American Indian Today*, pp. 133, 143; see statements by H. W. McGill and John Collier, respectively. Harper, "The Canadian Indian Administration: Basic Concepts," pp. 127–28.

39. Schmeckebier, *Office of Indian Affairs*, p. 66.

40. Prucha, *Americanizing the American Indians, Writings by the Friends of the Indian, 1880–1910* (Cambridge, Mass.: Harvard University Press, 1973), p. 335.

41. Otis, *Dawes Act*, pp. 7, 5, 14–15. *SI* 1914, vol. 1, p. 12. *CIA* 1911, p. 23.

42. Cited in *SI* vol. 2, 1899, pp. 236–37. *CIA* 1906, p. 27. 34 Stat. L. 182.

43. Janet McDonnell, "Competency Commissions and Indian Land Policy," *South Dakota History* 11 (Winter 1980). *SI* 1912, p. 53. *CIA* 1906, pp. 27–31.

44. McDonnell, "Competency Commissions," p. 33. *CIA* 1907, pp. 63–65.

45. *CIA* 1913, p. 15.

46. *CIA* 1917, pp. 3–4. *CIA* 1919, pp. 3–4.

47. *CIA* 1920, p. 49. *CIA* 1911, p. 49. Estimates of land loss are from Felix S. Cohen, *Handbook of Federal Indian Law* (Washington: Government Printing Office, 1942), p. 216.

48. *DIA* 1889, p. 165.

49. *DIA* 1889, pp. 165–66.

50. Abbott, *Administration of Indian Affairs*, p. 23. *An Act for the Gradual Enfranchisement of Indians, the Better Management of Indian Affairs, and to Extend the Provisions of the Act 31 Vict. Chapter 42.* S. C. 1869, c. 6, s. 13 (32–33 Vict.).

51. *DIA* 1889, p. x.

52. *The Indian Act, 1880.* S. C. 1880, c. 28, s. 19 (43 Vict.). *The Indian Act.* R. S. C. 1886, c. 43, s. 39 (49 Vict.).

53. *An Act to Amend the Indian Act, 1880.* S. C. 1884, c. 27, s. 99 (47 Vict.). Section 100 of this act describes the location ticket, which is similar to the trust patent issued in the United States.

54. *DIA* 1917, pp. 20–22. *CIA* 1917, p. 178.

55. Scott, "Some Features," p. 98. The Reverend John McDougall, a prominent Canadian missionary, advocated this move at the 1912 Lake Mohonk meeting; *Lake Mohonk*, (1912), pp. 97–98.

56. Jennings, "The Plains Indians and the Law," in *Men in Scarlet*, ed. Hugh A. Dempsey, pp. 51, 54.

57. Scott, "Some Features," p. 97

58. *Leasing of Indian Lands.* Senate Doc. 212, 57th Cong., 1st sess., 1912, serial 4234. E. B. Linnen, "Our Indian People," *The Red Man* 8 (October 1915):62.

59. John H. Warketin, "Western Canada in 1886," *Transactions of the Historical and Scientific Society of Manitoba* 3 (1965):85–86. R. G. Riddell, "A Cycle in the Development of the Canadian West," *The Canadian Historical Review* 21 (September 1940):286. Ewers, *Blackfeet Indians*, p. 293.

60. Robert J. Surtees, "The Development of an Indian Policy in Canada," *Ontario Historical Society* 61 (June 1969):92.

61. Alexander Morris, *The Treaties of Canada with the Indians* (Toronto: Coles Publishing Co., 1979), p. 10. John L. Tobias, "Indian Reserves in Western Canada: Indian Homelands or Devices for Assimilation?" (1975), Treaties and Historical Research Center, DIAND, pp. 3–4.

62. John L. Taylor, "Canada's North-West Indian Policy in the 1870s, Traditional Premises and Necessary Innovations," in *Approaches to Native History*, ed. D. A. Muise, pp. 107–8.

63. Loram and McIlwraith, *North American Indian Today*, pp. 4–5. Harper, "Canada's Indian Administration: The Treaty System" pp. 129–30. Tobias, "Indian Reserves," pp. 5–6. Taylor, "Two Views of the Meaning of Treaties 6 and 7," in *The Spirit of Alberta Treaties*, ed. Richard Price (Montreal: Institute for Research on Public Policy and Indian Association of Alberta, 1980), pp. 9–43.

64. Warketin, "Western Canada in 1886," p. 115. Chester Martin, *Dominion Lands Policy*, ed. Louis H. Thomas (Toronto: McClelland and Stewart, 1973). L. H. Thomas, "The North-West Territories, 1870–1905," *The Canadian Historical Association Booklets*, no. 26 (Ottawa: Canadian Historical Association, 1970). Jennings, "Plains Indians and the Law," p. 50.

65. Leighton, "A Victorian Civil Servant at Work: Lawrence Vankoughnet and the Canadian Indian Department, 1874–1893" (paper presented to the Canadian Historical Association, London, Ontario, 30 May 1978), pp. 4–5. Hall, "Clifford Sifton," pp. 130, 135.

66. Hall, "Clifford Sifton," p. 146. *DIA* 1908, p. xxxv. Grant, "Indian Affairs under Duncan Campbell Scott," pp. 24, 36.

67. "A Brief Account of the Indians of Canada, 1920," PAC, Blue Books, v. 10020, p. 107, C11059.

68. Loram and McIlwraith, *North American Indian Today*, p. 198.

Chapter 2

1. Morris, *Treaties*, p. 203.

2. Quoted in Schmeckebier, *Office of Indian Affairs*, p. 289. One Indian commissioner who recognized the thankless position of agents was Francis E. Leupp, *The Indian and His Problem* (New York: Arno Press, 1971), pp. 103–4.

3. There is no single satisfactory study of American Indian agents. See William E. Unrau, "The Civilian as Indian Agent, Villain or Victim," *Western Historical Quarterly* 3 (October 1972). Langdon Sully, "The Indian Agent: A Study in Corruption and Avarice," *The American West* 10 (March 1973).

4. John Young to Col. Thomas R. Ruger, 4 May 1880; John Young to J. W. Powell, 10 November 1880, Denver FARC, MPI–A, v. 3, pp. 250–51, 338.

5. Ewers, *Blackfeet Indians*, p. 151.

6. Tobias, "Indian Reserves," p. 4. A. J. Looy, "Saskatchewan's First Indian Agent, M. G. Dickienson," *Saskatchewan History* 32 (Autumn 1979):110.

7. Looy, "Saskatchewan's First Indian Agent," p. 104.

8. Leighton, "Victorian Civil Servant," pp. 22–23.

9. P. B. Waite, *Canada, 1874–1896* (Toronto: McClelland and Stewart, 1976), p. 71. *CIA* 1878, pp. 89–91. Jean Larmour, "Edgar Dewdney, Indian Commissioner in the Transitional Period of Indian Settlement, 1879–1884," *Saskatchewan History* 33 (Winter 1980):20. Looy, "Saskatchewan's First Indian Agent," p. 111. The number of American Indian refugees was estimated from six to eight thousand. J. Young to Commissioner E. A. Hayt, 10 January 1879, Denver FARC, MPI–A, v. 2, p. 316.

10. Dempsey, *Crowfoot*, pp. 104, 110.

11. C. Scollen to A. G. Irvine, 13 April 1879, pp. 5–7, 11, PAC, v. 3671, f. 10836–2, C10118.

12. Dempsey, *Crowfoot*, p. 112. Looy, "Saskatchewan's First Indian Agent," p. 109.

13. Edgar L. Dewdney, "Memorandum of my Appointment as Indian Commissioner, 1879," pp. 1, 9, DP reel 1.

14. Larmour, "Edgar Dewdney," p. 20.

15. J. S. Dennis to E. Dewdney, 30 May 1879, PAC, v. 3635, f. 6567, C10111.

16. Dewdney, "Memorandum," p. 11. *DIA* 1881, p. 36. Dempsey, *Crowfoot*, pp. 116, 127.

17. Dempsey, *Crowfoot*, pp. 116, 127.

18. *DIA* 1882, pp. 168, 169. J. Young to T. Ruger, 7 June 1881, Denver FARC, MPI–A, v. 3, pp. 439–40.

19. Hugh A. Dempsey, "The First Indian Agent," in Dempsey, ed., *Scarlet and Gold*, 36th ed. (n.p., 1954), pp. 97–107. Looy, "Saskatchwan's First Indian Agent," p. 57.

20. Helen B. West, "Starvation Winter of the Blackfeet," *Montana* 9 (January 1959):10, 6.

21. West, "Starvation Winter," p. 10. J. Young to J. Q. Smith, 22 December 1876, Denver FARC, MPI–A, v. 1, pp. 249–50.

22. J. Young to J. Q. Smith, 13 August 1878, Denver FARC, MPI–A, v. 1, p. 427.

23. J. Young to E. A. Hayt, 25 February 1879, Denver FARC, MPI–A, v. 2, pp. 377–78.

24. J. Young to E. A. Hayt, 14 January 1880, Denver FARC, MPI–A, v. 3, pp. 164–66.

25. J. Young to R. E. Trowbridge, 11 March 1880, Denver FARC, MPI–A, v. 4, pp. 18–22.

26. L. T. Kirkwood to CIA, 15 September 1881; H. Price to J. Young, 19 September 1881, Denver FARC, BAC, Miscellaneous Letters 1880–81, folder 40, July–September 1881.

27. *The Fort Benton Weekly Record* (Fort Benton, Montana), 28 April 1883.

28. J. Young to Alex C. Botkin, U.S. Marshal, 1 May 1883; J. Young to H. Price, 1 May 1883; J. Young to General John R. Brooke, 7 May 1883, Denver FARC, MPI–A, v. 5, pp. 463–66 and 449–50, respectively.

29. *Indian Tribes of Northern Montana*, Senate Doc. 255, 58th Cong., 2d sess., 1904, serial 4592.

30. *The New North-West* (Deer Lodge, Montana), 27 June 1884.

31. H. Price to J. Young, 4 February 1884, Denver FARC, BAC, Miscellaneous Letters 1884–86, folder 53, January–March 1884.

32. A. C. Warner to E. A. Hayt, 16 December 1878, Denver FARC, MPI–A, v. 2, pp. 295–301.

33. Herbert Walsh report on the Blackfeet reservation, 23 December 1884, IRA Papers, A28, A31, reel 102.

34. R. A. Allen to H. Price, 4 June 1884, Denver FARC, MPI–A, v. 6, pp. 346–48.

35. R. A. Allen to E. L. Stevens, 11 August 1884, Denver FARC, MPI–A, v. 6, pp. 401–3.

36. *DIA* 1881, p. xxiv.

37. Deputy Superintendent General (DSG) to Thomas P. Wadsworth, (?) July 1879, PAC, v. 3695, f. 14748, C10121.

38. J. S. Dennis to Edward Hooper, 21 May 1879, PAC, v. 3695, f. 14763, C10121. McQuillan, "Creation of Indian Reserves," p. 389.

39. One such employee was James Patterson, who worked at Blackfoot Crossing. An elderly gentleman from Ontario, he required a cane and a crutch to get around. He stayed among the Blackfeet for about six months and was allegedly so frightened of the Indians that he refused to venture onto the reserves. He opted to return "to Canada." J. F. Mcleod to E. Dewdney, 17 June 1880, v. 3695, f. 14763, C10122.

40. Dempsey, *Crowfoot*, pp.139–45.

41. Dempsey, *Crowfoot*, p. 146.

42. Information on file in DIA, PAC, v. 3695, f. 14748, C10121.

43. Memorandum regarding reorganization of Treaty 7, 23 March 1883, PAC, v. 3635, f. 6567, C10111; C. E. Denny to D. Dewdney, 15 June 1882, p. 1135, DP, reel 2.

44. C. E. Denny to T. P. Wadsworth, 27 June 1882; T. P. Wadsworth to A. T. Galt, 29 July 1882, PAC, v. 3609, f. 3334, C10106.

45. L. Vankoughnet to Indian Agents, 23 November 1883; E. Dewdney to William B. Pocklington, 13 December 1883; C. E. Denny to E. Dewdney, 1 and 10 January 1884; see protest of Battleford agent I. M. Rea to E. Dewdney, 18 January 1884, PAC, v. 3664, f. 9843, C10116. Rea was Poundmaker's agent.

46. Orders of the DIA, 28 October 1884, and Clerk of Privy Council to Superintendent, 23 January 1885, PAC, v. 2277, f. 55412–1, C11193. For subsequent orders see D. C. Scott, Departmental Order, 9 December 1895, and Order of December 14, 1907, PAC, v. 2277, f. 55412–1, C11193.

47. Leighton, "Victorian Civil Servant," pp. 3, 4. Sue Baptie, "Edgar Dewdney," *Alberta History* 16 (Autumn 1968):10. Stanley, *The Birth of Western Canada*, p. 390. Isabel Andrews, "Indian Protest against Starvation: The Yellow Calf Incident, 1884," *Saskatchewan History* 28 (Spring 1975):41–50.

48. L. Vankoughnet to E. Dewdney, 5 December 1884; E. Dewdney to L. Vankoughnet, 12 December 1884, pp. 1104–16, DP, reel 2.

49. E. Dewdney to John A. Macdonald, ? February 1885, pp. 537–39, DP, reel 1.

50. Cecil Edward Denny, *The Riders of the Plains* (Calgary: Herald Co., 1905), pp. 177, 201. Larmour, "Edgar Dewdney," p. 110. Dempsey, *Crowfoot*, pp. 168–70. C. E. Denny to E. Dewdney, 26 June 1885, PAC, v. 3715, f. 21984, C10125. Hayter Reed to E. Dewdney, 25 November 1885, PAC, v. 3727, f. 25167–1, C10126. See also Andre N. Lalonde, "The North-West Rebellion and Its Effects on Settlers and Settlement in the Canadian West," *Saskatchewan History* 27 (Autumn 1974). F. C. Cornish, "The Blackfeet and the Rebellion, Experiences of an Agency Clerk in 1885," *Alberta Historical Review* 6 (Spring 1958).

51. House of Commons (Canada), Debates (1886), pp. 753–54, 758–59.

52. Cited in House of Commons Debates, p. 772.

53. Warketin, "Western Canada in 1886," p. 114. Leighton, "Federal Indian Policy," vol. 2, p. 541.

54. For details, see Steell's appointment file. NA, RG 48, Appointments Division, Montana, Blackfeet Indian Agency. Steele, *Forty Years in Canada*, p. 137.

55. G. Steell to CIA, 3 May 1892, Seattle FARC, MPI–A, v. 59, pp. 113–15, reel 70. G. Steell to W. C. Pollock, 6 February 1896, Denver FARC, MPI–A, v. 19, p. 121.

56. L. W. Cooke to CIA, 28 November 1893, Seattle FARC, MPI–A, v. 60, p. 160, reel 70; Cooke to CIA, 15 May 1894, Seattle FARC, MPI–A, v. 61, p. 63, reel 70.

57. For salary information, see Denver FARC, BAC, Miscellaneous Letters, folder 118, July 1895. Steell to CIA, 27 December 1890, Seattle FARC, MPI–A, v. 58, p. 119, reel 70. *CIA 1894*, p. 161.

58. C. A. Churchill to CIA, 13 July 1909, Seattle FARC, MPI–A, v. 77, p. 321, reel 73.

59. "Copy of a Report of a Committee of the Honorable Privy Council, 30 October 1887," PAC, v. 2392, f. 80222, C19213.

60. D. J. Hall, *Clifford Sifton, The Young Napoleon, 1861–1900*, vol. 1 (Vancouver: University of British Columbia Press, 1981), pp. 127–28.

61. Memorandum for the DSG, 3 March 1904, PAC, v. 3877, f. 91839–1, C10155.

62. *DIA 1897*, pp. xxix–xxx.

63. D. C. Scott to DSG, 3 March 1904, PAC, v. 3635, f. 6567, C10111. DSG to A. F. Forget, 27 September 1895, PAC, v. 3877, f. 91839–1, C10155.

64. "Reorganization of North West Territories, 1897," PAC, v. 3877, f. 91839–1, C10155. D. C. Scott to DSG, 3 March 1904, PAC, v. 3635, f. 6567, C10111. Memorandum for the DSG, 3 March 1904, PAC, v. 3877, f. 91839–1, C10155.

65. Memorandum to DSG from Assistant Commissioner A. McKenna, 12 January 1904, PAC, v. 3635, f. 6567, C10111.

66. Memorandum of the DSG to D. C. Scott, 23 February 1904, PAC, v. 3635, f. 6567, C10111. D. C. Scott to DSG, 3 March 1904, PAC, v. 3877, f. 91839–1, C10155.

67. David Laird to the Secretary of the DIA, 9 November 1905; Assistant Commissioner to Secretary of the DIA, 7 March 1905, PAC, v. 3086, f. 279222–1, C11322. A rather popular account of Laird's career is John W. Chalmers, *Laird of the West* (Calgary: Detseling Enterprises, 1981).

68. Robert M. Kvasnicka and Herman J. Viola, *The Commissioners of Indian Affairs, 1824–1977* (Lincoln: University of Nebraska Press, 1979), p. 237. Meriam, *The Problem of Indian Administration*, pp. 140–41. Interestingly enough, F. A. Abbott felt that there was no centralized administration of Indian reservations from Washington and praised Canada for her centralized system. Abbott, *The Administration of Indian Affairs*, p. 33.

69. *Surplus Lands, Indian Blackfeet Reservation, Montana*, hearings before the Senate Committee on Indian Affairs on S. 793, 64th Cong., 1st sess., April 11, 15, 1916, p. 48.

70. *Granting the Indians the Right to Select Agents and Superintendents*, hearings before Senate Committee on Indian Affairs on S. 3904, 64 Cong., 1st sess., 9 March 1916.

71. Ponting and Gibbins, *Out of Irrelevance*, p. 17.

72. Meriam, *Problem of Indian Administration*, pp. 143–45.

73. See DIA files, PAC v. 2908, f. 185723–A, 1909–1910, C11296.

74. "A Visit to the Blood Reserve," *The Macleod Gazette* (Ft. Macleod, Alberta), 13 August 1891, repr. in the *Kainai News*, 1 December 1972, ed. Hugh A. Dempsey.

75. Hugh L. Scott, "Blackfeet Indian Agency, Montana," *BIC 1925*, pp. 23–24.

76. Hugh L. Scott, "Blackfeet Reservation, Montana," *BIC 1919*, p. 34.

Chapter 3

1. E. E. Hagan and Louis C. Shaw, *The Sioux on Reservations: the American Colonial Problem* (Cambridge, Mass.: Center for International Studies, 1960). See also *Economic Development in American Indian Reservations*, Native American Studies (Albuquerque: University of New Mexico Press, 1979).

2. The development of dependency among several Indian tribes has recently been examined by Richard White, *The Roots of Dependency, Subsistence, Environment, and Social Change among the Choctaws, Pawnees, and Navajos* (Lincoln: University of Nebraska Press, 1983).

3. Thomas R. Wessell, "Agriculture, Indians, and American History," *Agricultural History* 50 (January 1976):9.

4. John Martin, "John Hamilton Gooderham," p. 244, GAI.

5. Kappler, *Indian Laws and Treaties*, vol. 1, p. 738, 999. Ewers, *The Blackfeet*, pp. 231–32.

6. Morris, *Treaties*, p. 371.

7. See the Blackfeet treaties in Kappler, *Indian Laws and Treaties*, vol. 4, p. 1135, and vol. 1, pp. 738, 1001.

8. Morris, *Treaties*, p. 371.

9. Abbott, *Administration of Indian Affairs*, p. 22.

10. Ibid., pp. 29, 84.

11. *DIA* 1883, pp. ix, xv.

12. Acting Commissioner William M. Leeds to U.S. Indian Agents, Circular no. 23, 22 August 1878, Denver FARC, BAC, Miscellaneous Letters 1878, folder 23, July–August 1878.

13. J. D. C. Atkins to R. A. Allen, 15 March 1886, Denver FARC, BAC, Miscellaneous Letters 1884–88, folder 59, January–April 1886.

14. Frank Pedley to Clifford Sifton, 24 March 1904, PAC, v. 3635, f. 6567, C10111.

15. Harper, "Canada's Indian Administration: Basic Concepts," pp. 120, 123.

16. *DIA* 1883, p. 83.

17. IRA Papers, A31, p. 17, reel 102.

18. Schmeckebier, *Office of Indian Affairs*, p. 253. U.S. Department of the Interior, Census Office, *Report on Indians Taxed and Not Taxed in the United States (except Alaska), at the 11th Census, 1890* (Washington: Government Printing Office, 1894), p. 76.

19. J. Young to E. A. Hayt, 10 April 1878, Denver FARC, MPI–A, v. 2, p. 30. J. Young to CIA, 6 May and 14 June 1878, Denver FARC, MPI–A, v. 2, pp. 68–69, 106–8. R. A. Allen to CIA, 3 October 1884, Denver FARC, MPI–A, v. 6, pp. 444–45.

20. G. Steell to CIA, 6 February 1896, Denver FARC, MPI–A, v. 19, p. 121.

21. *CIA* 1900, p. 5. *BIC* 1901, p. 648. *SI* 1904, p. 28.

22. *CIA* 1902, p. 227.

23. CIA to Blackfeet Indian Agent, 6 September 1900, Denver FARC, BAC, Miscellaneous Letters 1900–1901, folder 171, September 1900, box 56.

24. CIA to J. H. Monteath, 6 December 1901, and CIA to Blackfeet Indian Agent, 5 November 1901, Denver FARC, BAC, Miscellaneous Letters 1900–1901, folder 180, November–December 1901.

25. *CIA* 1901–1902, p. 227. J. H. Monteath to CIA, 31 December 1903, Seattle FARC, MPI–A, v. 67, p. 408–9, reel 71. *CIA* 1903–1904, p. 223.

26. *CIA* 1905–1906, p. 237. J. Z. Dare to Blood Agent, 10 April 1905, BIAC, file 13, GAI.

27. C. A. Churchill to CIA, 3 April 1909, Denver FARC, MPI–A, v. 77, p. 126.

28. Superintendent, Blackfeet Agency to CIA, 12 April 1913, Denver FARC, BAC, Entry 5, folder: Reservation Industry.

29. Ibid.

30. Memorandum to the DSG, 3 March 1904, p. 3, PAC, v. 3635, f. 6567, C10111. "Instructions to Indian Agents, 1913," 25 October 1913, PAC, v. 3086, f. 279222–1, C11322. McQuillan, "Creation of Indian Reserves," p. 390.

31. *DIA* 1885, p. x. *DIA* 1884, p. 88. L. Vankoughnet to H. Reed, 10 March 1884, PAC, v. 3664, f. 9843, C10116. *DIA* 1885, p. 73. For the situation on other reserves, see Andrews, "Indian Protest against Starvation," pp. 41–51.

32. *DIA* 1890, pp. x, xxviii. Dempsey, ed., "A Visit to the Blood Reserve." R. Sinclair to Acting DSG, 2 January 1891, PAC, v. 3853, f. 78004, C10150.

33. House of Commons (Canada), Debates (1892), pp. 2668–90.

34. D. C. Scott, "Memorandum to the DSG," 3 March 1904, PAC, v. 3877, f. 91839–1, p. 8, 7–9, C10111.

35. Brian Titley, "W. M. Graham: Indian Agent Extraordinaire," *Plains Forum* 8 (Spring 1983):26–28.

36. *DIA* 1901, pp. xxii, 129.

37. *DIA* 1901–1902, p. 126. Scott, "Memorandum," p. 13.

38. J. A. McKenna to Blood Indian Agent, 12 June 1903, BIAC, file 2, GAI.

39. J. D. Maclean to R. N. Wilson, 3 and 23 February 1904, BIAC, file 2, GAI. J. D. Maclean to R. N. Wilson, 30 August 1905, BIAC, file 7, GAI.

40. Abbott, *Administration of Indian Affairs*, p. 84. *DIA* 1903, p. 148.

41. G. H. Gooderham, "Twenty-five Years as an Indian Agent to the Blackfoot Band" (28 January 1972), GAI.

42. *DIA* 1915, pt. 2, p. 78.

43. BIC 1920, p. 19. Ewers, *The Blackfeet*, p. 320.

44. *Annual Report of the Superintendent of Indian Schools, 1900* (Washington: Government Printing Office, 1900), p. 20. *DIA* 1890, p. xxvii, commented about the situation in the North West Territories this way: "It is most gratifying to find a response given in so pronounced a manner to the practical working out of the policies of the Department, namely, to render these Indians self-supporting contributors to the wealth of the country, instead of remaining consumers of it in perpetuity."

45. Hoxie, *A Final Promise*, p. 239, points out that the Indians' fundamental problem was their inability to become self-supporting.

Chapter 4

1. *CIA* 1911, p. 22. *CIA* 1920, p. 21. Thomas R. Wessell, "Agriculture, Indians, and American History," *Agricultural History* 50 (January 1976):16–18.

2. J. Young to CIA, 16 April 1878, Denver FARC, MPI–A, v. 2, pp. 44–49.

3. J. Young to CIA, 31 July 1881, Denver FARC, MPI–A, v. 4, p. 50.

4. *CIA* 1890–91, pp. 265–67. G. Steell to CIA, 26 August 1891, Seattle FARC, MPI–A, v. 58, p. 351, and 4 November 1891, MPI–A, v. 58, pp. 416–19, reel 70. *CIA* 1892, p. 279. After Young's departure, no other agent lasted as long. Between 1880 and 1920, nineteen agents came and went (one agent was appointed twice), and six agents lasted a year or less.

5. *CIA* 1895, p. 178. *CIA* 1899, p. 216. *CIA* 1901, p. 256. J. Z. Dare to CIA, (?) August 1905, Seattle FARC, MPI–A, v. 70, p. 79, reel 72.

6. W. D. Baldwin to CIA, 31 January and 7 May 1887, Denver FARC, MPI–A, v. 7, pp. 128–30, 186–87. See also J. B. Catlin to CIA, 28 August 1889, Denver FARC, MPI–A, v. 8, pp. 76–77. G. Steell to CIA, 23 February 1892, Seattle FARC, MPI–A, v. 59, p. 34, reel 70.

7. *CIA* 1885, p. xxiv. See the complaints of the CIA in *Investigation of Indian Affairs*, Sen-

ate Doc. 984, 63d Cong., 3d sess., 19 March 1915, p. 6, serial 6784. Schmeckebier, *Office of Indian Affairs*, p. 249. "The Indian as Farmer," *The Red Man* 8 (December 1915):111–13.

8. Dempsey, ed., "An Unwilling Diary," *Alberta Historical Review* 7 (Summer 1959):7–10.

9. C. A. Churchill to CIA, 27 January 1910, Seattle FARC, MPI–A, v. 78, p. 116, reel 73. Arthur E. McFatridge to CIA, 28 September 1910, Seattle FARC, MPI–A, v. 78, p. 495, reel 74.

10. A. E. McFatridge to CIA, 4, 15, 27 March 1911, Seattle FARC, MPI–A, v. 79, pp. 231, 267, 279; ibid., 20 October, 16 November 1911, MPI–A, v. 80, pp. 132, 200, reel 74.

11. Kappler, *Indian Laws and Treaties*, v. 1, pp. 604–7.

12. IRA Papers, A31, p. 16, reel 102.

13. G. Steell to CIA, 7 February 1891, Seattle FARC, MPI–A, v. 58, p. 186, reel 70. *CIA* 1906–7, p. 251. Wessell, "Agriculture on the Reservation: the Case of the Blackfeet, 1885–1935," *Journal of the West* 18 (October 1979):17–24. Most supervisors had praise for Indian workers. See "Blackfeet Irrigation Project, and the Employment of Indians Thereon," NA, RG 75, BIA Central Files 1907–1939, file 13546–08 Blackfeet 341.

14. *CIA* 1900, p. 264.

15. J. Z. Dare to CIA, 5 April, 1 July 1905, Seattle FARC, MPI–A, v. 69, pp. 70, 376–79, reel 72. *CIA* 1906–7, p. 251.

16. J. H. Monteath to Conrad Investment Company, 30 September 1904, and Monteath to Carl Rasch, U.S. District Attorney, 14 October 1904, Denver FARC, MPI–A, v. 26, pp. 172, 174, 190. J. Z. Dare to C. Rasch, 18 April 1906, Denver FARC, MPI–A, v. 31, pp. 300–301. C. A. Churchill to CIA, 17 November 1908, Seattle FARC, MPI–A, v. 76, p. 398, reel 73. Such challenges to the Indians' water rights in Montana and elsewhere were not unusual. In fact, in the same year a dispute between Indians and non-Indians over allotment of water from the Milk River in Montana led the Supreme Court to defend Indian water rights in the *Winters v. U.S.* decision.

17. *CIA* 1906, p. 84. J. Z. Dare to CIA, 1 May 1907, Seattle FARC, MPI–A, v. 73, p. 24, reel 73.

18. *The Montana Daily Record* (Helena, Montana), 7 July 1906.

19. *Surplus Lands, Blackfeet Indian Reservation, Montana*, pp. 88–90. These provisions were not unusual, however; before 1914, according to the BIA guidelines the cost of irrigation was to be paid from the proceeds of the sale of surplus lands. Schmeckebier, *Office of Indian Affairs*, p. 241. E. B. Linnen to Cato Sells, 30 August 1917, NA, RG 75, BIA Central Files 1907–39, file 85549–1917 Blackfeet 341; A. E. McFatridge to CIA, 4 May 1914, file 12791–1914 Blackfeet 341.

20. *Surplus Lands*, p. 9.

21. C. Gunderson to Thralls W. Wheat, 24 March 1911, Denver FARC, BAC, Entry 5, folder: Miscellaneous Letters. *CIA* 1911, p. 24.

22. *CIA* 1917, vol. 2. p. 25, 27–29. The optimism of the war's boom years ended in 1920, and with the end of war production Indian farming suffered commensurately. See Leonard A. Carlson, *Indians, Bureaucrats, and Land: The Dawes Act and the Decline of Indian Farming* (Westport, Conn.: Greenwood Press, 1981). See, also, Janet McDonnell, "The Disintegration of the Indian Estate: Indian Land Policy, 1913–1929" (Ph.D. diss., Marquette University, 1980), chap. 5. David L. Wood, "American Indian Farmland and the Great War," *Agricultural History* 55 (July 1981).

23. Warketin, "Western Canada in 1886," pp. 87, 108–9. Hall, *Clifford Sifton*, p. 252.

24. *DIA* 1882, pp. xvi–xvii. *DIA* 1881, p. 117. Denny, *Riders of the Plains*, p. 163.

25. *DIA* 1883, p. xi. *DIA* 1884, pp. 142, 143.

26. *DIA* 1884, p. 90. Leighton, "Federal Indian Policy," v. 2, pp. 368–69, 371. Denny, *Riders of the Plains*, p. 145.

27. *DIA* 1889, pp. 161–62.

28. A. G. Irvine to Indian Commissioner, 1 March 1892, PAC, v. 3871, f. 89071, C10154.

29. Denny, *Riders of the Plains*, pp. 163, 165. *DIA* 1896, p. xxiii. Memorandum to F. A. Forget, 9 July 1896, PAC, v. 3871, f. 91839–1, C10155.

30. *DIA* 1898, p. 160. See also *DIA* 1899, p. 170. *DIA* 1901, p. 166.

31. *DIA* 1898, p. 128. "Result of Expenditures for the Purpose of Making Indians in Manitoba and North West Territories Self-Supporting," PAC, v. 3993, f. 187224, C10169. *DIA* 1901, p. xxii. *DIA* 1909, p. 173.

32. F. A. Forget to F. Pedley, 25 November 1908, PAC, v. 4041, f. 334503, C10178. *DIA* 1910, p. 165. *DIA* 1909, pp. 173–74.

33. F. W. Godsal to D. Laird, 3 November 1909. Memorandum to Secretary of the DIA, 19 November 1909. Reply to Godsal, n.d. PAC, v. 4045, f. 352850–1, C10178.

34. J. A. Markle to Secretary of the DIA, 9 July 1910, PAC, v. 4045, f. 352850–1, C10178. Hanks, *Tribe Under Trust*, p. 34. Gooderham, "Twenty-Five Years as an Indian Agent," p. 1. Goldfrank, "Administrative Programs and Changes in Blood Society," pp. 20–21.

35. *DIA* 1918, pp. 10–12. Titley, "W. M. Graham," pp. 29–30.

36. Lawrence B. Lee, "The Canadian–American Irrigation Frontier, 1884–1914," *Agricultural History* 40 (October 1966):282. Hall, *Clifford Sifton*, p. 254.

37. Andy A. den Otter, "Irrigation in Southern Alberta, 1882–1901," *Great Plains Journal* 2 (Spring 1972):134.

38. *DIA* 1896, p. xxx. Memorandum to the Governor General in Council, 23 October 1893, PAC, v. 3907, f. 107178, C10159. Assistant Commissioner to W. H. Graves, 30 October 1894, PAC, v. 3582, f. 988, C10102.

39. Den Otter, "Irrigation," pp. 125, 133. Lee, "Canadian–American Irrigation Frontier," pp. 279–80. C. S. Burchill, "The Origins of Canadian Irrigation Law," *The Canadian Historical Review* 29 (September 1948).

40. Deputy Superintendent to the Commissioner of Indian Affairs, 8 December 1894, PAC, v. 3582, f. 988, C10102. R. N. Wilson to Secretary of the DIA, 6 February and 27 March 1905, PAC, v. 7603, f. 12013 pt. 1, C11571.

41. Memorandum to the DSG, 6 February 1906; Chief Surveyor to the DSG, 1 May 1906; Commissioner of Irrigation to the Secretary of the DIA, 26 March 1906, PAC, v. 7063, f. 12013 pt. 1, C11571.

42. R. N. Wilson to Secretary of the DIA, 14 February 1907, PAC, v. 7603, f. 12103 pt. 1, C11571.

43. J. D. Maclean to R. N. Wilson, 25 February 1907, PAC, v. 7603, f. 12103, C11571.

44. J. A. Markle to the Secretary of the DIA, 20 March 1907; Maclean to R. N. Wilson, 30 May 1907; E. F. Drake to W. W. Carey, 5 June 1914, PAC, v. 7603, f. 12103, C11571.

45. E. N. Peters, Commissioner of Irrigation to F. Pedley, 13 November 1912; J. A. Markle to G. H. Gooderham, 13 January 1913; G. H. Gooderham to J. A. Markle, 4 December 1913; J. A. Markle to E. N. Peters, 15 January 1913, PAC, v. 7604, f. 12104–2 pt. 2, C11571.

46. J. Young to H. Price, 3 July 1881, Denver FARC, MPI–A, v. 4, pp. 41–51. R. A. Allen to CIA, 28 June 1886, Seattle FARC, MPI–A, v. 57, p. 404, reel 60.

47. Kappler, *Indian Laws and Treaties*, vol. 1, p. 262. *SI* 1899, pt. 2, p. 302.

48. G. Steell to CIA, 7 February 1891, Seattle FARC, MPI–A, v. 58, p. 185, reel 70. L. W. Cooke to CIA, 20 October 1893, Seattle FARC, MPI–A, v. 60, p. 99, reel 70.

49. See the terms of the 1885 agreement. Kappler, *Indian Laws and Treaties*, v. 1, p. 262. L. W. Cooke posted such a notice prohibiting unauthorized butchering of cattle on 4 September 1893, Denver FARC, MPI–A, v. 13, p. 89. In 1898 the agent still complained that the

Blackfeet worshiped their horses and regarded cattle as secondary. T. P. Fuller to CIA, 8 March 1898, Seattle FARC, MPI–A, v. 64, p. 52, reel 71.

50. Malcolm McFee, *Modern Blackfeet, Montanans on a Reservation* (New York: Holt, Rinehart and Winston, 1972), p. 51.

51. J. Monteath to CIA, 29 July 1904, Seattle FARC, MPI–A, v. 68, pp. 123–24, reel 72.

52. CIA to J. Monteath; W. H. Jones to J. Monteath, 21 October 1901, Denver FARC, MPI–A, v. 23, p. 464.

53. J. Monteath to CIA, 8 October 1903, Seattle FARC, MPI–A, v. 67, p. 291, reel 71. J. R. Jensen to CIA, 2 March 1905, Seattle FARC, MPI–A, v. 68, p. 386, reel 72. McFee, *Modern Blackfeet*, p. 53, states that in the 1920s, 3 percent of the tribe owned 95 percent of the cattle. See also Inspection Report 1910, of E. A. Allen, NA, RG 75, BIA Central Files 1907–1939, file 17107–2/10 Blackfeet 150.

54. *Leasing of Indian Lands.* Senate Doc. 212, 57th Cong., 1st sess., 1912, serial 4234.

55. W. A. Jones to J. Monteath, 27 July 1901, Denver FARC, BAC, Miscellaneous Letters 1900–1901, folder 76, July–August 1901.

56. *CIA 1914*, p. 88. *BIC 1918*, pp. 353–54. *BIC 1920*, p. 21.

57. A. E. McFatridge to CIA, 29 August 1911, Seattle FARC, MPI–A, v. 80, p. 17, reel 74; ibid., 6 October 1911, MPI–A, v. 80, p. 138, reel 74; ibid., ? April 1911, MPI–A, v. 79, p. 369, reel 74.

58. *CIA* 1918, p. 351. *BIC 1920*, p. 19. T. R. Wessell, "Agriculture on the Reservation," p. 20.

59. For Indian agricultural production during World War I, see Wood, "American Indian Farmland and the Great War." *BIC 1920*, p. 19. McFee, *Modern Blackfeet*, p. 54.

60. Dewdney, "Story of My Life," p. 33, DP reel 1.

61. *DIA 1884*, p. 83. Simon M. Evans, "American Cattlemen on Canadian Range, 1874–1914," *Prairie Forum* 4 (Winter 1979):124–25.

62. *DIA 1890*, pp. xxix, 163.

63. *DIA 1886*, p. xlix.

64. *DIA 1891*, pt. 1, p. 95.

65. H. Reed to Superintendent General, 26 April 1891, PAC, v. 3853, f. 78004, C10150.

66. DSG to E. A. Forget, (?) November 1893, PAC, v. 3653, f. 6567, C10111. Report of Alex McGibbon, inspector, 12 February 1891, PAC, v. 3843, f. 72695–13, C10150.

67. *DIA 1889*, p. xxvi.

68. *DIA 1899*, pp. xxv, 191, 170, 130, 133.

69. *DIA 1901–2*, pp. xx, 125.

70. F. Pedley to Indian Agents, Circular, 11 May 1903, BIAC, file 9, GAI. *DIA 1899*, p. 170. J. A. Markle to James Wilson, 9 March 1901, BIAC, file 10, GAI. J. Wilson to P. C. H. Primrose, NWMP, 11 May 1909, BIAC, file 42, GAI. *An Act to Amend the Indian Act* S. C. 1906, c. 20, s. 43 (6 Ed. VII). J. Wilson to P. C. H. Primrose, 3 August 1906, BIAC, file 6, GAI. Blood Agent to Assistant Deputy Superintendent General, 6 June 1914, BIAC, file 97, GAI.

71. W. G. Conrad to F. Pedley, 28 May 1903 and Grazing Contract with Donald McEwen Co., 16 May 1903, PAC, v. 3571, f. 130, pt. 18 and pt. 19, C10101.

72. Campbell to W. T. Hyde, 6 December 1912; W. T. Hyde to Campbell, 13 December 1912, BIAC, file 97, GAI.

73. DIA 1918, p. 20. R.N. Wilson, "Our Betrayed Wards" (1921), repr. in *Western Canadian Journal of Anthropology* (January 1974):42.

74. Wilson, "Our Betrayed Wards," pp. 37, 40, 45, 47, 49, 52. Titley, "W. M. Graham," pp. 30–31.

75. Gooderham, "Twenty-Five Years," p. 2.

Chapter 5

1. IRA Papers, A113, reel 102.
2. Leslie and Maguire, *The Historical Development of the Indian Act*, pp. 107–9. *An Act to Amend the Indian Act*. S. C. 1911, c. 14, s. 49A (1–2 George V).
3. Tobias, "Indian Reserves," pp. 97–98.
4. Ewers, *Blackfeet Indians*, p. 142; idem., *Blackfeet*, pp. 270–72. This is the so-called Royce Area, restored by executive order of 15 April 1874.
5. L. J. Kirkwood to CIA, 15 September 1881; H. Price to J. Young, 19 September 1881, Denver FARC, BAC, Miscellaneous Letters 1880–1881, folder 40, July–September 1881.
6. J. Young to CIA, 17 January 1882, Denver FARC, MPI–A, v. 5, pp. 53–54.
7. J. Young to Martin Maginnis, 26 December 1882, Denver FARC, MPI–A, v. 5, pp. 357–58.
8. *The New North-West*, 15 June 1883 (repr. from *Chicago Times*, 30 May 1883).
9. *Indian Tribes of Northern Montana, Etc.* Senate Doc. 255, 58th Cong., 2d sess., 1904, serial 4592, p. 19.
10. Ibid.
11. *The New North-West*, 7 December 1883.
12. W. D. Baldwin to CIA, 1 March 1884, Denver FARC, MPI–A, v. 7, p. 156. *CIA 1888*, pp. 150, 536. Kappler, *Indian Laws and Treaties*, v. 1, p. 262.
13. G. Steell to Lt. James A. Irons, 29 May 1893, Denver FARC, MPI–A, v. 12, p. 383.
14. L. W. Cooke to CIA, 29 January, 11 June 1894, Seattle FARC, MPI–A, v. 60, pp. 255, 408, reel 70.
15. G. B. Grinnell to G. Steell, 28 October 1895, Denver FARC, BAC, Miscellaneous Letters 1884–88, folder 62. *CIA 1896*, p. 34. G. Steell to C. E. Conrad, 27 July 1896, Denver FARC, MPI–A, v. 19, p. 355. G. B. McLaughlin to Chas. Frost, 30 July 1897, Denver FARC, MPI–A, v. 20, p. 288. G. Steell to T. H. Carter, 19 March 1897, Denver FARC, MPI–A, v. 20, p. 165. *CIA 1898*, p. 182.
16. W. A. Jones to G. H. Monteath, 23 July 1900, Denver FARC, BAC, Miscellaneous Letters 1900–1901, folder 169, July 1900.
17. *Leasing of Indian Lands*. Senate Doc. 212. 57th Cong., 1st sess., 1902, serial 4234.
18. Kappler, *Indian Laws and Treaties*, vol. 1, p. 606.
19. Hall, *Clifford Sifton*, p. 143.
20. *DIA 1908*, p. xxxiv. *DIA 1909*, p. xxxiv.
21. PAC, v. 3145, f. 343777, C11330.
22. *DIA 1910*, p. 462, 175. Memorandum to D. C. Scott, 20 April 1909, PAC, v. 4034, f. 302340–1, C10176.
23. "Peigan Surrender," PAC, "Blue Books," v. 10030, pp. 84–85, C11060. J. A. Markle to the Secretary of the DIA, 24 May 1909, PAC, v. 4034, f. 302340–1, C10176.
24. J. A. Markle to the Secretary of the DIA, 16 July 1900, PAC, v. 4034, f. 302340–1, C10176.
25. "Peigan Surrender," pp. 84–87.
26. These signs are on file in PAC, v. 4034, f. 302340–1, C10176.
27. Hanks and Hanks, *Tribe Under Trust*, pp. 37–38.
28. Stocken, *Among the Blackfoot and Sarcee*, pp. 63–64.
29. Malcolm Western Canneries Ltd. to D. Laird, 1 February 1907, PAC, v. 3563, f. 82, pt. 18, C10099. Petition of the town of Gleichen, 2 March 1909, PAC, v. 3202, f. 17537–3, C10123. Memorandum of D. C. Scott, 20 April 1909, PAC, v. 4034, f. 302340–1, C10176. J. A. Markle to the Secretary of the DIA, 28 September 1909, v. 3702, f. 17537–3, C10123.

30. J. A. Markle to Secretary of the DIA, 29 March 1910, PAC, v. 3701, f. 17537–3, C10123. Of the 133 votes cast, 69 were for and 64 against the sale. J. A. Markle to the Secretary of the DIA, 15 June 1910, v. 3701, f. 17537–3, C10123. For the history of the sale, see Hanks and Hanks, *Tribe Under Trust*, pp. 35–47.

31. F. Pedley to J. A. Markle, 16 May 1910, PAC, v. 3701, f. 17537–3, C10123.

32. The terms of land sales were originally one-fifth in cash, with the balance payable in four years. In the West the department extended the period to ten years, over the protest of the head of the Indian Lands and Timber Branch. Memorandum from Land and Timber Branch, 15 February 1912, PAC, Blue Books, v. 10021, p. 260, C11059. D. C. Scott, Memorandum, 22 February 1912; D. C. Scott to the DSG, 11 November 1912; D. C. Scott to R. B. Bennett, 26 January 1914, PAC, v. 3702, f. 17537–3, C10123. D. C. Scott, Memorandum, 15 January 1913, PAC, v. 3702, f. 17537–3, C10123.

33. Blackfoot Petition, 25 March 1913; Chief Wolf Collar to J. A. Markle, 7 March 1913, D. C. Scott to J. H. Gooderham, 14 June 1915, PAC, v. 3702, v. 17537–3, C10123. D. C. Scott to J. A. Markle, 12 May 1915, PAC, v. 3706, f. 17537, C10123.

34. Blackfoot Petition, 30 April 1915, PAC, v. 3702, f. 17537–3, C10123. Blackfoot Memorandum, 22 April 1916; Wolf Collar to J. A. Markle, 4 May 1916, PAC, v. 3702, f. 17537–3, C10123. Newspaper clipping in the DIA files, n.d., PAC, v. 4063, f. 406557, C10182.

35. J. A. Markle to D. Laird, 20 May 1904; R. N. Wilson to J. McKenna, 25 March 1904, PAC, v. 3571, f. 130, pt. 18 and pt. 19, C10101.

36. J. A. Markle to R. N. Wilson, 7 March 1907, BIAC, file 64, GAI.

37. J. A. Markle to Secretary of the DIA, 6 June 1907, PAC, v. 3939, f. 121698–3, C10164. Dempsey, *Red Crow, Warrior Chief* (Lincoln: University of Nebraska Press, 1980), p. 53.

38. J. A. Markle to the Secretary of the DIA, 6 June 1907, PAC, v. 3939, f. 121698–3, C10164.

39. Crop Eared Wolf to D. Laird, 28 May 1907; D. Laird to Crop Eared Wolf, 30 May 1907, PAC, v. 3939, f. 121698–3, C10164.

40. R. N. Wilson to Indian Commissioner, 6 June 1907, PAC, v. 7451, f. 29103–1, pt. 1, C14811.

41. J. A. Markle to Commissioner, 7 June 1907, PAC, v. 3939, f. 12169–3, C10164. These provisions are in *An Act to Further Amend the Indian Act*. S. C. 1895, c. 35, s. 75 (2 and 4), (58–59 Vict.). J. A. Markle to Secretary of the DIA, 6 June 1907; F. Pedley to Commissioner, 9 March 1907, PAC, v. 3939, f. 121698–4, C10164.

42. Assistant Indian Commissioner to the Secretary of the DIA, 11 June 1907, PAC, v. 3939, f. 121698–3, C10164.

43. R. N. Wilson to J. D. Maclean, 30 June 1910, BIAC, file 64, GAI.

44. R. N. Wilson to the Secretary of the DIA, 30 June 1910, BIAC, file 64, GAI.

45. "Instructions for the Guidance of Indian Agents in Connection with the Surrender of Indian Reserves," PAC, v. 7541, f. 29103–1, pt. 1, C14811.

46. D. C. Scott to W. J. Dilworth, 19 June 1917, PAC, v. 7541, f. 29103–1, pt. 1, C14811.

47. *An Act to Amend the Indian Act*, S. C. 1918, c. 26, s. 4(3), (8–9 George. V).

48. Titley, "W. M. Graham," pp. 29–31. Wilson, "Our Betrayed Wards," p. 41.

49. D. C. Scott, Memorandum to Sir Arthur Meighen, 8 June 1920, PAC, v. 7102, f. 773/3–1–1 pt. 2, C9679.

50. D. C. Scott to W. M. Graham, 7 April, 6 May 1921; D. C. Scott to the Blood Chiefs, 17 August 1922; W. M. Graham to D. C. Scott, 21 February 1921, PAC, v. 7102, f. 773/3–1–1 pt. 2, C9679.

51. Leslie and Maguire, *Historical Development of the Indian Act*, pp. 109–10, cite speech by Robert Borden and others on behalf of the Indians.

52. Editor, "The White Man's Greed," *The Red Man* 8 (December 1915). Editor, "Mohonk and the Indians," *The Red Man* 5 (November 1911).

53. Abbott, *Administration of Indian Affairs*, p. 23. H. Reed to Indian Agents, 21 November 1889, PAC, v. 3865, f. 85679–26, C10153. *DIA* 1889, p. ix, 165.

54. *DIA* 1892, p. xix. *DIA* 1910, p. xxxii. *DIA* 1918, p. 28. My conclusion differs from that of Tobias.

55. Meriam, *Problem of Indian Administration*, p. 19. During the same period, however, some tribes in the Southwest, such as the Navajos and the Pueblos, had their reservations enlarged by executive orders at the behest of the Bureau of Indian Affairs. The extensions of these reservations over public domain by executive orders was eventually blocked by congressional opposition.

56. Kappler, *Indian Laws and Treaties*, vol. 3, p. 286. *CIA* 1907, pp. 148, 251.

57. G. Steell to CIA, 1 November 1890, Seattle FARC, MPI–A, v. 48, p. 41, reel 70. *CIA* 1891, p. 265. G. Steell to CIA, 31 May 1892, Seattle FARC, MPI–A, v. 59, p. 231, reel 70. J. H. Monteath to CIA, 7 and 9 January 1904, Seattle FARC, MPI–A, v. 67, pp. 421–22, 429, reel 71.

58. J. Saunders to CIA, 28 July 1908, Seattle FARC, MPI–A, v. 76(?), p. 2, reel 77. C. A. Churchill to CIA, 21 June 1909, Seattle FARC, MPI–A, v. 77, p. 295, reel 77.

59. *SI* 1912, vol. 2, pp. 57–58. A. McFatridge to CIA 23 April 1912, Seattle FARC, MPI–A, v. 80, pp. 382, 376, reel 74.

60. *Cost of Survey and Allotment Work, Indian Service, 1913*, House Doc. 331, 63d Cong., 2d sess., 1913, serial 6756.

61. A. McFatridge to CIA, 13 December 1913, Seattle FARC, MPI–A, v. 82, p. 448, reel 74.

62. A. McFatridge to CIA, 9 February 1914, Seattle FARC, MPI–A, v. 83, p. 78, reel 74. McFatridge to O. H. Lipps, 27 February 1914, Seattle FARC, MPI–A, v. ?, p. 43, reel 69.

63. *Surplus Lands*, p. 29. For details of the House hearings, see *Disposal of Surplus Lands of Blackfeet Indian Reservation, Montana*, hearings before a Subcommittee of the Committee on Indian Affairs of the House of Representatives on H. R. 14739, 64th Cong., 1st sess., 12 July 1916.

64. *Surplus Lands*, p. 46.

65. Ibid., p. 54.

66. Ibid., pp. 61, 68.

67. *CIA* 1913, pp. 208, 212. *CIA* 1919, p. 78. Ewers, *Blackfeet*, p. 319. J. H. Dortch to F. C. Campbell, 24 April 1918, Denver FARC, BAC, Entry 5, folder 121, Patents in Fee.

68. "Heart Butte Survey," Seattle FARC, MPI–A, v. 102, reel 75. Ewers, *Blackfeet*, p. 319.

69. D. J. Hall, "The Half-Breed Claims Commission," *Alberta History* 25 (Spring 1977). One notable exception to this principle was the issuance of land scrip to the mixed-bloods. After the second Riel Rebellion, mixed-bloods were issued money and land scrip to the public domain to settle their claims against Canada. The land scrip, essentially a fee patent to 160 acres, soon found its way into the hands of speculators in a way similar to what happened to the fee patents of the American Indians.

70. See, for example, Carlson, "Federal Policy and Indian Land: Economic Interests and the Sale of Indian Allotments, 1900–1934," *Agricultural History* 57 (January 1983).

Chapter 6

1. Leighton, "Federal Indian Policy," vol. 2, p. 330.

2. Abbott, "*Administration of Indian Affairs*, p. 38.

3. John Maclean, *The Indians of Canada, Their Manners and Customs* (London: Charles H. Kelly, 1892), p. 273.

4. John Young to CIA, 3 July 1881, Denver FARC, MPI–A, v. 4, p. 40.

5. Harrod, *Mission among the Blackfeet* (Norman: University of Oklahoma Press, 1971), pp. 29–33, 55–57. Wilfred P. Schoenberg,

S. J., "Historic St. Peter's Mission: Landmark of the Jesuits and Ursulines among the Blackfeet," *Montana* 11 (January 1961):74.

6. H. H. Walsh, *The Christian Church in Canada* (Toronto: Ryerson Press, 1956), pp. 254, 250. An excellent account of the mission is Ian A. L. Getty, "The Church Missionary Society among the Blackfoot Indians of Southern Alberta, 1880–1895" (Master's thesis, University of Calgary, 1970.

7. Getty, "The Failure of the Native Church Policy of the CMS in the North-West," in *Religion and Society in the Prairie West*, ed. Richard Allen (Canadian Plains Research Center, University of Regina, 1974), pp. 19, 25. David J. Carter, "The Rev'd. Samuel Trivett," pt. 1, *Alberta Historical Review* 21 (Spring 1973); idem. pt. 2, *Alberta Historical Review* 21 (Summer 1973). J. W. Tims, "Anglican Beginnings in Southern Alberta," *Alberta Historical Review* 15 (Spring 1967):1, 2. Harrod, *Mission among the Blackfeet*, p. 24.

8. John Young to CIA, 3 July 1881, Denver FARC, MPI–A, v. 4, pp. 46–47. CIA 1881, p. 112.

9. The Imoda–Young episode is described by Harrod, "The Blackfeet and the Divine Establishment," *Montana* 22 (January 1972). C. Imoda to John Young, 27 May and 16 June 1880, Denver FARC, BAC, Miscellaneous Correspondence, 1880–81, folder 35, April–June 1881; R. E. Trowbridge to John Young, 15 July 1880, folder 36, July–September 1880; J. L. Dryden to E. K. Raynar, 12 January 1881, folder 38, January–March 1881.

10. Young to CIA, 27 December 1881, 3 January 1882, Denver FARC, MPI–A, v. 5, pp. 38–44. Harrod, *Mission among the Blackfeet*, p. 80. Schoenberg, "Historic St. Peter's Mission," p. 82.

11. W. D. Baldwin to CIA, 30 August 1887, Denver FARC, MPI–A, v. 7, pp. 247–48.

12. George Steell to Rev. E. S. Dutcher, 19 December 1892, Denver FARC, MPI–A, v. 12, p. 209.

13. Harrod, *Mission among the Blackfeet*, pp. 110, 114–15.

14. Robert F. Berkhofer, *Salvation and the Savage: An Analysis of Protestant Missions and Indian Response, 1787–1862* (Lexington: University of Kentucky Press, 1965).

15. Gresko, "White 'Rites' and Indian 'Rites'," p. 179; Getty, "Failure of the Native Church," p. 28. Stocken, *Among the Blackfoot and Sarcee*, p. xi.

16. Getty, "Failure of the Native Church," p. 28.

17. J. W. Tims to (?), 21 February 1892, Letterbook of the Reverend J. W. Tims, pp. 107–8, 13–14, Calgary Indian Mission Papers, GAI.

18. *Ottawa Journal* (Ottawa, Ontario), 26 November 1900, clipping on file in BIAC, file 197, GAI.

19. Abbott, *Administration of Indian Affairs*, pp. 29–30.

20. *An Act to Further amend the "Indian Act, 1880," S. C. 1884, c. 27 (47 Vict.), clause 3.*

21. *CIA 1896*, p. 174.

22. *George Steell to E. D. Weld, 17 June 1891, Denver FARC, MPI–A, v. 10, pp. 201–2.*

23. *For calls for regulation of Indian marriages see CIA 1901, pp. 630–33; CIA 1902, pp. 42–44; BIC 1901, p. 640. Schmeckebier, Office of Indian Affairs, p. 258.*

24. James Wilson to Secretary of the DIA, 23 July 1898; Commissioner of Indian Affairs to J. Wilson, 18 August 1898, PAC, v. 3559, f. 74, pt. 1, C10188. This file is restricted. It is not clear whether the seventy-four polygamous marriages were already existing or whether they were contracted that year. *DIA 1903*, p. 148. *The Indian Act* (1906), section 92, author-

ized the superintendent general to withhold payments of annuities or interest from tribal funds to those husbands or wives who deserted their families. Stocken, *Mission among the Blackfoot and Sarcee*, p. 50.

25. *DIA* 1907, pp. xxix–xxx. *DIA* 1910, pp. xxix–xxx.

26. *DIA* 1909, p. xxx. Schmeckebier, *Office of Indian Affairs*, p. 258. R. N. Wilson to Secretary of the DIA, 4 June 1909, GAI, BIAC, file 59.

27. Frank Pedley to R. N. Wilson, 12 June 1909, GAI, BIAC, file 59.

28. John Young to G. W. A. Stanch; Young to CIA, 23 September 1881, Denver FARC, MPI–A, v. 3, pp. 472, 474–79. H. Price to John Young, 3 November 1881, Denver FARC, BAC, Miscellaneous Correspondence 1880–81, folder 41, October–December 1881. W. D. Baldwin to CIA, 31 January 1881, Denver FARC, MPI–A, v. 7, p. 385.

29. Report of Father Lacombe to Edgar Dewdney, 25 November 1889, DP, frame 2187, reel 3. Memo of the Deputy Superintendent General, 4 December 1889, DP, frame 2193, reel 3. M. Beggs to Commissioner, 2 August 1889, PAC, v. 3770, f. 33952, C10135.

30. *DIA* 1891, pt. 1, p. 83. M. Beggs to Commissioner, 3 July 1890, PAC, v. 3770, f. 33952, C10135. P. C. Shaw, "I Saw the Last Brave," *Alberta Historical Review* 24 (Autumn 1976). Ewers, *Indian Life on the Upper Missouri* (Norman: University of Oklahoma Press, 1968), pp. 83–84, 153, states that the ceremony was banned in 1891. The ban, however, did not end the ceremony.

31. Notice of 22 January 1901, Denver FARC, MPI–A, v. 23, p. 360. W. J. Jones to Blackfeet Agent, 21 January 1902, Denver FARC, BAC, Miscellaneous Letters 1902–1909, folder 181, 1902, box 57.

32. Petition of Indians, 7 June 1909, GAI, BIAC, file 15.

33. Rev. A de B. Owen to Major (?) Howe, 26 June 1902, GAI, BIAC, file 23.

34. J. H. Gooderhan to R. N. Wilson, 14 June 1905, GAI, BIAC, file 21.

35. *DIA* 1908, p. xxi.

36. D. Laird (?) to Corporal (?) Armer, 14 June 1910, GAI, BIAC, file 58. D. Laird to W. J. Dilworth, 23 March 1914, GAI, BIAC, file 98.

37. Titley, "W. M. Graham," pp. 28–29. Gresko, "White 'Rites' and Indian 'Rites'," pp. 176–78. D. Laird to Blood Agent, 16 July 1902, GAI, BIAC, file 25.

38. J. Z. Dare to Tim No Runner, 17 March 1905, Denver FARC, MPI–A, v. 27, p. 12. J. H. Monteath to J. R. Jensen, 21 January 1902, Denver FARC, v. 24, p. 75. Ewers, *Blackfeet*, pp. 310–11. C. Churchill to CIA, 22 November 1909, Seattle FARC, MPI–A, v. 78, pp. 18–19, reel 78. A. McFatridge to CIA, 17 August 1912, Seattle FARC, MPI–A, v. 181, pp. 87–88, reel 74.

39. Ewers, *Blackfeet*, pp. 320–21.

40. *Report on Indians Taxed and not Taxed*, p. 360. *Lake Mohonk* (1899), p. 62.

41. *DIA* 1898, p. 161. *DIA* 1899, pp. 133, xxxi. In 1905, former agent Cecil Denny wrote in his memoirs about the Blackfeet: "Missionary labor among the Blackfeet has proved . . . a failure, and I know of no instance where a full grown man or woman among the Blackfeet has been converted to Christianity." *Riders of the Plains*, p. 67.

42. Maclean, *Indians of Canada*, p. 266. S. Blake to the Archbishop of Rupert's land, 22 June 1909, PAC, v. 4024, f. 289032–2, C10174.

43. *DIA* 1909, p. 172, Goldfrank, *Changing Configuration*, p. 4.

44. Stocken, *Among the Blackfoot and Sarcee*, p. 86. Getty, "The Failure of the Native Church Policy," p. 27.

45. Stocken, *Among the Blackfoot and Sarcee*, pp. 52, 58–59.

46. G. H. Gooderham, "Northern Plains Tribes," vol. 1, Blackfeet, GAI, p. 137.

47. Harrod, *Mission among the Blackfeet*, p. 68. C. Churchill to CIA, 12 November 1909, Seattle FARC, MPI–A, v. 77, p. 497, reel 73.

48. Getty, "Failure of the Native Church Policy," pp. 21, 19, 30.

49. Grant, *Moon of Wintertime*, pp. 264–66.

50. Stocken, *Among the Blackfoot and Sarcee*, p. xv.

51. *CIA* 1902, p. 9. *DIA* 1917, p. x. There are numerous studies of Indian education in the United States. See, for example, Francis P. Prucha, *The Churches and the Indian Schools, 1888–1912* (Lincoln: University of Nebraska Press, 1979); and idem, *American Indian Policy in Crisis*. Margaret Szasz, *Education and the American Indian: The Road to Self-Determination since 1928* (Albuquerque: University of New Mexico Press, 1977). An early study of Indian education is Alice C. Fletcher, *Indian Education and Civilization*, Bureau of Education Special Report 1888 (Washington: Government Printing Office, 1888). See, also, Meriam, *Problem of Indian Administration*, pp. 11–14, 32–37, 346–428. Frederick E. Hoxie, "Redefining Indian Education, Thomas J. Morgan's Program in Disarray," *Arizona and the West* 24 (Spring 1982). Canadian studies include Gerald A. Falk, "Missionary Education Work among the Prairie Bands, 1870–1914" (Master's thesis, University of Western Ontario, 1973). Jacqueline Gresko, "White 'Rites' and Indian 'Rites,' " pp. 163–81. Eric R. Porter, "The Anglican Church and Native Education: Residential Schools and Assimilation" (Ph.D. diss., University of Toronto, 1981). Andre Renaud, *Education and the First Canadians* (Toronto: Gage Educational Publications, 1971).

52. Pliny Earle Goddard, "The Indian Problem in Canada," *The Red Man* 4 (December 1911):135. Abbott, *Administration of Indian Affairs*, p. 38.

53. Fletcher, *Indian Education*, pp. 167–68. Prucha, *American Indian Policy in Crisis*, p. 290.

54. Ponting & Gibbins, *Out of Irrelevance*, p. 20. Falk, "Missionary Education Work," p. 1.

55. Prucha, *Churches and the Indian Schools*, p. 25.

56. D. C. Scott, "Indian Affairs, 1867–1912," in *Canada and Its Provinces*, vol. 7, ed. Adam Shortt and Arthur Daugherty (Toronto: Glasgow, Brook and Co., 1914), p. 613. Memorandum of 21 March 1908, PAC, v. 6001, f. 1–1–1 pt. 2, C8134. Only the Province of Canada had maintained an Indian School Fund from contributions by several Indian bands.

57. *CIA* 1890, p. viii.

58. Richard Henry Pratt, *Battlefield and Classroom, Four Decades with the American Indian, 1865–1904*, ed. Robert Utley (New Haven: Yale University Press, 1964).

59. *CIA* 1902, p. 2. *Annual Report of the Superintendent of Indian Education, 1891* (Washington: Government Printing Office, 1891), p. 15. *CIA* 1901, p. 17. *CIA* 1907, pp. 20, 17. See discussion of the industrial schools in Robert A. Trennert, "Educating Indian Girls in Nonreservation Boarding Schools, 1878–1920," *Western Historical Quarterly* 13 (July 1982). Trennert concludes that girls educated in these schools did not assimilate into white society, nor did they manage to bring civilization to reservation Indians. Many Indian children spent their summer vacations away from their homes working and living with white families in a program called "outing." See Trennert, "From Carlisle to Phoenix: The Rise and Fall of the Indian Outing System, 1878–1930," *Pacific Historical Review* 52 (November 1983).

60. *CIA* 1906, p. 46. Day schools for Indian students were the dream of Commissioner Thomas J. Morgan. See Hoxie, "Redefining Indian Education," p. 10. Public school education found favor with many commissioners because the cost of public school education was much less than for government schools. *CIA* 1918, pp. 27–28.

61. N. F. Davin, "Indian Education," p. 4, PAC, v. 6001, f. 1–1–1 pt. 2, C8134.

62. N. F. Davin, "Report on Industrial Schools for Indians and Half-Breeds" (Ottawa: 14 March 1879), p. 13, DP Papers, file 1, box 4281. For a discussion of Indian education in the West, see Grant, *Moon of Wintertime*, p. 158.

63. Memorandum from J. A. Macdonald, 19 October 1880, PAC, v. 6001, v. 1–1–1 pt. 1, C8134. The prime minister expected to save on the construction of these schools by build-

ing them with Indian labor. The department would contribute no more than one hundred dollars for completion and for furnishings.

64. Memorandum to A. Meighen, "Notes on Indian Education," p. 2, PAC, v. 6001, f. 1–1–1 pt. 2, C8431.

65. L. G. Vankoughnet, "Indian Schools," 26 August 1887, pp. 1, 49, DP Papers, file 1, box 4281. Scott, "Indian Affairs," p. 614.

66. In 1895, High River (St. Joseph's) school owed 1,616 dollars, Regina school 880 dollars, and Qu'Appelle 1,431 dollars, Extract from the Report of the Committee of the Honorable Privy Council, 27 March 1895, PAC, v. 6001, f. 1–1–1 pt. 1, C8134.

67. H. Reed to Superintendent General, 14 May 1889, PAC, v. 3818, f. 57799, C10143. Clipping on file in PAC, n.d., v. 6001, f. 1–1–1 pt. 1, C8131.

68. *DIA* 1897, p. xxvi. The deputy superintendent general recommended using day schools in the older provinces and expanding boarding schools on reserves in the West. Falk, "Missionary Education Work," pp. 208, 47, 35.

69. Falk, "Missionary Education," p. 92. See also Grant, *Moon of Wintertime*, pp. 191–92.

70. Falk, "Missionary Education Work," pp. 107–9. Extract from the Hansard, 18 July 1904, on file in PAC, v. 6001, f. 1–1–1 pt. 1, C8134.

71. Memorandum to A. Meighen, "Notes on Indian Education," PAC, v. 6001, f. 1–1–1, pt. 2, C8134. Falk, "Missionary Education Work," pp. 46–78.

72. See, for example, comments of Dr. Alex Hrdlicka, *Lake Mohonk* (1916), p. 30. *CIA* 1907, p. 49.

73. *CIA* 1899, p. 4. Hoxie, *A Final Promise*, pp. 115–45, discusses the emergence at the end of the century of scientific racism and its impact on Indian education.

74. *DIA* 1897, p. xxvii. *DIA* 1899, p. xxvii. James Gladstone, a Blood Indian who became the first Canadian Indian senator, praised the education he received at St. Paul's Mission School and at Calgary Indian Industrial School, both operated by Anglicans. See James Gladstone, "Indian School Days," *Alberta Historical Review* 15 (Winter 1967):24.

75. Ewers, *Blackfeet*, pp. 219, 268. J. Young to CIA, 3 September 1878, Denver FARC, MPI–A, v. 2, pp. 171, 175. A very general survey is by Robert E. Howard, "A Historical Survey of the Foundation and Growth of Education on the Blackfeet Indian Reservation, 1872–1964" (Master's thesis, Western Montana College of Education, 1965.)

76. E. A. Hayt to J. Young, 10 October 1879, Denver FARC, BAC, Miscellaneous Correspondence, September–October 1879, folder 31. J. Young to CIA, 1 March 1881, Denver FARC, MPI–A, v. 3, pp. 381–82.

77. Morris, *Treaties*, p. 371.

78. Carter, "The Rev'd Samuel Trivett," pt. 1, p. 14. Maurice C. Lewis, "The Anglican Church and Its Mission Schools in Dispute," *Alberta Historical Review* 14 (Autumn 1966):7.

79. Fr. A. Lacombe to H. Reed, 7 September 1888; E. A. Forget to A. Lacombe, 26 September 1888; E. A. Forget to A. Lacombe 24 October 1888; A. Lacombe to E. A. Forget, 1 November 1888, PAC, v. 3833, f. 65138 pt. 2, C10146. C. Pinkham to H. Reed, 27 May 1887, PAC, v. 3833, f. 65138, pt. 4, C10146.

80. J. A. Macrea, "Report of Indian Schools," 21 March 1888, PAC, v. 3796, f. 40738, C10139. H. Reed (?) to J. Springett, 6 January 1888; J. Springett to H. Reed, 31 October 1887, PAC, v. 3833, f. 65138 pt. 4, C10146.

81. Superintendent Almon C. Cox to Superintendent of Indian Schools, 30 September 1889, Seattle FARC, MPI–A, v. 127, pp. 64–65, reel 77.

82. J. Z. Dare to CIA, 29 August 1905, Seattle FARC, MPI–A, v. 70, p. 66, reel 72. J. Saunders to CIA, 16 September 1908, Seattle FARC, MPI–A, v. 76, v. 252, reel 73. C. Churchill to CIA, 28 June 1909, Seattle FARC, v. 77, p. 303, reel 73.

83. These day schools were Cut Finger, Burd, Browning, and Milk River. A. McFatridge

to CIA, 11 December 1911, Seattle FARC, v. 80, p. 231, reel 74. Statistics on church attendance are from C. Churchill's annual report for 1909, Seattle FARC, MPI–A, v. 77, p. 496, reel 73. C. Churchill to CIA, 8 February 1910, Seattle FARC, MPI–A, v. 78, p. 129, reel 73. Of the 771 children between the ages of five and eighteen, only 401 attended school. Efforts to admit Blackfeet children to public schools failed because state officials refused to admit them, even though the state collected taxes on property within the reservation. A. McFatridge to CIA, 29 September 1913, Seattle FARC, MPI–A, v. 82, p. 314, reel 74. C. L. Ellis to CIA, 14 February 1916, Seattle FARC, MPI–A, reel 75; volume and page number illegible.

84. E. Legal to D. Laird, 9 March 1899; M. Bensen to Secretary of the DIA, 7 December 1899, PAC, v. 6362, v. 759–1 pt. 1, C8715.

85. D. C. Scott to the DSG, 23 April 1909, PAC, v. 6348, f. 752–1 pt. 1, C8705. *DIA 1910*, p. 477.

86. S. Stewart to E. H. Yeoman, 24 October 1912; J. D. Maclean to J. W. Tims, 22 January 1913; School Superintendent to Assistant Deputy Secretary, 26 March 1913, PAC, v. 6369, f. 763–1 pt. 1, C8720.

87. For a brief summary of this protracted episode, see Lewis, "Anglican Church and Its Mission Schools in Dispute."

88. J. C. Maclean to J. W. Tims, 17 October 1916, PAC, v. 6358, f. 758–1 pt. 1, C8713. Memorandum of D. C. Scott to J. Lougheed, 11 December 1920, PAC, v. 6348, f. 752–1 pt. 1, C8705.

89. Dr. Z. T. Daniels to G. Steell, 20 March 1892, Seattle FARC, MPI–A, v. 59, p. 72, reel 70.

90. W. R. Logan to CIA, 8 August 1899, Seattle FARC, MPI–A, v. 65, p. 69, reel 71. A. McFatridge to CIA, 19 February 1913, Seattle FARC, MPI–A,v. 81, p. 486, reel 74. W. H. Matson to W. R. Logan, 1 February 1900, Denver FARC, BAC, Miscellaneous Correspondence, folder 164, February 1900. *CIA 1900*, p. 265. R. A. Allen to CIA, 29 July 1885, Seattle FARC, MPI–A, v. 57, p. 178, reel 70. C. Churchill to CIA, 10 February 1910, Seattle FARC, MPI–A, v. 78, p. 190, reel 73.

91. A. McFatridge to E. E. McKean, 30 September and 26 October 1912, Seattle FARC, MPI–A, v. (?), pp. 52–53, 156, reel 69.

92. W. A. Jones to J. H. Monteath, 27 June 1901, Denver FARC, BAC, Miscellaneous Correspondence, 1900–1904, folder 177, May–June 1901.

93. L. W. Cooke to CIA, 1 October 1893; G. Steell to CIA, 1 January 1893, Seattle FARC, MPI–A, v. 59, p. 304, reel 70. G. Steell to CIA, 3 March 1892, Seattle FARC, MPI–A, v. 59, pp. 43–45. G. Steell to CIA, 29 January 1895, Denver FARC, BAC, Miscellaneous Correspondence, folder (?), January 1895, C. Churchill to CIA, 10 February 1910, Seattle FARC, MPI–A, v. 78, p. 190, reel 73. L. W. Cooke to CIA, 10 October 1893, Seattle FARC, MPI–A, v. 60, p. 69, reel 70.

94. T. Graham to W. M. Graham, 1 December 1919; W. M. Graham to D. C. Scott, 23 December 1919; Cannon S. Gould to D. C. Scott, 26 December 1920; W. M. Graham to D. C. Scott, 10 June 1920; J. B. R. Westgate to D. C. Scott, 4 May 1921; G. R. Gooderham to the Assistant Deputy and Secretary of the DIA, 21 June 1922, PAC, v. 6358, f. 758–1 pt. 1, C8713.

95. Corporal G. S. Stevens to T. Graham, 7 November 1920; T. Graham to the Secretary of the DIA, 15 November 1920; J. Middleton to Cannon S. Gould, 20 November 1920, PAC, v. 6369, f. 763–1, pt. 1, C8720.

96. D. C. Scott to Fr. E. Rioux, 16 December 1921; Fr. E. Rioux to D. C. Scott, 10 January 1922, PAC, v. 6348, f. 752–1, pt. 1, C8705.

97. Wilbert H. Ahern, " 'The Returned Indians': Hampton Institute and Its Indian Alumni, 1879–1893," *Journal of Ethnic Studies* 10 (Winter 1983), presents a generally positive evaluation of the graduates' lives and contributions after leaving Hampton, but his study depends

heavily on CIA reports which tend to be, to say the least, too optimistic. D. C. Scott, "Indian Affairs," p. 610. Gresko, "White 'Rites' and Indian 'Rites,' " p. 172. On the File Hill colony, see Titley, "W. M. Graham," pp. 27–28. J. D. M McLean to W. J. Dilworth, 16 March 1914, BIAC, file 97, GAI. D. C. Scott to Principal, Sarcee Boarding School, 12 March 1914, Calgary Indian Mission Papers, file 3, GAI.

98. W. R. Haynes to J. W. Tims (?), 6 December 1904, BIAC, file 2, GAI. Frank Red Crow et al. to Frank Oliver, 11 April 1911, BIAC, file 91, GAI. Abbott, *Administration of Indian Affairs,* p. 51. G. Steell to N. H. Hailman, Superintendent of Indian Schools, 28 May 1896, Denver FARC, MPI–A, v. 19, pp. 273–75.

99. A. McFatridge to CIA, 30 July 1913, Seattle FARC, MPI–A, v. 82, p. 215, reel 74. Hugh L. Scott, "Report on the Blackfeet Indian Reservation, Montana," *BIC* 1920, pp. 19–20. The commissioner discussed the need for compulsory education in his annual report *CIA* 1890, pp. xiv–xvi. In theory, compulsory education for Indian children was introduced in 1892, and in 1921 Indian agents were instructed to cooperate with state officials in the enforcement of their states' compulsory education laws on Indian reservations. Schmeckebier, *Office of Indian Affairs,* p. 223. In Canada, school attendance for Indian children was made compulsory in 1894 with little success. See Leslie and Maguire, *The Historical Development of the Indian Act,* pp. 97–98.

100. Blood agent to the Principal of Dunbow Industrial School, R. C. Mission Blood reserve, and St. Paul's Mission School, 8 August 1914, BIAC, file 91, GAI. Report of W. J. Dilworth, 1919 (?), BIAC, file 91, GAI.

101. H. A. Gunn to Superintendent of Indian Education, 5 April 1918, PAC, v. 6362, f. 759–1, pt. 1, C8715. Report of J. H. Hutchinson, 5 October 1922, PAC, v. 6342, f. 750–1 pt. 1, C8966.

102. Meriam, *Problem of Indian Administration,* pp. 11, 358, 399.

103. Extract from report of W. J. Dilworth on the Catholic boarding schools, May 1915; Assistant Deputy Secretary to Fr. E. Rioux, 13 July 1915, PAC, v. 6342, f. 750–1 pt. 1, C8960.

Chapter 7

1. Felix S. Cohen, *Handbook of Federal Indian Law* (Washington: Government Printing Office, 1942), pp. 363–65. *CIA* 1883, pp. x, xiv.

2. For the origins of Apache police, see Michael L. Tate, "Apache Scouts, Police, and Judges as Agents of Acculturation, 1865–1920" (Ph.D. diss., University of Toledo, 1974.)

3. *CIA* 1882, p. xlix. William T. Hagan, *Indian Police and Judges, Experiments in Acculturation and Control,* (Lincoln: University of Nebraska Press, 1980), p. 43. *CIA* 1884, pp. xvi–xvii.

4. Prucha, *American Indian Policy in Crisis,* p. 208. *CIA* 1883, p. xv. *CIA* 1884, p. ix. *CIA* 1890, p. lxxxiii.

5. Cohen, *Handbook,* p. 363.

6. *CIA* 1916, vol. 2, p. 63. Hagan, *Indian Police and Judges,* pp. 141–53.

7. *CIA* 1877, p. 2.

8. E. C. Morgan, "The North-West Mounted Police, Internal Problems and Public Criticism, 1874–1883," *Saskatchewan History* 26 (Spring 1973). The best treatment of the North West Mounted Police and its relations with the Indians is John Jennings, "North West Mounted Police."

9. Macleod, *North-West Mounted Police,* pp. 73–88. Jennings, "North West Mounted Police," pp. 97–98. See also Turner, *Across the Medicine Line,* for a description of the relations between Police Superintendent James M. Walsh and Sitting Bull.

10. Samuel B. Steele, *Forty Years in Canada* (Toronto: McClelland, Goodchild and Stewart, 1914), pp. 256–57. Macleod, *North-West Mounted Police*, p. 46.

11. *The Indian Act, 1876*. S. C. 1876, c. 18 (39 Vict.), s. 24.

12. *An Act to Further Amend the Indian Act, 1880*. S. C. 1882, c. 30 (45 Vict.), s. 3. Abbott, *Administration of Indian Affairs*, pp. 24–25.

13. *DIA* 1889, pp. xiii–xiv.

14. C. E. Denny to E. Dewdney (?), 1882, DP, frame 1140, reel 2. Looy, "The Indian Agent," p. 155. *DIA* 1889, pp. xiii–xiv. H. Reed to Superintendent General, 3 July 1889, PAC, v. 3818, f. 57798, C10143.

15. Memorandum of H. Reed, 30 November 1891; F. White to L. Vankoughnet, 18 February 1892, PAC, v. 3865, f. 84815, C10152.

16. Macleod, *North-West Mounted Police*, pp. 148–50. Jennings, "North West Mounted Police," p. 80.

17. J. Young to E. A. Hayt, 3 Febraury 1880, Denver FARC, MPI–A, v. 3, pp. 179–80; J. Young to CIA, 12 April 1883, Denver FARC, MPI–A, v. 5, pp. 445–48.

18. Hugh A. Dempsey, "Final Treaty of Peace," *Alberta Historical Review* 10 (Winter 1962).

19. W. B. Pocklington to H. Reed, 17 May 1889; H. Reed to DSG, 3 July 1889, PAC, v. 3818, f. 57798, C10148.

20. M. D. Baldwin to CIA, 7 May 1887, Denver FARC, MPI–A, v. 7, pp. 187–88. J. Colton to R. A. Allen, 7 December 1885, Denver FARC, BAC, Miscellaneous Correspondence, 1884–85, folder 58, January–December 1885. Evidence also shows, however, that the relations between Canadian and American authorities were less than cooperative. See Stan D. Hanson, "Policing the International Boundary Area in Saskatchewan, 1890–1910," *Saskatchewan History* 19 (Spring 1966).

21. G. Steell to S. B. Steele, 26 October 1881, Denver FARC, MPI–A, v. 10, pp. 314–15.

22. *CIA* 1882, p. x. J. Young to CIA, 17 January and 20 May 1882, Denver FARC, MPI–A, v. 5, pp. 54–59, 167–73.

23. S. B. Steele to Comptroller of NWMP, 1 December 1891, PAC, v. 3863, f. 83757, C10152. *CIA* 1894, p. 159. *DIA* 1894, p. 89.

24. G. Steell to J. Wilson, 20 August 1895, Denver FARC, MPI–A, v. 18, p. (?).

25. G. Steell to Indian Commissioners (Regina), 8 June 1897, Denver FARC, MPI–A, v. 20, p. 432. J. Z. Dare to Blood Agent, 10 April 1905, GAI, BIAC, file 13. G. B. McLaughlin to J. Wilson, 11 October 1897, Denver FARC, MPI–A, v. 20, p. 432. J. Z. Dare to Blood agent, 10 April 1905, GAI, BIAC, file 13.

26. C. Hilliard to J. Wilson, 30 November 1899; D. Laird to Blood Agent, 14 December 1899, GAI, BIAC, file 15; D. Laird to Blood Agent, 29 April 1905, GIA, BIAC, file 44; D. Laird to Blood Agent, 2 June 1900, GAI, BIAC, file 25. W. A. Jones to Secretary of the DIA, 5 December 1902, GAI, BIAC, file 14. L. D. Maclean to R. N. Wilson, 23 August 1908; R. N. Wilson to Secretarty of the DIA, 23 June 1908, GAI, BIAC, file 60.

27. G. Steell to CIA, 2 December 1891, 1 February 1892, Seattle FARC, MPI–A, v. 55, p. 448, reel 70.

28. *CIA* 1914, v. 2, p. 65.

29. W. M. Leeds to J. Young, 28 October 1878, Denver FARC, BAC, Miscellaneous Correpondence, 1878, folder 24, September–October 1878. R. N. Allen to CIA, 14 August 1884, Denver FARC, MPI–A, v. 116, pp. 42–49.

30. *CIA* 1899, p. 217. *CIA* 1886, pp. 160–72.

31. William H. Ketcham, "Report on the Blackfeet Indian Reservation," *BIC* 1919, p. 41, in *CIA* 1919.

32. *CIA* 1892, pp. 25–26.

33. *CIA* 1890, p. lxxxiv.

34. No court was established as of 1884. See R. N. Allen to CIA, 14 August 1884, Denver FARC, MPI–A, v. 116, p. 45. *CIA 1891*, pt. 1, p. 267, states that no judges were called until George Steell assumed office. G. Steell to CIA, 1 November 1890, Seattle FARC, MPI–A, v. 58, p. (?), reel 70. J. B. Baldwin to CIA, 16 September 1889, Denver FARC, MPI–A, v. 8, pp. 100–103. *CIA 1899*, p. 217.

35. *Lake Mohonk* (1899), p. 63. Cohen, *Handbook*, pp. 352–53.

36. D. M. Macleod, "Liquor Control in the North-West Territories: the Permit System, 1870–1891," *Saskatchewan History* 16 (Summer 1963). Dempsey, ed., *William Parker, Mounted Policeman* (Edmonton: Hurting Publishers, 1973), p. 39.

37. See Circular no. 13, of Commissioner E. A. Hayt, 30 March 1878, Denver FARC, BAC, Miscellaneous Correspondence, 1878, folder 21, March–April 1878. *CIA 1881*, pp. xxx–xxxi.

38. Ewers, *Blackfeet*, p. 273. For the impact of whiskey sales on the Blackfoot Confederacy, see Jennings, "The North West Mounted Police," pp. 84–85.

39. Cato Sells,"The Greatest Present Menace to the American Indians," *The Red Man* 6 (March 1914). *Lake Mohonk* (1907), p. 27. *CIA 1902*, p. 51. *CIA 1920*, pp. 46–47.

40. *The Indian Act*. R. S. C. 1886, c. 42, s. 94. *DIA 1907*, p. xxxi.

41. For a description of the problems in obtaining liquor convictions, see G. B. Grinnel, "The Enforcement of Liquor Laws, A Necessary Protection of the Indians," IRA Papers, B8, reel 102. G. Steell to CIA, 11 November 1892, and 1 January 1893, Seattle FARC, MPI–A, v. 59, pp. 277, 299, reel 70. For a history of Robare, see West, "Robare: Elusive Post in Blackfeet Country," *Montana* 15 (Summer 1965).

42. J. Z. Dare to CIA, 22 August 1905, Seattle FARC, MPI–A, v. 70 , p. 34, reel 72. A. McFatridge to CIA, 25 July 1910, Seattle FARC, MPI–A, v. 78, p. 459, reel 74.

43. J. Z. Dare to CIA, 31 December 1906, Seattle FARC, MPI–A, v. 72, p. 417, reel 72.

44. D. Laird to Blood Agent, 15 February 1901, GAI, BIAC, file 15.

45. *DIA 1899*, pp. xxx, 134. D. Laird to R. N. Wilson, 8 March 1904; F. Pedley to R. N. Wilson, 10 March 1905; J. A. Markle to R. N. Wilson, 26 June 1905, GIA, BIAC, file 13.

46. F. Pedley to R. N. Wilson, 12 April 1905, file 13; L. D. Maclean to R. N. Wilson, 31 May 1910, file 58, GIA, BIAC.

47. Transcript on file in GIA, BIAC, file 12.

48. G. Steell to W. K. Flowree, 15 February 1897, Denver FARC, MPI–A, v. 20, pp. 112–13.

49. G. Steell to CIA, 1 November 1891, Denver FARC, MPI–A, v. 10, pp. 325–30. W. A. Jones to J. A. Monteath, 21 June 1900, Denver FARC, BAC, Miscellaneous Correspondence, 1900–1901, folder 168, June 1900.

50. Jennings, "North West Mounted Police," pp. 180, 209, 357. Denny, *Riders of the Plains*, p. 177. L. W. Herchmer to Comptroller, NWMP, 7 (?) November 1887, PAC, v. 3787, f. 42389, C10135. Jennings, "North West Mounted Police," pp. 306–11, discusses several of the incidents between Mounties and the Indians.

51. W. B. Pocklington to Indian Commissioner, 9 July 1889, PAC, v. 3818, f. 57798, C10143.

52. E. Dewdney to Superintendent General, 12 September 1887, PAC, v. 3770, f. 42389, C10138.

53. (?) to Comptroller, NWMP, 8 March 1893; S. B. Steele to H. Reed, 7 (?) March 1893, PAC, v. 3900, f. 99482, C10196. This file is restricted. *DIA 1895*, p. xviii.

54. Dempsey, *Charcoal's World* (Scarborough, Ontario: McMillan–NAL Publishing, 1979), pp. 59, 18–19, 39, 153, deal with this episode in great detail.

55. Baldwin to CIA, 7 May 1887, Denver FARC, MPI–A, v. 7, pp. 188–95.

56. J. A. Monteath to CIA, 9 March 1901, Seattle FARC, MPI–A, v. 66, p. 259, reel 71. C. A. Churchill to CIA, 13 August 1909, Seattle FARC, MPI–A, v. 77, p. 364, reel 77. Legal and administrative difficulties arising out of allowing white men to receive allotments and receiv-

ing control over his Indian wife's property came to light following allotment of the reservations. See E. B. Merritt to Secretary of the Interior, 2 September 1916, NA, RG 75, BIA Central Files 1909–1939, file 11526–1916 Blackfeet 314. Also see correspondence in file 89686–1911 Blackfeet 314.

57. A. McFatridge to CIA, 20 September 1913, Seattle FARC, MPI–A, v. 82, p. 293, reel 74. *The Indian Act* R. S. C. 1886, c. 43, s. 23. For a brief discussion of the trespass problem and government complicity, see Donald R. Englund, "Indians, Intruders, and the Federal Government," *Journal of the West* 13 (April 1974).

58. J. Young to CIA, 14 May 1883, Denver FARC, MPI–A, v. 5, pp. 483–84. L. W. Cooke to CIA, 30 June 1894, Seattle FARC, MPI–A, v. 60, p. 434, reel 70; ibid., 14 August 1894, Seattle FARC, MPI–A, v. 61, p. 64, reel 70. Problems of trespass by American herds on Canadian side occurred frequently; see Hanson, "Policing the International Boundary," pp. 63–65.

59. W. A. Jones to J. A. Monteath, 2 (?) June 1900, Denver FARC, BAC, Miscellaneous Correspondence 1900–1901, folder 168, June 1900. J. A. Monteath to CIA, 24 December 1900, Seattle FARC, MPI–A, v. 66, p. 183, reel 71. The BIA authorized reservation fencing in the next several years.

60. Memorandum of E. H. Yeomans, 1 December 1911, PAC, Blue Books, p. 81, v. 10030, C11060.

61. Macleod, *North-West Mounted Police*, p. 44. Hanson, "Policing the International Boundary," p. 61. Jennings, "North West Mounted Police," pp. 303–4, 308. J. A. Monteath to CIA, 8 June 1900, Seattle FARC, MPI–A, v. 78, p. 238, reel 73. A. McFatridge to CIA, 21 November 1910 and 28 June 1911, Seattle FARC, MPI–A, v. 79, pp. (?), 402, reel 74.

62. A. McFatridge to CIA, 18 April 1912, Seattle FARC, MPI–A, v. 80, p. 348, reel 74.

Chapter 8

1. Hoxie, *Final Promise*, pp. 115–45.

2. This theme is discussed in Dippie, *The Vanishing American*. Anthropologist Alice Fletcher commented on the decline of Indian population in *Indian Education and Civilization*, p. 152. See also J. Nixon Hadley, "The Demography of the American Indian," *Annals of the American Academy of Political and Social Sciences* 311 (May 1957):23–24. Denny, *Riders of the Plains*, p. 67. Maclean, *Canada's Savage Folk*, p. 298. Schmeckebier, *Office of Indian Affairs*, pp. 231, 229; statistics are on p. 232. Death-rate statistics are from Charles A. Eastman, "The Indian's Health," *The Popular Science Monthly* 86 (January 1915):49. Meriam, *Problem of Indian Administration*, p. 189.

3. Schmeckebier, *Office of Indian Affairs*, pp. 231, 229; statistics are on p. 232. Death-rate statistics are from Eastman, "The Indian's Health," p. 45. Meriam, *Problem of Indian Administration*, p. 189.

4. Frederick L. Hoffman, "Medical Problems of our Indian Population," *The Eastern Association on Indian Affairs* (5 February 1925), Bulletin no. 6.

5. Anna F. Gough, "Public Health in Canada, 1867–1967," *Medical Services Journal, Canada* 23 (January 1967):33. Frank Pedley stated in 1912 that the department employed two hundred physicians. Most physicians were probably not working on a full-time basis. See Frank Pedley,"The Indian Question from a Canadian Standpoint," *Lake Mohonk* (1912), p. 96. Information on the history of Indian health care is from G. Graham-Cummings, "Health of the Original Canadians, 1867–1967," *Medical Services Journal, Canada* 23 (February 1967):117, 122–25. Graham-Cummings cites extensively a Master's thesis on Indian health by Lt. C.

R. Maundrell, written before World War II. Maundrell states that Bryce worked for the DIA from 1905 to 1910. However, Peter H. Bryce, *The Story of a National Crime, An Appeal for Justice to the Indians of Canada* (Ottawa: James Hope and Sons, 1922), p. 8, uses the dates I have cited.

6. Bryce, *Report on the Indian Schools of Manitoba and the North-West Territories* (Ottawa: Government Printing Bureau, 1907), p. 18. *DIA 1913*, p. 296. See, also, Bryce, *Story of a National Crime*.

7. Accurate statistics about diseases among the Indians during this period are virtually impossible to obtain. For example, reporters at the Lake Mohonk conference in 1911 placed the Indian death rate due to tuberculosis at 40.1 percent per thousand. See Dr. Joseph A. Murphy, "Health Conditions among the Indians," *Lake Mohonk* (1911), p. 41. *Contagious and Infectious Diseases among the Indians*, Senate Doc. 1038, pp. 40, 19, 62d Cong., 3d sess., 27 January 1913, serial 6365. Blacks had a tuberculosis death rate of 33.9 percent per thousand, nearly as high as that of the Indians.

8. *Conduct and Management of Indian Schools*, Senate Doc. 201, 57th Cong., 1st sess., 7 February 1902, serial 4234. *CIA 1902*, pp. 29–30, contains the innoculation order. *Contagious and Infectious Diseases*, p. 79.

9. *Contagious and Infectious Diseases*, pp. 66, 61.

10. *CIA 1892*, p. 282. *CIA 1898*, p. 182. *Conduct and Management of Indian Schools*, pp. 4–6. A. McFatridge to W. K. Moorehead, 20 April 1914, Seattle FARC, MPI–A, v. (?), p. 299, reel 69. A. McFatridge to CIA, 6 October 1913, Seattle FARC, MPI–A, v. 82, p. 332, reel 74.

11. In 1877 the BIA announced the appointment of a physician to the Blackfeet reservation at 1,200 dollars annually. See memorandum of 13 September 1877, Denver FARC, Blackfoot Miscellaneous Correspondence, 1877, folder 17, September–October. *CIA 1898*, p. 182. *Conduct and Management of Indian Schools*, p. 4. This hospital did not operate continuously.

12. C. Churchill to CIA, 9, 13 July 1909, Seattle FARC, MPI–A, v. 77, p. 312, 321, reel 73. C. Churchill to CIA, 7, 26 March 1910, Seattle FARC, MPI–A, v. 82, p. 407, reel 74. A. McFatridge to CIA, 8 February 1913, Seattle FARC, MPI–A, v. (?), p. 405, reel 69. A. McFatridge to CIA, 13 January 1914, Seattle FARC, MPI–A, v. 82, p. 490, reel 74.

13. *Indian Appropriation Bill*, hearings before the Committee on Indian Affairs, on H. R. 10385, 64th Cong., 1st sess., 16 February 1916, pp. 146, 156.

14. Elsie Eaton Newton, "A Health Campaign among the Blackfeet Indians," *Lake Mohonk* (1916).

15. Jenness, "Canada's Indian Problems," *America Indigena* 11 (January 1941):32.

16. Peigan Census, 1 December 1888, PAC, v. 3804, f. 50774–12, C10140. *DIA 1899*, p. 169. *DIA 1901*, p. 166. *DIA 1909*, p. 186.

17. Blackfoot Census, 1 January 1889, PAC, v. 3804, f. 50774–14, C10140. *DIA 1896*, p. 151. *DIA 1901*, p. 128. *DIA 1910*, p. 162. *DIA 1886*, p. 138. Dempsey, *Crowfoot*, pp. 196–200.

18. J. B. Lash to Blood agent, 6 July 1899, BIAC, file 15, GAI.

19. J. McKenna to R. N. Wilson, 19 March 1904, BIAC, file 21, GAI. *DIA 1883*, p. xvi. *DIA 1889*, p. xxix. *DIA 1900*, p. 138. *DIA 1910*, p. 163. *DIA 1891*, p. xv. *DIA 1909*, p. xxiv.

20. *DIA 1884*, p. liii.

21. Stocken, *Among the Blackfoot and Sarcee*, pp. 13, 38, 34, 68–69, 47, 55. The DIA eventually built a larger hospital on the reserve. DIA *1915*, pt. 2, p. 75. The Catholics had operated a hospital on the Blood reserve. *DIA 1899*, p. 132. *DIA 1909*, p. 172.

22. Abbott, *Administration of Indian Affairs*, p. 81.

23. Franz Boaz, "The Half Blood Indian, an Anthropological Study," *Popular Science Monthly* 45 (May–October 1894).

24. G. Steell to CIA, 4 August 1891, Seattle FARC, MPI-A, v. 58, p. 340, reel 70. See also Moorehead, *The American Indian*, pp. 379, 381. Leupp, *Indian and His Problem*, p. 345.

25. *SI* 1912, vol. 2, p. 76. *CIA* 1905–6, p. 237.

26. Ewers, *Blackfeet*, p. 320.

27. *BIC* 1921, p. 56.

28. W. Everard Edmonds, "Canada's Red Army," *Canadian Magazine of Politics, Science, Art and Literature* 56 (February 1921):341. *SI* vol. 2, 1918, p. 5.

29. Verne de Witt Rowell,"Canadian Indians at the Front," *Current History* 6 (August 1917):290–92. *DIA* 1917, pt. 2, p. 17. James Dempsey, "The Indians and World War One," *Alberta History* 31 (Summer 1983):4. *SI* 1918, vol. 2, p. 16.

30. *The Winnipeg Free Press*, 13 October 1920, clipping on file in PAC, v. 3181, f. 452, 124–1A, C11335. James Dempsey, "The Indians and World War One," pp. 1–8. *The Sun* (New York), 9 April 1919, clipping on file in the PAC, v. 3181, f. 452–1A, C11335. See, for example, *The Globe* (Toronto, Ontario), 27 September 1918; and *The Intelligencer* (Belleville, Ontario), 24 February 1919, clipping on file, PAC, v. 3181, f. 452, 124–1A, C11335.

31. *SI* 1919, vol. 2, p. 8. *DIA* 1918, p. 14.

32. McFee, *Modern Blackfeet*, p. 53. James Dempsey, "Indians and World War One," p. 3. W. J. Dilworth to Assistant Department Secretary, 27 November 1915, PAC, v. 3182, f. 452, 124–6, C11335. J. A. Markle to Secretary, 30 November 1915, PAC, v. 3182, f. 452, 124–6, C11335. "Canadian Indians Showing their Loyalty in This War," n.d., clipping on file in PAC, v. 3180, f. 452, 124–1, C11335.

33. See, for example, Edmonds, "Canada's Red Army," p. 342. J. D. Maclean to Thomas Deasy, 8 September 1922, PAC, v. 3181, f. 452, 124–1A, C11335.

34. Hanks and Hanks, *Tribe under Trust*, pp. 51–52, 103–9. Roma Standefer, "A Program of Directed Economic Change for the Northern Blackfoot Reservation," p. 18, GAI.

Conclusion

1. White, *The Roots of Dependency*.

2. Several anthropologists studied the question of Blackfeet acculturation. The Hankses had observed this about the Canadian Blackfoot: "Yet by 1920 more than a generation of Indians had passed, and despite the decades of exposure to the obvious benefits of white civilization, the inhabitants of the reserve remain largely Indian in outlook." Hanks and Hanks, *Tribe Under Trust*, p. 51. Esther Goldfrank, who studied the Bloods in 1939, noted social conflicts and aggressiveness that displaced the former need for cooperation during buffalo-hunting days, but concluded that reserve life had not altered generally the general characteristics of the Bloods. Goldfrank, *Changing Configuration*, pp. 3, 12, 71. A somewhat similar conclusion is reached by Clayton Denman, "Cultural Change among the Blackfeet Indians of Montana" (Ph.D. diss., University of California, Berkeley, 1968). McFee, in "The 150% Man, A Product of Blackfeet Acculturation," *American Anthropology* 70 (December 1968), and in *Modern Blackfeet*, discusses Blackfeet society in terms of "white-oriented" and "Indian-oriented" individuals rather than in terms of simply a progressive scale toward full assimilation. There does not appear to be a similar study of the North Peigans, the smallest group of the Confederacy. Although they had made

a successful early transition to a ranching economy, their population declined until they were on the verge of extinction.

3. House of Commons (Canada), *Report of the Special Committee on Indian Self-government in Canada*, 12 and 20 October, 1983; also called the Penner Report. The study of aboriginal policies of other countries is in "The Government of Aboriginal Peoples, An Executive Summary," report courtesy of Dr. John Leslie, Historical Treaties and Research Center, DIAND.

4. A. Harper to J. Collier, 24 October 1944, Collier Papers II–151, frame 205.

5. Ponting and Gibbins, *Out of Irrelevance*, p. x.

Selected Bibliography

Books

Allen, Richard, ed. *Religion and Society in the Prairie West*. Canadian Plains Studies 3, Canadian Plains Research Center, University of Regina. Regina: University of Saskatchewan, 1974.

Barsch, Russell L., and James Youngblood Henderson. *The Road, Indian Tribes and Political Liberty*. Berkeley: University of California Press, 1980.

Beaver, R. P. *Church, State and the American Indian*. St. Louis: Concordia Publishing House, 1966.

Berkhofer, Robert F. *Salvation and the Savage: An Analysis of Protestant Missions and Indian Response, 1787–1862*. Louisville: University of Kentucky Press, 1965.

Bryce, Peter H. *The Story of a National Crime, An Appeal for Justice to the Indians of Canada*. Ottawa: James Hope and Sons, 1922.

Cardinal, Harold. *The Unjust Society*. Edmonton: Hurting, 1969.

Carlson, Leonard A. *Indians, Bureaucrats, and Land: The Dawes Act and the Decline of Indian Farming*. Westport, Conn.: Greenwood Press, 1981.

Carter, David J. *Where the Wind Blows: A History of the Anglican Diocese of Calgary*. Calgary: Kyle Printers, 1968.

Chalmers, John W. *Laird of the West*. Calgary: Detseling Enterprises, 1981.

Chamberlain, J. E. *The Harrowing of Eden, White Attitudes toward Native Americans*. New York: Seabury Press, 1975.

Cross, Michael S., ed. *The Frontier Thesis and the Canadas: The Debate on the Impact of the Canadian Environment*. Toronto: The Capp Clark Publishing Co., 1970.

Dempsey, Hugh A. *Charcoal's World*. Scarborough, Ontario: McMillan–NAL Publishing, 1979.

———. *Crowfoot, Chief of the Blackfeet*. Norman: University of Oklahoma Press, 1972.

———. *Men in Scarlet*. Calgary: McClelland-Stewart West, 1974.

———. *Red Crow, Warrior Chief*. Lincoln: University of Nebraska Press, 1980.

———. *Scarlet and Gold*. 36th ed. N. p., 1954.

———. *William Parker, Mounted Policeman*. Edmonton: Hurting Publishers, 1973.

Denny, Cecil Edward. *The Law Marches West*. Toronto: Dent Co., 1939.

———. *The Riders of the Plains*. Calgary: Herald Co., 1905.

Dippie, Brian. *The Vanishing American, White Attitudes and U.S. Indian Policy*. Middleton, Conn.: Wesleyan University Press, 1982.

Economic Development in American Indian Reservations, Native American Studies, Albuquerque: New Mexico, 1979.

Ewers, John C. *The Blackfeet Indians, Ethnological Report of the Blackfeet and Gros Ventre Tribes of Indians*. American Indian Ethnohistory Series. New York: Garland Publishing Co., 1974.

———. *The Blackfeet, Raiders of the Northwestern Plains*. Norman: University of Oklahoma Press, 1958.

———. *Indian Life on the Upper Missouri*. Norman: University of Oklahoma Press, 1968.

Getty, Ian A. L., and Donald B. Smith, eds. *One Century Later: Western Canadian Reserve Indians since Treaty 7*. Vancouver: University of British Columbia Press, 1978.

Goldfrank, Esther. *Changing Configuration in the Social Organization of a Blackfoot Tribe during the Reserve Period. The Bloods of Alberta, Canada*. American Ethnological Society Monograph Series, no. 8. Seattle: University of Washington Press, 1966.

Graham, Elizabeth. *Medicineman to Missionary: Missionaries as Agents of Change among the Indians of Southern Ontario. 1784–1867*. Toronto: P. Martin Associates, 1975.

Grant, John Webster. *Moon of Wintertime, Missionaries and the Indians of Canada in Encounter since 1534*. Toronto: University of Toronto Press, 1984.

Gray, James H. *Booze: The Impact of Whiskey on the Prairie West*. Toronto: Macmillan of Canada, 1972.

Hagan, E. E., and Lewis C. Shaw. *The Sioux on Reservations: The American Colonial Problem*. Cambridge, Mass.: Center for International Studies, 1960.

Hagan, William T. *Indian Police and Judges, Experiments in Acculturation and Control*. Lincoln: University of Nebraska Press, 1980.

———. *The Indian Rights Association, The Herbert Welsh Years, 1882–1904*. Tucson: University of Arizona Press, 1985.

Hall, D. J. *Clifford Sifton, The Young Napoleon, 1861–1900*. Vol. 1. Vancouver: University of British Columbia Press, 1981.

Handy, Robert T. *A Christian America: Protestant Hopes and Historical Realities*. New York: Oxford University Press, 1971.

Hanks, Lucien M., and Jane Richardson. *Observations on Northern Blackfoot Kinship*. Monographs of the American Ethnological Society, no. 9. Seattle: University of Washington Press, 1945.

———. *Tribe under Trust, A Study of the Blackfoot Reserve of Alberta*. Toronto: University of Toronto Press, 1950.

Harrod, Howard L. *Mission among the Blackfeet*. Norman: University of Oklahoma Press, 1971.

Hoxie, Frederick H. *A Final Promise, The Campaign to Assimilate the Indians, 1880–1920*. Lincoln: University of Nebraska Press, 1983.

Jackson, Helen Hunt. *A Century of Dishonor, A Sketch of the United States Government's Dealings with Some of the Indian Tribes*. Minneapolis: Ross and Haines, 1964.

Jamieson, Kathleen. *Indian Women and the Law in Canada: Citizens Minus*. Ottawa: Minister of Supply and Services Canada, 1978.

Jenness, Diamond. *The Indians of Canada*. Toronto: University of Toronto Press, 1977.

Kammen, Michael, ed. *The Past Before Us: Comparative Historical Writings in the United States.* Ithaca: Cornell University Press, 1980.

Keller, Robert H. *American Protestantism and United States Indian Policy, 1869–1882.* Lincoln: University of Nebraska Press, 1983.

Kvasnicka, Robert M., and Herman J. Viola. *The Commissioners of Indian Affairs, 1824–1977.* Lincoln: University of Nebraska Press, 1979.

LaFarge, Oliver, ed. *The Changing Indian.* Norman: University of Oklahoma Press, 1942.

Leupp, Francis E. *The Indian and His Problem.* New York: Arno Press, 1971.

Lewis, Oscar. *The Effects of White Contact upon Blackfoot Culture with Special Reference to the Role of the Fur Trade.* American Ethnological Society Monograph Series, no. 6. Seattle: University of Washington Press, 1942.

Little Bear, Leroy, Menno Boldt, and J. Anthony Long. *Pathways to Self-Determination: Canadian Indians and the Canadian State.* Toronto: University of Toronto Press, 1984.

Lora, Roland, ed. *The American West, Essays in Honor of W. Eugene Hollon.* Toledo, Ohio: University of Toledo Press, 1980.

Loram, C. T., and T. L. McIlwraith, eds. *The North American Indian Today: University of Toronto–Yale University Seminar–Conference, Toronto, September 4–16, 1939.* Toronto: University of Toronto Press, 1943.

McFee, Malcolm. *Modern Blackfeet, Montanans on a Reservation.* New York: Holt, Rinehart and Winston, 1972.

Macleod, R. C. *The North-West Mounted Police and Law Enforcement, 1873–1905.* Toronto: University of Toronto Press, 1976.

Maclean, John. *Canadian Savage Folk.* Toronto: William Briggs, 1896.

———. *The Indians of Canada, Their Manners and Customs.* London: Charles H. Kelly, 1892.

Martin, Chester. *Dominion Lands Policy.* Edited by Louis H. Thomas. Toronto: McClelland and Stewart, 1973.

Meriam, Lewis, et al. *The Problem of Indian Administration.* Institute for Government Research, Studies in Administration. Baltimore: Johns Hopkins Press, 1929.

Miller, David H., and Jerome O. Steffen, eds. *The Frontier: Comparative Studies.* Norman: University of Oklahoma Press, 1977.

Moorehead, Warren K. *The American Indian in the United States Period, 1850–1914.* Andover, Mass.: The Andover Press, 1914.

———. *Plan of Reorganization of the Indian Service.* Andover, Mass.: n. p., 15 December 1925.

Morris, Alexander. *The Treaties of Canada with the Indians.* Toronto: Coles Publishing Co., 1979.

Muise, D. A., ed. *Approaches to Native History in Canada: Papers of a Conference Held at the National Museum of Man, October 1975.* Ottawa: National Museum of Man, 1975.

Nix, James E. *Mission among the Buffalo: The Labours of the Reverends George M. and John C. McDougall in the Canadian North West, 1860–1876.* Toronto: Ryerson Press, 1963.

Otis, D. S. *The Dawes Act and the Allotment of Indian Lands.* Edited by F. P. Prucha. Norman: University of Oklahoma Press, 1973.

Patterson, E. Palmer. *The Canadian Indian: A History since 1500.* Don Mills, Ontario: Collier–Macmillan, 1972.

Ponting, J. Rick, and Roger Gibbins. *Out of Irrelevence: A Socio-Political Introduction to Indian Affairs in Canada.* Toronto: Butterworth, 1980.

Pratt, Richard Henry. *Battlefield and Classroom, Four Decades with the American Indian, 1865–1904.* Edited by Robert Utley. New Haven: Yale University Press, 1964.

Price, Richard, ed. *The Spirit of Alberta Treaties.* Montreal: Institute for Research on Public Policy and Indian Association of Alberta, 1980.

Prucha, Francis Paul. *American Indian Policy in Crisis: Christian Reformers and the American Indian, 1865–1900.* Norman: University of Oklahoma Press, 1976.

———. *American Indian Policy in the Formative Years.* Lincoln: University of Nebraska Press, 1962.

———. *Americanizing the American Indians, Writings by the Friends of the Indian, 1880–1910.* Cambridge, Mass.: Harvard University Press, 1973.

———. *The Churches and the Indian Schools, 1888–1912.* Lincoln: University of Nebraska Press, 1979.

———. *The Great Father, The United States Government and the American Indians.* Lincoln: University of Nebraska Press, 1984.

———. *Indian Policy in the United States, Historical Essays.* Lincoln: University of Nebraska Press, 1981.

Rasporich, Anthony W., ed. *Western Canada: Past and Present.* Calgary: McClelland and Stewart West, 1975.

Ray, Arthur J. *Indians in the Fur Trade.* Toronto: University of Toronto Press, 1974.

Renaud, Andre. *Education and the First Canadians.* Toronto: Gage Educational Publications, 1971.

Schmeckebier, Lawrence F. *The Office of Indian Affairs, Its History, Activities and Organization.* Baltimore: Johns Hopkins Press, 1927.

Sharp, Paul. *Whoop Up Country, The Canadian--American West, 1865–1885.* Norman: University of Oklahoma Press, 1978.

Shortt, Adam, and Arthur G. Daugherty, eds. *Canada and Its Provinces.* 8 vols. Toronto: Glasgow, Brook and Co., 1914.

Stanley, George F. G. *The Birth of Western Canada, A History of the Riel Rebellions.* Toronto: University of Toronto Press, 1961.

Steele, Samuel B. *Forty Years in Canada.* Toronto: McClelland, Goodchild and Stewart, 1914.

Stocken, H. W. Gibbon. *Among the Blackfoot and Sarcee.* Calgary: Glenbow–Alberta Institute, 1976.

Stuart, Paul. *The Indian Office, Growth and Development of an American Institution, 1865–1900.* Ann Arbor, Mich.: University Microfilms International Research Press, 1978.

Surtees, Robert J. *Canadian Indian Policy, A Critical Bibliography.* Bloomington: Indiana University Press, 1982.

Szasz, Margaret. *Education and the American Indian: The Road to Self-Determination since 1928.* Albuquerque: University of New Mexico Press, 1977.

Tanner, Adrian, ed. *The Politics of Indianness, Case Studies of Native Ethnopolitics in Canada.* St. Johns's Newfoundland: Memorial University of Newfoundland, 1983.

Thomas, L. H. *The Struggle for Responsible Government in the North West Territories, 1870–1897.* Toronto: University of Toronto Press, 1956.

Thompson, Leonard, and Howard Lamar, eds. *The Frontier in History, North America and Southern Africa Compared.* New Haven: Yale University Press, 1981.

Turner, Frank C. *Across the Medicine Line, The Epic Confrontation between Sitting Bull and the North West Mounted Police*. Toronto: McClelland and Stewart, 1973.

Waite, Peter B. *Canada, 1874–1896, An Arduous Destiny*. Toronto: McClelland and Stewart, 1976.

Wallace, W. ed. *The Macmillan Dictionary of Canadian Biography*. 3rd ed. Toronto: Mcmilland Co. of Canada, 1963.

Walsh, H. H. *The Christian Church in Canada*. Toronto: Ryerson Press, 1956.

Weaver, Sally M.*Making of Canadian Indian Policy, The Hidden Agenda, 1968–1979*. Toronto: University of Toronto Press, 1981.

White, Richard. *The Roots of Dependency: Subsistence, Environment, and Social Change among the Choctaws, Pawnees, and Navajos*. Lincoln: University of Nebraska Press, 1983.

Wyman, Walker D., and Clifton B. Kroeber, eds.*The Frontier in Perspective*.Madison: University of Wisconsin Press, 1957.

Periodicals

Ahern, Wilbert H. " 'The Returned Indians': Hampton Institute and Its Indian Alumni, 1879–1893." *Journal of Ethnic Studies* 10 (Winter 1983): 101–24.

Andrews, Isabel, "Indian Protest against Starvation: The Yellow Calf Incident, 1884." *Saskatchewan History* 28 (Spring 1975):41–50.

Annual Reports of the Lake Mohonk Conference of Friends of the Indian and Other Dependent People. (Lake Mohonk, N.Y.: 1883–1916).

Baker, Donald G. "Color, Culture, and Power: Indian–White Relations in Canada and America." *The Canadian Review of American Studies* 3 (Spring 1972): 3–20.

Baptie, Sue. "Edgar Dewdney." *Alberta Historical Review* 16 (Autumn 1968):1–10.

Barrass, Georgeen, "A Friend of the Indians." *Glenbow* 2 (March 1969):6–8.

Barry, Edward E., Jr. "From Buffalo to Beef:Assimilation on Fort Belknap Reservation." *Montana* 26 (January 1976):38–51.

Berens, John F. "Old Campaigns, New Realities: Indian Policy Reform in the Progressive Era, 1900–1912." *Mid-America* 59 (January 1977):51–64.

Boaz, Franz, "The Half Blood Indian, An Anthropological Study." *Popular Science Monthly* 45 (May–October 1894):761–70.

Burchill, C. S. "The Origins of Canadian Irrigation Law." *The Canadian Historical Review* 29 (September 1948):353–62.

Cameron, Bleasdale. "The North West Redman and His Future." *The Canadian Magazine* 14 (January 1900):23–26.

Careless, J. M. S. "Frontierism, Metropolitanism, and Canadian History." *The Canadian Historical Review* 35 (March 1954):1–21.

Carlson, Leonard A. "Federal Policy and Indian Land: Economic Interests and the Sale of Indian Allotments, 1900–1934." *Agricultural History* 57 (January 1983):33–45.

Carter, David J. "The Rev'd. Samuel Trivett." part l, *Alberta Historical Review* 21 (Spring 1973):13–19.

———. "The Rev'd Samuel Trivett." part 2, *Alberta Historical Review* 21 (Summer 1973):18–27.

Cornish, F. C. "The Blackfeet and the Rebellion, Experiences of an Agency Clerk in 1885," *Alberta Historical Review* 6 (Spring 1958):20–26.

Cummings, Peter A., et al. "The Rights of Indigenous People," *American Society of International Law* 68 (1974):265–301.

Dempsey, Hugh A. "Blackfoot or Blackfeet?" *Glenbow:* 4 (May–June 1971):7–8.

———. "Final Treaty of Peace." *Alberta Historical Review* 10 (Winter 1962):8–16.

———. "The 'Thin Red Line' in the Canadian West." *American West* 7 (January 1970):24–30.

———. "An Unwilling Diary." *Alberta Historical Review* 7 (Summer 1959):7–10.

Dempsey, James. "The Indians and World War One," *Alberta History* 31 (Summer 1983):1–8.

Den Otter, Andy A. "Irrigation in Southern Alberta, 1882–1901." *Great Plain Journal* 11 (Spring 1972):125–37.

Dinwiddie, Peter W. "The Nature of the Relationship between the Blackfeet Indians and the Men of the Fur Trade." *Annals of Wyoming* 46 (Spring 1974):123–35.

Downes, Randolph C. "A Crusade for Indian Reform, 1927–1934." *Mississippi Valley Historical Review* 32 (December 1945):331–45.

Eastman, Charles A. "The Indians' Health Problem." *The Popular Science Monthly* 86 (January 1915):49–54.

Editor. "The White Man's Greed," *The Red Man* 8 (December 1918) :113–15.

———. "Mohonk and the Indians." *The Red Man* 5 (November 1911) :123.

Edmonds, W. Everard. "Canada's Red Army." *Canadian Magazine of Politics, Science, Art, and Literature* 56 (February 1921):340–42.

Englund, Donald R. "Indians, Intruders, and the Federal Government." *Journal of the West* 13 (April 1974):97–105.

Evans, Simon M. "American Cattlemen on Canadian Range, 1874–1914." *Prairie Forum* 4 (Winter 1979):121–35.

Fair Play (pseudonym). "The Future of Our Indians." *The Canadian Indian* 1 (March 1891):157–60.

Fritz, Henry E. "The Last Hurrah of Christian Humanitarian Indian Reform: The Board of Indian Commissioners, 1909–1918." *The Western Historical Quarterly* 16 (April 1985):147–62.

Furman, Necah. "Seed Time for Indian Reform: An Evaluation of the Administration of Commissioner Francis Ellington Leupp." *Red River Valley Historical Review* 2 (Winter 1975):495–517.

Gladstone, James. "Indian School Days." *Alberta Historical Review* 15 (Winter 1967):18–24.

Goddard, Pliny Earle. "The Indian Problem in Canada." *The Red Man* 4 (December 1911):133–36.

Goldfrank, Esther. "Administrative Programs and Change in Blood Society during the Reserve Period." *Applied Anthropology* 2 (January–March 1943):18–23.

Gough, Anna F. "Public Health in Canada, 1867–1967." *Medical Services Journal, Canada* 23 (January 1967):32–41.

Graham-Cummings, G. "Health of the Original Canadians, 1867–1967." *Medical Services Journal, Canada* 23 (February 1967):115–66.

Grant, S. D. "Indian Affairs under Duncan Campbell Scott, the Plains Cree of Saskatchewan, 1913–1930." *Journal of Canadian Studies* 18 (Fall 1983):21–37.

Hadley, J. Nixon. "The Demography of the American Indians." *Annals of the American Academy of Political and Social Sciences* 311 (May 1957):23–30.

Hagan, William T. "Civil Service Commissioner T. Roosevelt and the Indian Rights Association." *Pacific Historical Review* 44 (May 1975):187–200.

Hall, D. J. "Clifford Sifton and Canadian Indian Administration, 1896–1905." *Prairie Forum* 2 (November 1977):127–51.

———. "The Half-Breed Claims Commission." *Alberta History* 25 (Spring 1977): 1–8.

Hanson, Stan D. "Policing the International Boundary Area in Saskatchewan, 1890–1910." *Saskatchewan History* 19 (Spring 1966):61–73.

Harper, Allan G. "Canada's Indian Administration: Basic Concepts and Objectives." *America Indigena* 5 (April 1945):118–32.

———. "Canada's Indian Administration: The Indian Act." *America Indigena* 6 (October 1946):296–313.

———. "Canada's Indian Administration: The Treaty System." *America Indigena* 7 (April 1947):129–43.

Harrod, Howard. "The Blackfeet and the Divine Establishment." *Montana* 22 (January 1972):42–51.

Hoffman, Frederick L. "Medical Problem of our Indian Population." *The Eastern Association on Indian Affairs*, 5 February 1925, Bulletin no. 6.

Hoxie, Frederick. "The End of the Savage, Indian Policy and United States Senate, 1880–1900." *Chronicles of Oklahoma* 55 (Summer 1977):157–79.

———. "Redefining Indian Education: Thomas J. Morgan's Program in Disarray." *Arizona and the West* 24 (Spring 1982):5–18.

Hutton, Paul A. "Phil Sheridan's Pyrrhic Victory: The Peigan Massacre, Army Politics and the Transfer Debate." *Montana* 32 (Spring 1982):32–43.

"The Indian as Farmer," *The Red Man* 8 (December 1915):111–13.

"The Indian Difficulty." *The Nation* (31 December 1868):545.

Jackson, W. Turrentine. "A Brief Message to the Young and/or Ambitious: Comparative Frontier as Field for Investigation." *Western Historical Quarterly* 9 (January 1978):5–18.

Jenness, Diamond. "Canada's Indian Problems." *America Indigena* 11 (January 1941) :29–38.

Joyner, Christopher. "The Hegira of Sitting Bull to Canada: Diplomatic Realpolitic, 1876–1881." *Journal of the West* 13 (April 1974) :6–18.

Knapp, Roland G., and Lawrence M. Hauptman. "'Civilization over Savagery': the Japanese, the Formosan Frontier, and United States Indian Policy, 1895–1915." *Pacific Historical Review* 49 (November 1980):647–52.

Kolchin, Peter. "Comparing American History." *Reviews in American History* 10 (December 1982):64–81.

Kutzleb, Charles R. "Educating the Dakota Sioux, 1876–1890." *North Dakota History* 32 (October 1965):197–215.

Lalonde, Andre N. "The North-West Rebellion and Its Effects on Settlers and Settlement in the Canadian West." *Saskatchewan History* 27 (Autumn 1974) :95–112.

Larmour, Jean. "Edgar Dewdney and the Aftermath of the Rebellion." *Saskatchewan History* 23 (Autumn 1970):106–17.

———. "Edgar Dewdney, Indian Commissioner in the Transitional Period of Indian Settlement, 1879–1884." *Saskatchewan History* 33 (Winter 1980):13–24.

Lee, Lawrence B. "The Canadian-American Irrigation Frontier, 1884–1914." *Agricultural History* 40 (October 1966):271–83.

Leupp, Francis E. "Outlines of an Indian Policy." *Outlook* 79 (15 April 1905):946–50.

———. "Spoilsmen and Indian Agencies." *The Nation* 65 (28 October 1897):333–34.
Lewis, Maurice C. "The Anglican Church and Its Mission Schools in Dispute." *Alberta Historica Review* 14 (Autumn 1966):7–13.
Linnen, E. B. "Our Indian People." *The Red Man* 8 (October 1915):61–66.
Looy, A. J. "Saskatchewan's First Indian Agent, M. G. Dickieson." *Saskatchewan History* 32 (August 1979):104–15.
McDonnell, Janet. "Competency Commissions and Indian Land Policy." *South Dakota History* 11 (Winter 1980):21–34.
McFee, Malcolm. "The 150% Man, a Product of Blackfeet Acculturation." *American Anthropologist* 70 (December 1968):1096–1103.
MacInnes, T. R. L. "History of Indian Administration in Canada." *Canadian Journal of Economics and Political Science* 12 (1946):387–94.
McQuillan, D. Aidan, "Creation of Indian Reserves on the Canadian Prairies, 1870–1885." *The Geographical Review* (Canada) 70 (October 1980):379–96.
Macleod, D. M. "Liquor Control in the North-West Territories: The Permit System, 1870–1891." *Saskatchewan History* 16 (Summer 1963):81–89.
Mallory, Garrick. "The Indian Systems of Canada and the United States." *The Nation* 636 (6 September 1877):147–49.
Mickenberg, Neil H. "Aboriginal Rights in Canada and the United States." *Osgood Hall Law Review* 9 (1971):119–55.
Miles, Nelson A. "The Indian Problem" (1879). The North American Review 10 (Winter 1973):40–44.
Montgomery, Malcolm. "The Six Nations and the Macdonald Franchise." *Ontario History* 57 (March 1965):13–25.
Morgan, E. C. "The North-West Mounted Police: Internal Problems and Public Criticism, 1874–1883." *Saskatchewan History* 26 (Spring 1973):41–62.
Morton, Desmond. "Cavalry or Police: Keeping Peace on Two Adjacent Frontiers." *Journal of Canadian Studies* 12 (December 1977):27–37.
Murphy, Joseph A. "Health Conditions among the Indians." *Lake Mohonk* (1911):41–46.
———. "Health Problems of the Indians." *Annals of American Academy of Political and Social Science* 37 (March 1911):347–53.
Newton, Elsie Eaton. "Health Campaign among the Blackfeet Indians." *Lake Mohonk* (1916):107–11.
Patterson. E. Palmer. "The Poet and the Indian: Indian Themes in the Poetry of D. C. Scott and John Collier." *Ontario History* 59 (June 1967):69–78.
Pedley, Frank. "The Indian Question from a Canadian Standpoint," *Lake Mohonk* (1912):89–97.
Riddell, R. G. "A Cycle in the Development of the Canadian West." *The Canadian Historical Review* 21 (September 1940):268–84.
Robbins, William G. "Herbert Hoover's Indian Reformers under Attack: The Failure of Administrative Reform." *Mid-America* 63 (October 1981):157–70.
Rowell, Verne de Witt. "Canadian Indians at the Front." *Current History* 6 (August 1917):290–92.
Schoenberg, Wilfred P. "Historic St. Peter's Mission, Landmark of the Jesuits and Ursulines among the Blackfeet." *Montana* 11 (January 1961):68–85.
Schurz, Carl. "Present Aspects of the Indian Problem" (1881). *The North American Review* 19 (Winter 1973):45–54.
Scott, D. C. "Civil Service in Its Relation to Indian Administration." *Lake Mohonk* (1914), pp. 42–48.

————. "Some Features of Indian Administration in Canada." *Lake Mohonk* (1916), pp. 95–100.

Sells, Cato. "The Greatest Present Menace to the American Indians." *The Red Man* 6 (March 1914):249.

Sharp, Paul F. "Three Frontiers: Some Comparative Studies of Canadian, American, and Australian Settlement." *Pacific Historical Review* 24 (November 1955) :369–77.

Shaw, P. C. "I Saw the Last Brave." *Alberta Historical Review* 24 (Autumn 1976) :28–29.

Stacey, C. P. "The Military Aspects of Canada's Winning of the West, 1870–1885." *The Canadian Historical Review* 21 (March 1940):1–24.

Stanley, George F. G. "Western Canada and the Frontier Thesis." *The Canadian Historical Association Paper* (1940):105–17.

Stuart, Paul. "Administrative Reform in Indian Affairs." *The Western Historical Quarterly* 16 (April 1985) :133–46.

Sully, Langdon. "The Indian Agent: A Study in Corruption and Avarice." *The American West* 10 (March 1973) :4–9.

Surtees, Robert J. "The Development of an Indian Policy in Canada." *Ontario History* 61 (June 1969) :87–98.

Svensson, Frances, "Comparative Ethnic Policy on the American and Russian Frontiers." *Journal of International Affairs* 36 (Spring–Summer 1982) :83–103.

Szasz, Margaret Garretson. "Federal Boarding Schools and the Indian Child, 1920–1960." *South Dakota History* 7 (Fall 1977) : 371–84.

————. "Indian Reform in a Decade of Prosperity," *Montana* 20 (Winter 1970) :16–27.

Thomas, L. H. "The North West Territories, 1870–1905." *The Canadian Historical Association Booklets.* no. 26. (Ottawa: Canadian Historical Association, 1970).

Tims, J. W. "Anglican Beginnings in Southern Alberta." *Alberta Historical Review* 15 (Spring 1967) :1–11.

Titley, Brian. "W. M. Graham, Indian Agent Extraordinaire." *Prairie Forum* 8 (Spring 1983) :24–41.

Tobias, John L. "Canada's Subjugation of the Plains Cree, 1879–1885." *The Canadian Historical Review* 64 (December 1983) :519–58.

————. "Protection, Civilization, Assimilation: An Outline of Canada's Indian Policy." *The Western Canadian Journal of Anthropology* 6 (1976) :13–30.

Trant, William. "The Treatment of the Canadian Indians." *Westminster Review* 144 (July–December 1895) :506–27.

Trennert, Robert A. "Educating Indian Girls at Nonreservation Boarding Schools, 1878–1920." *Western Historical Quarterly* 13 (July 1982) :271–90.

————. "From Carlisle to Phoenix: The Rise and Fall of the Indian Outing System, 1878–1930." *Pacific Historical Review* 52 (November 1983) :267–91.

Unrau, William E. "An International Perspective on American Indian Policy: The South Australian Protector and Aborigines Protection Society." *'Pacific Historical Review* 45 (November 1976) :519–38.

————. "The Civilian as Indian Agent: Villain or Victim." *Western Historical Quarterly* 3 (October 1972) :405–20.

Upton, L. F. S. "The Origins of Canadian Indian Policy." *Journal of Canadian Studies* 7 (November 1973) :51–61.

Valentine, Robert G. "Address of the Honorable Robert G. Valentine." *Lake Mohonk* (1912), pp. 80–84.

Walker, James W. St. G. "The Indian in Canadian Historical Writing." *Canadian Historical Association History Papers* (1971) :20–51.

Ward, W. Peter. "Western Canada: Recent Historiography." *Queen's Quarterly* 85 (Summer 1978) :272–74.

Warketin, John H. "Western Canada in 1886." *Transactions of the Historical and Scientific Society of Manitoba* 3 (1965) :85–116.

Washburn, William S. "The Application of the Civil Service Law Examinations." *Lake Mohonk* (1914) :51–56.

Wessell, Thomas R. "Agriculture, Indians, and American History." *Agricultural History* 50 (January 1976) :9–20.

———. "Agriculture on the Reservation: The Case of the Blackfeet, 1885–1935." *Journal of the West* 18 (October 1979) :17–24.

West, Helen B. "Robare: Elusive Post in Blackfeet Country." *Montana* 15 (July 1965) :44–57.

———. "Starvation Winter of the Blackfeet." *Montana* 9 (January 1959) :2–19.

White, Bruce W. "The American Indian as Soldier, 1890–1919." *Canadian Review of American Studies* 7 (Spring 1976) :15–25.

Wilson, R. N. "Our Betrayed Wards" (1921). *Western Canadian Journal of Anthropology* (January 1974) :21–59.

Wilson, Wesley C. "The U.S. Army and the Peigans, The Baker Massacre of 1870." *North Dakota History* 32 (January 1965) :40–58.

Wood, David L. "American Indian Farmland and the Great War." *Agricultural History* 55 (July 1981) :249–65.

Young, Egerton R. "The Indian Question in Canada." *Lake Mohonk* (1900), pp. 131–32.

Zaslow, Morris. "The Frontier Hypothesis in Recent Historiography." *The Canadian Historical Review* 24 (June 1948) :153–68.

Government Documents

Canada. House of Commons. Debates.

Codification, Annotation, and Revision of Indian Laws. Prepared in Compliance with House Resolution 134. Congressional Committee Prints, House 2793, 1917.

Conduct and Management of Indian Schools. Senate Document 201. 57th Cong., 1st sess., 27 February 1902. Serial 4234.

Cost of Survey and Allotment Work, Indian Service, 1913. House Document 331. 63d Cong., 2d sess. Serial 6756.

Contagious and Infectious Diseases among the Indians. Senate Document 1038. 62d Cong., 3d sess. 27 January 1913. Serial 6365.

Disposal of Surplus Lands of Blackfeet Indian Reservation, Montana. Hearings before a Subcommittee of the Committee on Indian Affairs of the House of Representatives on H.R. 14739. 64th Cong., 1st sess., 12 July 1916.

Granting the Indians the Right to Select Agents and Superintendents. Hearings before the Senate Committee on Indian Affairs on S. 3904. 64th Cong., 1st sess., 9 March 1916.

Indian Appropriation Bill. Hearings before the House Committee on Indian Affairs on H.R. 10385. 64th Cong., 1st sess., 16 February 1916.

Indian Tribes of Northern Montana. Senate Document 255. 58th Cong., 2d sess., 1904. Serial 4592.

Investigation of Indian Affairs. Senate Document 984. 63d Cong., 3d sess., 19 March 1915. Serial 6784.

Leasing of Indian Lands. Senate Document 212. 57th Cong., 1st sess., 1912. Serial 4234.

Report on the Management of Indians in British North America by the British Government. House Miscellaneous Document 35. 41st Cong., 2d sess., 1870. Serial 1433.

Surplus Lands, Blackfeet Indian Reservation, Montana. Hearings before the Senate Committee on Indian Affairs on S. 793. 64th Cong., 1st sess., 11 and 15 April 1916.

Government Publications

Abbott, Frederick H. *The Administration of Indian Affairs in Canada, Report of an Investigation Made in 1914 under the Direction of the Board of Indian Commissioners*. Washington: Government Printing Office, 1915.

Annual Reports of the Board of Indian Commissioners. Washington: Government Printing Office, 1870–1920.

Annual Reports of the Commissioner of Indian Affairs to the Secretary of the Interior. Washington: Government Printing Office, 1870–1920.

Annual Report of the Department of Indian Affairs. Ottawa: Queen's Printers, 1870–1920.

Annual Report of the Secretary of the Department of the Interior. Washington: Government Printing Office, 1870–1920.

Annual Report of the Superintendent of Indian Education. Washington: Government Printing Office, 1891, 1900.

Bryce, P. H. *Report on the Indian Schools of Manitoba and the North-West Territories*. Ottawa: Government Printing Bureau, 1907.

Cohen, Felix S. *Handbook of Federal Indian Law*. Washington: Government Printing Office, 1942.

Davin, Nicholas Flood. *Report on Industrial Schools for Indians and Half-Breeds*. Ottawa: Queen's Printers, 14 March 1879.

Fletcher, Alice C. *Indian Education and Civilization*. Bureau of Education Special Report, 1888. Washington: Government Printing Office, 1888.

House of Commons. *Indian Self-Government in Canada*. Report of the Special Committee, October 1983.

Indian Acts and Amendments, 1868–1950. Treaties and Historical Research Center, DIAND, 1981.

Kappler, Charles I., ed. *Indian Laws and Treaties*. 5 vols. Washington: Government Printing Office, vol 1–2, 1904; vol. 3, 1919; vol. 4, 1929; vol. 5, 1941.

Leslie, John, and R. Maguire, eds. *The Historical Development of the Indian Act*. 2d ed. Ottawa: Department of Indian and Northern Affairs, 1978.

U.S. Department of the Interior, Census Office. *Report on Indians Taxed and Not Taxed in the United States (except Alaska), at the 11th Census, 1890*. Washington: Government Printing Office, 1894.

Theses and Dissertations

Denman, Clayton. "Cultural Change among the Blackfeet Indians of Montana." Ph.D. diss., University of Berkeley, 1968.

Dyck, N. E. "The Administration of Federal Indian Aid in the North-West Territories, 1879–1885." Master's thesis, University of Saskatchewan, 1970.

Falk, Gerald A. "Missionary Education Work among the Prairie Bands, 1870–1914." Master's thesis, University of Western Ontario, 1973.

Getty, Ian A. L. "The Church Missionary Society among the Blackfoot Indians of Southern Alberta, 1880–1895." Master's thesis, University of Calgary, 1970.

Howard, Robert E. "A Historical Survey of the Foundation and Growth of Education on the Blackfeet Indian Reservation, 1872–1964." Master's thesis, Western Montana College of Education, 1965.

Jennings, John. "The North West Mounted Police and Indian Policy 1874–1896." Ph.D. diss., University of Toronto, 1979.

Leighton, James Douglas. "The Development of Federal Indian Policy in Canada, 1840–1890." 2 vols. Ph.D. diss., University of Western Ontario, 1975.

Looy, Anthony J. "The Indian Agent and His Role in the Administration of the North-West Superintendency, 1876–1893." Ph.D. diss., Queen's University, 1977.

McDonnell, Janet. "The Disintegration of the Indian Estate: Indian Land Policy, 1913–1929." Ph.D. diss., Marquette University, 1980.

Olsen, John A. "Comparative Changes in the Status of Indians in Canada and the United States since World War II." Ph. D. diss., University of Western Ontario, 1979.

Owram, Douglas Robb. " 'White Savagery': Some Canadian Reaction to American Indian Policy, 1867–1885." Master's thesis, Queen's University, 1971.

Porter, Eric R. "The Anglican Church and Native Education: Residential Schools and Assimilation." Ph.D. diss., University of Toronto, 1981.

Regular, W. K. "The Plains Indians and the Application of the Federal Government's Indian Policy during the Laurier Era." Master's thesis, University of Calgary, 1980.

Simons, G. S. "Attitude of the Western Canadian Press to the Indian Affairs Department, 1880–1896." Master's thesis, Queen's University, 1978.

Tate, Michael. "Apache Scouts, Police, and Judges as Agents of Acculturation, 1865–1920." Ph.D. diss., University of Toledo, 1974.

Taylor, J. L. "The Development of an Indian Policy for the Canadian North-West, 1869–1879." Ph.D. diss., Queen's University, 1975.

Unpublished Sources

Department of Indian and Northern Affairs. "The Government of Aboriginal Peoples, An Executive Summary." Treaties and Historical Research Center, 1983.

Gooderham, G. H. "Northern Plains Tribes," Vol. 1. Blackfeet. Manuscript, Glenbow–Alberta Institute.

———. "Twenty-Five Years as an Indian Agent to the Blackfeet Band." Manuscript, 28 January 1972, Glenbow–Alberta Institute.

Leighton, Douglas J. "A Victorian Civil Servant at Work: Lawrence Vankoughnet and the Canadian Indian Department, 1874–1893." Paper presented to the Canadian Historical Association, London, Ontario, 30 May 1978.

McNab, David T. "Research Report on the Royal Proclamation of 1763 and British Indian Policy, 1750–1795." Treaties and Historical Research Center, DIAND, 1979.

Martin, John. "John Hamilton Gooderham." Manuscript, Glenbow–Alberta Institute.

Standefer, Roma. "A Program of Directed Economic Change for Northern Blackfoot Reservation." Manuscript, Glenbow–Alberta Institute.

Tobias, John L. "Indian Reserves in Western Canada: Indian Homelands or Devices for Assimilation?" Treaties and Historical Research Center, DIAND, 1975.

Newspapers

The Fort Benton Weekly Record, Ft. Benton, Montana.
The New North-West, Deer Lodge, Montana.
The Montana Daily Record, Helena, Montana.

Collections and Archives

John Collier Papers.
Edgar L. Dewdney Papers.
Indian Rights Association Papers.
Denver Federal Archives and Records Center, Denver.
Glenbow–Alberta Institute, Calgary.
National Archives, Washington, D. C.
Public Archives of Canada, Ottawa.
Seattle Federal Archives and Records Center, Seattle.

Index

Abbott, Frederick H., 9, 21, 30, 59, 66, 67, *89*, 120, 124, 128, 147, 152, 173

aboriginal title, 17

Administration of Indian Affairs in Canada, The (Abbott), 9

agents, 36, 41–53, 71, 152–56

agriculture: agricultural policies, 56–60; cattle economy, 64, 66– 68, 71, 74–76, 80–86, 117, 164; farming, 40, 45–47, 56, 70–77, 128; irrigation, 72–74, 78

Alberta, 11–15, 75, 77, 78, 85, 164

Allen, R. A., 45, 156

allotment, 18, 27–30, 64, 68, 72, 82, 106–22, 129, 179, 204 n 69

Almighty Voice, 162

American Liberty Bonds, 176

Anglican Church, 125, 127, 128, 134, 139, 141, 146

Apache, the, 150

assimilation, 16–20, 25, 34, 181; enfranchisement, 26–30, 176

Assinibiones, the, 13

Badger Creek, 41, 141

Baker, Hugh, *97*

Baker Massacre, 12

Baldwin, M. D., 163

Battleford, 138

Battle River, 65

Begg, Magnus, *87*, 131, 172

Belly River, 78

Birch Creek, 13, 73

Blackfeet Allotment Act, 72, 74

Blackfeet Stock Protection Association, 165

Blackfeet, the, 11, 13, 57, 61, 68, 107–9, 119–22, 125, 144, 154, 161, 163

Blackfeet War, 12, 125

Blackfoot Confederacy, 11–15

Blackfoot Crossing, 153

Blackfoot, the, 11, 13, 37–40, 49, 52, 55, 66, 67, 75, 78, 79, 83–86, 112–14, 125, 143, 144, 171

Black Hills, 6

Black Looking, 155

Black Soldiers, 46

Blake, Samuel, 134

Bloods, the, 11, 13, 39, 45, 49, 52, 54, 59, 63, 65, 67, 75–79, 84–86, 114–18, 125, 134, 142, 153, 154, 156, 160, 172, 176

Board of Indian Commissioners, 9, 20, 38. *See also* Abbott, Frederick H.

boundaries, 11–15

Bourgis, P. C., 133

Bourne, H. T., 142

British North America Act, 31

Browning, 51, 135

Bryce, Peter H., 168

buffalo, 37–42

Bull Shield, 132

Story of a National Crime, The,
   (Bryce), 168
Sun Dance, 127–33
Sun River, 57

Tatsey, Joe, 121
taxation, 28–30, 209 n 83
Teton River, 12, 141
Three Bears, 120
Three Suns, 135
Tims, John W., *97*, 125, 127, 135,
   142, 173
Toronto Conference, 11
Toronto Women's Auxiliary, 173
trachoma, 167, 171
treaties, 12–18, 33, 39, 57, 58, 66, 80,
   115, 118, 141
"Treatment of the Canadian
   Indians, The," 8
trespass, 163–65
tribal councils, 26, 120, 152
tribal income, 59, 64, 73, 77, 81, 82
Trivett, Samuel, *94, 95*, 125, 127, 142
tuberculosis, 143, 168–73
Two Foxes, 162
typhoid, 173

Uintah reservation, 109
Upham, William, *98*

Valentine, Robert G., 20, 53
Vankoughnet, Lawrence G., 22, 24,
   34, 38, 47, 48, 59, 138
Victoria Home, 143, 146

Wadsworth, Thomas P., 46, 47, 52
Walsh, Thomas J., 121
water rights, 73, 78–79, 119
wealth, 80–81
weather, 76–79, 82
Whipple, H. B., 7
White Eagle school, 144
Willow Creek, 141–43
Wilson, James, 129, 155, 160
Wilson, R. N., 78, 79, 85, 114, 117,
   130, 172
Winnipeg, 51, 66
Winters, 199 n 16
Wood, John, 159
worldview, 53, 57, 127, 128
World War I (the Great War), 68, 74,
   77, 82, 85, 117, 140, 175–77

Yeomans, E. H., 164, 171
Young, Egerton, 8
Young, John, 41–45, 55, 61, 70, 71,
   106, 107, 124–26, 141, 163
Young Pine, 153, 154